JEREMIAH AND
LAMENTATIONS

Michael Wilcock

Michael Wilcock's thorough and creative exposition of the books of Lamentations and Jeremiah is a joy to read. His clear style and pastoral perspective provide a valuable resource for preachers in the pulpit, teachers in the classroom, and other students of this important, and at times, difficult prophetic pair. I recommend it to those who would encounter Jeremiah's message in light of its ancient context, the redemptive work of Christ, and its application into the contemporary Christian life.

Scott Redd, Jr.
President and Associate Professor of Old Testament
Reformed Theological Seminary, Washington, D.C.

In this book, Michael Wilcock has done a real service to students of Scripture: he has made Jeremiah and Lamentations accessible and applicable. From page 1, it is clear that the reader is in the hands of a careful scholar and faithful guide to the life and writings of the prophet Jeremiah. In short, this is a wonderful resource for anyone who wants to preach, teach, or simply study these sometimes intimidating books. When people in my church ask for a resource to help them read Jeremiah and Lamentations, this book will be at the top of my list!

Michael McKinley
Senior Pastor, Guilford Baptist Church, Sterling, Virginia

It is a pleasure to commend this fine piece of commentary writing by Michael Wilcock. Over the years he has produced many commentaries on both Testaments, including some fine examples in the BST series. Here he has lost none of his touch as with sure-footed exegesis, spiritual insight and elegant writing he tackles the difficult books of Jeremiah and Lamentations. All Bible readers will profit from reading these books with a sympathetic and knowledgeable guide. However, they will also be of great use to preachers who will find themselves stimulated, enlightened and emboldened to tackle these often neglected books in the company of an experienced and erudite preacher.

Bob Fyall
Senior Tutor in Ministry
Cornhill Training Course, Scotland

JEREMIAH AND LAMENTATIONS

The death of a dream, and what came after

Michael Wilcock

CHRISTIAN
FOCUS

Michael Wilcock is a respected author and Bible teacher. He has spent many years in pastoral ministry, including his most recent charge, St Nicholas, Durham. He was formerly Director of Pastoral Studies at Trinity College, Bristol. He also wrote *In the Days of the Kings* (ISBN 978-1-84550-508-0).

Copyright © Michael Wilcock 2013

ISBN 978-1-78191-148-8

10 9 8 7 6 5 4 3 2 1

First published in 2013
by
Christian Focus Publications Ltd.,
Geanies House, Fearn, Ross-shire,
IV20 1TW, Scotland, UK.

www.christianfocus.com

Cover design by Daniel van Straaten

Printed and bound by
Bell & Bain, Glasgow

MIX
Paper from responsible sources
FSC
www.fsc.org
FSC® C007785

Contents

To

Gordon McConville,
Leslie McFall,
John Mackay,
Alec Motyer,

four giants, to all of whom this book is deeply indebted

SIMPLIFIED TIMELINE
From the call of Jeremiah to the destruction of Jerusalem

This outline of the main events of those 41 years is based on the comprehensive work of Leslie McFall, chiefly in his extended article (with detailed accompanying charts), *Do the sixty-nine weeks of Daniel date the Messianic mission of Nehemiah or Jesus?* (Journal of the Evangelical Theological Society 52/4 [December 2009], pp. 673-718). It is designed to set Jeremiah's ministry in the framework of the reigns of the last five kings of Judah, and their contemporaries in Egypt and Babylon.

To

Gordon McConville,
Leslie McFall,
John Mackay,
Alec Motyer,

four giants, to all of whom this book is deeply indebted

SIMPLIFIED TIMELINE
From the call of Jeremiah to the destruction of Jerusalem

This outline of the main events of those 41 years is based on the comprehensive work of Leslie McFall, chiefly in his extended article (with detailed accompanying charts), *Do the sixty-nine weeks of Daniel date the Messianic mission of Nehemiah or Jesus?* (Journal of the Evangelical Theological Society 52/4 [December 2009], pp. 673-718). It is designed to set Jeremiah's ministry in the framework of the reigns of the last five kings of Judah, and their contemporaries in Egypt and Babylon.

627 BC	13th year of Josiah's reign. Call of Jeremiah.	600	
626		599	
625		598	Jehoiakim dies. Jehoiachin reigns for 3 months, until –
624		597	– Nebuchadnezzar invades again. Second deportation. Accession of Zedekiah.
623			
622	Finding of the Book of the Law.	596	
621		595	Accession of Psamtek II in Egypt.
620			
619		594	Anti-Babylonian conference of western states in Jerusalem.
618			
617		593	
616		592	
615		591	
614		590	
613		589	Accession of Hophra in Egypt. Nebuchadnezzar returns. Siege begins, December.
612			
611			
610	Accession of Neco II in Egypt.	588	
609	Josiah killed in 31st year. Jehoahaz reigns for 3 months. Accession of Jehoiakim.	587	
		586	Siege ends, July/August. Zedekiah captured. Third deportation. Jerusalem destroyed. Jeremiah taken to Egypt.
608	Jehoiakim a vassal of Egypt until –		
607		—	
606		561	Accession of Evil-Merodach in Babylon. Jehoiachin released from prison.
605	– accession of Nebuchadnezzar in Babylon, who invades. First deportation.		
604	Baruch's scroll read and burned.	—	
		536	Cyrus captures Babylon, First repatriation (70th year since first deportation)
603			
602			
601	Jehoiakim rebels against Nebuchadnezzar.		

627 BC	13th year of Josiah's reign. Call of Jeremiah.	600	
		599	
626		598	Jehoiakim dies. Jehoiachin reigns for 3 months, until –
625			
624		597	– Nebuchadnezzar invades again. Second deportation. Accession of Zedekiah.
623			
622	Finding of the Book of the Law.		
		596	
621		595	Accession of Psamtek II in Egypt.
620			
619		594	Anti-Babylonian conference of western states in Jerusalem.
618			
617		593	
616		592	
615		591	
614		590	
613		589	Accession of Hophra in Egypt. Nebuchadnezzar returns. Siege begins, December.
612			
611			
610	Accession of Neco II in Egypt.	588	
609	Josiah killed in 31st year. Jehoahaz reigns for 3 months. Accession of Jehoiakim.	587	
		586	Siege ends, July/August. Zedekiah captured. Third deportation. Jerusalem destroyed. Jeremiah taken to Egypt.
608	Jehoiakim a vassal of Egypt until –		
607		—	
606		561	Accession of Evil-Merodach in Babylon. Jehoiachin released from prison.
605	– accession of Nebuchadnezzar in Babylon, who invades. First deportation.		
604	Baruch's scroll read and burned.	—	
		536	Cyrus captures Babylon, First repatriation (70th year since first deportation)
603			
602			
601	Jehoiakim rebels against Nebuchadnezzar.		

Preface

Much the greater part of this exposition is devoted to that remarkable Old Testament document, the prophecy of Jeremiah; and behind it lies the conviction that the order in which we read his book today is not, as many hold, the result of much rearranging after his time by anonymous editors, but the order in which he actually meant us to read it. This view is, as I say, far from universal, but I believe a good case can be made for it, as I hope will become apparent.

The order of the Old Testament as a whole, however, is a different matter. That has varied considerably over the years. It might seem natural that in our Bibles (as in the Septuagint, the Greek version of the Old Testament) the book commonly known as the Lamentations of Jeremiah should follow closely after the other book that bears his name. But as our Lord says in a different connection, 'from the beginning it was not so'. In the Hebrew Bible it belongs not with the Prophets, but in the section known as the Writings. And to assume that its position in our Christian Bible is its 'natural place', as a kind of appendix to Jeremiah, can have an unfortunate effect. It can seem to be little more than an afterthought, a 'poor relation', of no great significance, readily overlooked. This is seriously to undersell its spiritual value. If we are aware of the tragic tale that is about to unfold in the pages of Jeremiah, there is no reason why we should not first deliberately expose ourselves to the emotional impact of these agonized poems,

even if the literary style which made them memorable for their original readers may be rather off-putting to us, with our very different language and culture. They set the tone, as it were, for the fifty-two chapters of the longer book, which will climax in the death of Israel as a kingdom. (We note, by the way, that 'Israel' in the sense of the breakaway northern half of the Hebrew monarchy had already perished in 722 B.C., and in that respect it was 'Judah' that finally expired in 586 B.C.; but the broader sense of 'Israel' as the nation to which both kingdoms belonged also figures often in these Scriptures).

So I have treated the shorter book as an introduction, not as an appendix, to the longer one. As my writing proceeded, a curious fact emerged, which I had not expected. Noting the three points at which Jeremiah's ministry to the nations is highlighted, I gave the relevant sections appropriate titles: 'The View from Anathoth' (ch. 1), 'The View from Jerusalem' (chs. 24–25), and 'The View from Tahpanhes' (chs. 46–51). It seemed reasonable next to divide chapters 2–23 into five sections of roughly equal length, and the same process suited chapters 26–45. Then I realized that to introduce the whole with a treatment of Lamentations, and to round it off with chapter 52 of Jeremiah, produced as neat a chiasmus (readers unfamiliar with the term will find it explained in section 1) as you could wish for. As follows:

1. Lamentations
   2. The View from Anathoth
      3-7. Judgments/Delusions/Protests I & II/ Betrayals
        8. The View from Jerusalem
      9-13. Intentions/Promises/Failures/Endings/Continuations
   14. The View from Tahpanhes
15. Destinies

I would not set as much store by this scheme as I have done, were it not that the chiastic pattern, which is of the essence in the shorter book, crops up repeatedly in the longer one as well, and indeed seems to come as second nature to many others of the Bible writers.

Lamentations, then, will provide the way in to our reading of Jeremiah. But I am treating the exposition of the two books

Preface

Much the greater part of this exposition is devoted to that remarkable Old Testament document, the prophecy of Jeremiah; and behind it lies the conviction that the order in which we read his book today is not, as many hold, the result of much rearranging after his time by anonymous editors, but the order in which he actually meant us to read it. This view is, as I say, far from universal, but I believe a good case can be made for it, as I hope will become apparent.

The order of the Old Testament as a whole, however, is a different matter. That has varied considerably over the years. It might seem natural that in our Bibles (as in the Septuagint, the Greek version of the Old Testament) the book commonly known as the Lamentations of Jeremiah should follow closely after the other book that bears his name. But as our Lord says in a different connection, 'from the beginning it was not so'. In the Hebrew Bible it belongs not with the Prophets, but in the section known as the Writings. And to assume that its position in our Christian Bible is its 'natural place', as a kind of appendix to Jeremiah, can have an unfortunate effect. It can seem to be little more than an afterthought, a 'poor relation', of no great significance, readily overlooked. This is seriously to undersell its spiritual value. If we are aware of the tragic tale that is about to unfold in the pages of Jeremiah, there is no reason why we should not first deliberately expose ourselves to the emotional impact of these agonized poems,

even if the literary style which made them memorable for their original readers may be rather off-putting to us, with our very different language and culture. They set the tone, as it were, for the fifty-two chapters of the longer book, which will climax in the death of Israel as a kingdom. (We note, by the way, that 'Israel' in the sense of the breakaway northern half of the Hebrew monarchy had already perished in 722 b.c., and in that respect it was 'Judah' that finally expired in 586 b.c.; but the broader sense of 'Israel' as the nation to which both kingdoms belonged also figures often in these Scriptures).

So I have treated the shorter book as an introduction, not as an appendix, to the longer one. As my writing proceeded, a curious fact emerged, which I had not expected. Noting the three points at which Jeremiah's ministry to the nations is highlighted, I gave the relevant sections appropriate titles: 'The View from Anathoth' (ch. 1), 'The View from Jerusalem' (chs. 24–25), and 'The View from Tahpanhes' (chs. 46–51). It seemed reasonable next to divide chapters 2–23 into five sections of roughly equal length, and the same process suited chapters 26–45. Then I realized that to introduce the whole with a treatment of Lamentations, and to round it off with chapter 52 of Jeremiah, produced as neat a chiasmus (readers unfamiliar with the term will find it explained in section 1) as you could wish for. As follows:

1. Lamentations
   2. The View from Anathoth
      3-7. Judgments/Delusions/Protests I & II/ Betrayals
        8. The View from Jerusalem
      9-13. Intentions/Promises/Failures/Endings/Continuations
   14. The View from Tahpanhes
15. Destinies

I would not set as much store by this scheme as I have done, were it not that the chiastic pattern, which is of the essence in the shorter book, crops up repeatedly in the longer one as well, and indeed seems to come as second nature to many others of the Bible writers.

Lamentations, then, will provide the way in to our reading of Jeremiah. But I am treating the exposition of the two books

as an integrated whole, and Jeremiah takes up fourteen-fifteenths of it; so he takes pride of place on the title page, to say nothing of the fact that Jeremiah comes before Lamentations both in biblical order and in alphabetical order!

I should stress that this is an exposition, not a commentary, and does not contain a lengthy bibliography. It values the work of behind-the-scenes academics, certainly, and several such scholars figure in footnotes, but I have been more concerned with the front-of-house public, the people in the pew. And with them in mind, I have tried to set forth not only what Scripture says but also what it is for.

I do want, all the same, to pay tribute where tribute is especially due; hence the four names that figure on the dedication page. What they have in common, besides an initial M to their names and their ancestral roots in the more exotic parts of the British Isles, is great experience in the field of Old Testament studies, far beyond my abilities. Gordon McConville helped me to see Jeremiah's book whole, in the shape in which it has come down to us, clarifying its themes and its purpose. Leslie McFall gave me an astonishingly detailed and coherent grid of the dating of events in Jeremiah's day, anchoring the prophet's life and work in their historical context. John Mackay provided me with the most thorough and up-to-date commentary I could have wished for, leaving not a stone unturned in the quest for what the text actually says. And Alec Motyer's deep love of the Old Testament, of the Hebrew language, of the structure of Scripture and of the ministry of preaching, has rubbed off on me through a friendship of many years.

Here then is a preacher's overview of one of the greatest books in the Bible. Overviews, they say, are a privilege given to dwarfs standing on the shoulders of giants. If you can cope with the bizarre image of my jumping across frequently from one giant to another, these are the learned people who have provided my main vantage points. My thanks to all of them.

Michael Wilcock
Eastbourne, 2013

I

Lamentations

(Lamentations 1–5)

'O happy band of pilgrims'?

The first line of John Mason Neale's once-popular hymn is emphatically not the right title for the little drama with which we begin. True, it is about a 'band of pilgrims', but as these people are nearing their goal, the first distant glimpse of the holy place to which they are travelling will warn them that they will scarcely recognize it: the very skyline has changed. In a sombre mood they make their way towards the devastated suburbs of the city. Even if the great temple at its heart is now a blackened ruin, they can at least pay their respects there to the God whose house it used to be.

They never reach it. A marauding gang of ex-soldiers which has survived the war sets upon them, and soon another heap of carcases is left for the crows to pick, dumped in a pit at Mizpah.

The incident was recorded centuries ago, in the Book of Jeremiah.[1] But the image of *die tote Stadt*, the dead city, is as real today as ever it was. The elegant streets of Melbourne, intact, but empty of every living thing, at the end of the 1959 movie *On the Beach*. New York, in the imagination of later film-makers flooded (*Deep Impact*) or frozen (*The Day After Tomorrow*). The bombing of Hiroshima and Nagasaki, 1945: that actually happened. So did the burning of Moscow, 1812. These images haunt the world's dreams, as did the fall of

---

1   Jeremiah 41:1-7.

Constantinople in 1453 and that of Rome a thousand years before. Babylon fell, too, a thousand years earlier still, though its final destruction is even today a vision yet to be fulfilled.[2] But the sack of Jerusalem in 586 B.C.[3], the background to the massacre just described, has a significance greater than them all.

It is the theme of five songs, written at the time or soon after, which appear in our Bibles as the Book of Lamentations, and will be for us a way in to Jeremiah's book. They are as much about Jerusalem dying as about Jerusalem dead: the siege as well as the sack of the city, a tale of suffering, starvation and despair, till finally the walls are breached, the survivors deported, the goods looted and the city torched.

Traditionally these songs have been thought of as Jeremiah's work. More recently, differences between them and the bigger book (and indeed between them themselves) have been thought to indicate one or more anonymous authors, though there is no reason why Jeremiah should not have written in different styles and from different viewpoints at different times. At all events, the 'voices' vary in the course of the five poems, so that the speaker is at one point the city of Jerusalem, at another a particular person involved in its suffering, and at yet others an observer describing these events.

A lamentable state of affairs (1:1-22)

Every part of the Bible, not least its poetry, repays the effort of working out how it is put together. 'Structural analysis' is the name of the game. Looked at in this way, the most obvious feature of these songs is the number of verses in each: either 22 or a multiple of 22. Since the Hebrew alphabet has 22 letters, we may not be surprised to learn that Lamentations 1 is an acrostic, like several of the psalms (most notably Psalm 119); that is to say, the first letter of the first word of the first verse of

---

2 See Revelation 18.

3 The year has generally been reckoned to be 587 B.C., but recent research seems to point rather to the following year, 586 BC. See John L. Mackay, *Jeremiah* (Tain: Christian Focus 2004), vol. 2, pp. 588-9, 612-13; Leslie McFall, 'The Sixty-Nine Weeks of Daniel', *Journal of the Evangelical Theological Society* 52/4 (December 2009), pp. 694-718; 'The Chronological Data in Kings and Chronicles', *Bibliotheca Sacra*, vol. 148 (1991); and other works available online at www.btinternet. com/~lmf12.

the first song is *aleph*, while *beth* begins verse 2, *gimel* verse 3, and so on – the equivalent of our ABC. So what we have in an acrostic is something akin to rhyme, except that it is the sounds at the beginning of lines, not those at the end of them, that follow a pattern.[4]

This song has another, more complicated, kind of 'rhyming' as well. Every verse contains an idea, usually an actual word or phrase, which reappears elsewhere, in a curious but regular fashion: the first verse is linked in this way with the last verse, the second with the next to last, and so forth.[5] That is, the acrostic is also a palindrome, like the words 'civic' and 'redder', or the sentences 'Madam, I'm Adam' and 'Rise to vote, sir'.[6] At the midpoint, therefore, these 'rhymes' come together: 'See and observe,' says verse 11, 'observe and see,' says verse 12;[7] and those words are in fact the keynote of the chapter – a view of the recent turmoils in Jerusalem, as they appear to an onlooker (call him the Writer) in the first half, and as they are experienced by the City herself in the second half. The Writer, and his 'rhymes', work up to verse 11, where he asks Yahweh too to look at these facts. The City, and her 'rhymes', begin from verse 12, there asking the passers-by – other nations, that is, uninvolved in the conflict – to look at what has happened.

First, then, the Writer's observations. They can be followed through in the text, a verse to each word or phrase. 'This place', he says, 'was once the home of many people; / now that it needs comforters there are only enemies, / there is deep distress, / the priests suffering, / the young taken captive – / such is the fate of Zion, / abandoned, / rejected; / where is God?' So the first nine verses, a panorama ending in verse 10

---

4 The Hebrew letters are occasionally mentioned in what follows. Readers unfamiliar with the Hebrew alphabet may like to check it out, and will find it in most English Bibles as the headings of the 22 sections of Psalm 119.

5 English versions often disguise these parallels, as we find from the very beginning, where 'full' in 1:1 is the same word (*rab*) as 'many' in 1:22. See also the next note.

6 Less artificial than these 22-verse palindromes, and underlying many parts of Scripture besides the poetry of the Old Testament, is the kind of palindromic structure called 'chiasmus', where ABA (or ABCBA, or any such sequence) have nothing to do with the letters of the Hebrew alphabet, but indicate the arrangement of topics.

7 Even the ESV lets us down here, giving 'look and see … look and see', which spoils the palindrome.

with an ominous hand stretched out to steal or destroy everything of value in Jerusalem. After the 'hinge' at verses 11-12, a parallel sequence of word-pictures will appear in reverse order in verses 13-22, beginning with a stretched-out net. But first, as the Writer has been 'seeing and observing' the facts of the case, he has put briefly into the mouth of the City (verses 9b, 11b) a plea that Yahweh will do the same.

Is there in this world of ours a lamentable state of affairs that corresponds to that one? Of course, we have to make all sorts of adjustments in order to see today the equivalent of what our Writer was seeing when the kingdom of Judah fell in ruins before his eyes. For one thing, that single image occupied all his attention, whereas innumerable tragedies from across the globe compete for ours. For another, to him everything seemed dark, whereas we are gratefully aware of light as well as darkness, the light both of the saving gospel and of common grace. For yet another, that gospel had not appeared in its fullness to him, whereas we know Christ the Lord of glory, the multi-national Israel of God, and the heavenly Jerusalem of which all His people are citizens: Old Testament buds that have now burst into New Testament bloom.[8]

Bearing these differences in mind, we have to say that if Jeremiah's Jerusalem has a modern equivalent, it is the church of Jesus Christ, which in our New Testament era is no longer tied to a particular place in the Middle East, though it is not yet sinless as it will be in the world to come. And we have to ask whether three basic facts about that Jerusalem and its relation to its God are true of the church today. All have been touched on already in the Writer's half of this song, and all are now confessed by the City herself in verses 12-22. 'Observe and see' is now her plea, as it was his, and now it is addressed to those 'who pass by'.

First and most obvious is the fact that she is in dire trouble. This is the background to the song (and indeed the book) as a whole. It is possible of course to react to the 'sufferings of Jerusalem' emotionally and unthinkingly. We must not automatically assume that for us that phrase simply means troubles that beset Christians (or indeed Jews) in today's world. Reports of the present persecution of Christian believers in

---

8 1 Corinthians 2:8; Galatians 6:16; Hebrews 12:22, Philippians 3:20.

many Asian and African countries may horrify us and stir us to action, for the trials of God's people anywhere should be the concern of God's people everywhere; 'if one member suffers, all suffer together.'[9] But they should not surprise us, for it is only 'through many tribulations' that Christ's people 'enter the kingdom of God,'[10] and we ourselves are not likely to be exempt. Persecution, however, is what Peter's first letter calls 'suffering *unjustly*'. He would put the City's distress in quite a different category, and tell her frankly, '*You sin* and are beaten for it.'[11] This is the second fact: that her suffering is her own fault. The Writer has simply said 'Jerusalem sinned' (v. 8), but the City is past pretending, and now admits repeatedly how she has rebelled and transgressed (vv. 14, 18, 20, 22).

The third fact is the hardest for the modern mind to accept. But significantly it is the City herself, not the Writer, who recognizes it and spells it out unambiguously. Her sufferings are, she says, 'my sorrow … *which the* LORD *inflicted*' (v. 12), and that is the first of a score of verbs that tell us God's part in these events. All that has happened to her is her fault, *and His doing*. Not only is she prepared to say so, but she wants all the nations to hear it too (v. 18). In her half of the song He is almost as often Adonai (Lord), the Sovereign, the Master of all peoples, as He is Yahweh (LORD), Israel's own covenant God. To these two names we shall return.

Three facts, then: the City is in trouble, she has deserved it, God has inflicted it. To take the last of them first, it was Yahweh who brought about the destruction of Jerusalem, and the *purpose* of that was twofold. In His scheme of things, His people had been for 450 years a nation-state ruled by kings of the line of David, but the 'shape' of Israel was about to change, just as it would change again even more radically six centuries later. In 586 B.C. He was putting an end not to Israel the nation,[12] but only to Israel the Davidic monarchy, for there were different lessons yet to be learned about what it means to be the people of God. All the events of that time, bad as well as

9 1 Corinthians 12:26.

10 Acts 14:22.

11 1 Peter 2:19-20.

12 The tree of Jesse would be cut down, but one day there would 'come forth a shoot from the stump' (Isa. 11:1).

good, were part of His comprehensive educational plan; and now as then His people find that that plan is often puzzling, sometimes shocking, and always far bigger (and eventually better) than they ever imagined.

And you cannot have education without discipline. This other aspect of His purpose for His people takes us back at once to the second of the facts, the *cause* of Jerusalem's downfall. The nation had to learn that privileges bring responsibilities, and sins have consequences. Even today, when deterrence and rehabilitation seem to be the chief aims of our penal system, there is still such a thing as punishment.[13] Some of our misfortunes are the penalty for our misdeeds. So in Lamentations 1 the City admits that what God has been doing, she has richly merited. And we might conceivably come under the same condemnation. No Christians, and no Christian communities, can ever truthfully say they have no sins to confess, and (as the hymn puts it) 'they who fain would serve Thee best are conscious most of wrong within.'[14] It is a community called by God's name that is here deservedly going through the mill.

However, the divine justice is scrupulously fair. There are sins and sins, and the *experience* of the City's fall, the first of the three facts, was a consequence – terrible, but just – of the deep-seated, unrepentant, deliberate, continuous and far-reaching sins of the wicked Jehoiakim and the weak Zedekiah, the royal brothers whose follies the Book of Jeremiah will expose, and of others like them. There is no denying that such suffering may come also to those who practise daily repentance, faith and obedience, but for them it will be the 'fiery trial' of 1 Peter 4:12, not a punishment but a solemn privilege. Jeremiah himself was just such a one.

A lamentable chain of consequences (2:1-22)
It was with the plight of the City that the first song began; but soon, and then often thereafter, she had to confess that this was a punishment for her sin from the hand of her God. That, we shall find, is the theme of the second song from start

---

13 See C. S. Lewis's famous essay on 'The Humanitarian Theory of Punishment', in *Undeceptions* (London: Geoffrey Bles 1971).

14 Henry Twells, 'At even, when the sun was set.'

to finish. Being as regular an acrostic-cum-palindrome as the first was,[15] it both begins and ends with a God who 'in the day of his anger' (vv. 1 and 22) shows no pity (vv. 2 and 21), brings about a dreadful devouring in verse 3 and a worse one in verse 20, and so continues, in a strict poetic sequence that nevertheless trembles with mortification and horror.

Who says what in the course of the song? Commentators differ over headings and sub-headings for it. The simpler the better, in my view, given the genius that can express so much emotion with so much discipline. There is, as before, a hinge at the centre of the palindrome: 'bile poured out/ faint in the streets' (v. 11), 'faint in the streets/life poured out' (v. 12). Moving towards it are ten verses in which the Writer describes objectively what God has been doing to the City. Then all at once, in the two 'hinge' verses, he becomes one with its citizens, and 'sits where they sit'.[16] He has thus far been speaking *about* them; now for the remaining ten verses he speaks *to* them, with an inspired blend of deep fellow-feeling and prophetic ruthlessness. True, verses 20-22 are addressed to the Lord, but they need not form a separate section; they are still the Writer's words, in which he is giving the City a form of prayer that he and she together can use in these extreme circumstances.

If readers new to the Bible happened to open it at this chapter, they might wonder why (in most English translations) it refers to God sometimes as 'the Lord' and sometimes as 'the LORD' – in fact seven times each. The difference, which we noticed in chapter 1, gives us a line on why Jerusalem is suffering the miseries described here.

Jerusalem was an Israelite city, the capital of an Israelite kingdom, only because God had long before called Israel to be His own people, rescuing them from slavery in Egypt and making with them a covenant that detailed His promises to them and their obligations to Him. All of that was wrapped up in His covenant name Yahweh, the LORD. In consequence, they had been blessed with the leadership of Moses the lawgiver, Joshua his successor, and a line first of judges and

---

15 Except that for some reason v. 16 begins with *pe* and v. 17 with *ayin*, reversing the normal alphabetical order.

16 Cf. Ezekiel 3:15.

then of kings, together with a series of priests and prophets;
all this in a land flowing with milk and honey, in due course
centred on a city which was the joy of the whole earth, with at
its heart a temple for God's name.[17]

Since that name is 'the LORD', why do the opening verses of
Lamentations 2 repeatedly call him 'the Lord'? Why Adonai
first, and only later (and sporadically) Yahweh?

Alongside the rosy picture of Israel's history just outlined,
we have to be aware of a much more negative one. Not every
judge lived up to his calling, many a king led the nation astray,
the priests were often corrupt, the prophets self-serving. In
consequence, God's people had again and again reneged
on their covenant obligations, while expecting Yahweh
nonetheless to keep His side of the bargain. Repeatedly He
had warned them against such an attitude, and repeatedly
they had ignored the warnings. Every sin made the next one
easier, and restoration harder.

Now they are having to learn that their faithlessness
in its turn has consequences. It is as Adonai, the Master,
the Sovereign Lord of all nations, that God now comes to
Jerusalem (vv. 1-5). No more Mr Nice Guy; no more privilege.
It seems Israel must face His fury on the same footing as the
most wicked and godless of her heathen neighbours. He is
even prepared to destroy the throne and the temple which
represent His presence on Mount Zion – they, of course, bear
His name Yahweh, and there He is indeed Yahweh as well
as Adonai (vv. 6, 8). From Yahweh too had come the original
word that had warned this could happen one day (v. 17). But
the suffering City feels she has lost the old relationship and
can only cry out to Adonai (vv. 18-19).

The words which the Writer puts into the City's mouth in
verses 20-22 do remind her that this is still in fact Yahweh as
well as Adonai with whom she must plead. The consequences
of His original covenant will in the end override the
consequences of her sin.

Two lamentable cries of distress (3:1-66)

Like the first two songs, this third one has a three-line stanza
for each letter of the alphabet; it differs from them in that

17 Exodus 3:17; v. 15 here, with Psalm 48:2; 2 Chronicles 6:5-6.

it numbers every line, not every third line (hence 66 verses instead of 22), and begins all three lines of each stanza, not just its first line, with the letter in question.

There is another difference. While this chapter is an acrostic, it is not a palindrome. For one thing, there is no noticeable link between stanzas 1 and 22, stanzas 2 and 21, and so forth. For another, its midpoint, between the eleventh (*kaph*, vv. 31-33) and the twelfth (*lamed*, vv. 34-36), is in no way the kind of hinge that we have found in each of the two previous songs, drawing attention to something of central importance. Attempts are generally made, therefore, to find in this song a structure which has more to do with a train of thought and a development of theme than with the pattern of the poetry.

It does seem curious, though, that with such an accomplished use of both the acrostic and the palindromic forms in the first two songs, the Writer should here extend the one but abandon the other. In fact he creates something which is in a way even more elaborate, yet makes very good sense.[18] If we regard the chapter's midpoint not as a hinge, but simply as a division into two halves, *each half* turns out to have a central hinge. Five stanzas (vv. 1-15), then the sixth (*waw*, vv. 16-18), then five more (vv. 19-33); and again, five stanzas (vv. 34-48), then a sixth (*ayin*, vv. 49-51), then five more (vv. 52-66). We might think that such a preoccupation with poetic form would clog the flow of the Writer's passionate words; in fact, it channels it.

Unrelieved 'affliction' (v. 1) is the burden of the first five stanzas. They are a catalogue of sufferings – darkness, injury, imprisonment, chains, obstruction, wild beasts, arrows, ridicule, some literal, some metaphorical, and in no sort of order. And something else catches the eye. The Writer introduces himself in a way almost unique in Bible poetry: 'I am the man who …'. The words are so personal, yet so tantalizing – he both does, and does not, tell us who he is! We ask, like the Ethiopian eunuch in Acts 8:34, 'Does the prophet say this about himself, or about someone else?' And

---

18 John L. Mackay, *Lamentations* (Tain: Mentor 2008), pp. 19 and 123, following Johan Renkema's 'The Literary Structure of Lamentations (I-IV)', in *The Structural Analysis of Biblical and Canaanite Poetry*, JSOT-Sup 74, ed. Van der Meer and de Moor (Sheffield: JSOT Press 1988).

in the same breath, and in the same way, his antagonist too is introduced but not identified: simply 'he'.

What do this anonymous 'I' and 'he' have to do with the modern reader? At the time of writing, 'I the man' could have meant Jerusalem, or (since the City is regularly feminine) some representative citizen of it, or Judah the kingdom or Israel the nation (God's firstborn son).[19] The 'he' who has assailed him would then be the Babylonian invaders in 589–586 B.C. Or 'I' could have been Jeremiah, complaining about his enemies, fellow Israelites, at the court of King Zedekiah. Thus far, the modern parallel to 3:1-15 could be the reaction of any sufferer to any tormentor.

But the hinge stanza (vv. 16-18) reveals who the tormentor is. And lo and behold, it is Yahweh himself. These afflictions are 'the rod of *his* wrath'. The world of this song could be our world, with believers and unbelievers alike blaming God for the woes that afflict us.

The Writer hurries on, however, by way of the hinge, to the remaining five stanzas of this half (vv. 19-33), and at once the mood changes. Here is to be found the most (indeed for many readers the only!) memorable passage in the book, and from verse 23 come the opening words of not one but two of our classic English hymns, John Keble's 'New every morning' and Thomas Chisholm's 'Great is thy faithfulness.' It is not that the Writer's affliction has been erased from his mind; another of our hymns speaks of 'sinners whose love can ne'er forget the wormwood and the gall.'[20] But the four-times-repeated name, Yahweh, brings hope and confidence and peace of heart: 'Though he cause grief, he will have compassion … He does not willingly afflict,' as in ways that we may find puzzling and painful He carries forward plans that are more complex and more far-reaching, and (as I suggested earlier) not only bigger but better, than we can for the present understand.

From this point the second half of the song unfolds. Here, the first five stanzas survey the evil in our world, not now as we see it but as God sees it. Injustice is cited as an example of the bad things of which men are guilty and God disapproves (vv. 34-36). Punishment too is a 'bad thing', that is, a painful

---

19 Exodus 4:22.

20 Edward Perronet, 'All hail the power of Jesus' name.'

one; but in this case they deserve it and God inflicts it (vv. 37-39). In these stanzas, *lamed* and *mem*, he is Adonai, the Sovereign Lord of all nations. Then the Writer becomes a spokesman for the City; God is now Yahweh, the City's God, and in the next three stanzas the evil in view is first the City's sin, far less excusable than that of the world at large (*nun*), then God's anger against that sin (*samech*), and finally the destruction of the City (*pe*).

Like the first half of the song, this one hinges on a cry to Yahweh. Again the Writer testifies that there is no one else to whom he can turn in his distress. When he cried out like this in the *waw* stanza (v. 18), he was given a sight of the loving purposes of God that will infallibly come to pass in spite of all the temporary triumphs of evil. Should not God's answer to the cry of the *ayin* stanza (v. 50) be even more reassuring? Will it not show him again, in the words of William Cowper, 'the blessedness I knew when first I saw the Lord'?[21]

The answer, apparently, is no. The last five stanzas of Lamentations 3 seem very far from the 'soul-refreshing view' that both the English poet and the Hebrew poet are hoping for. As the psalmists find, the ups and downs of spiritual experience often come in that order, and similarly the author of these songs, uplifted by the reassurances of verses 19-33, is well and truly cast down again in verses 52-66.

Yet stand back from the song, look at it as a whole, compare verses 52-66 now with verses 1-15, and you will realize that there is after all something palindromic about it, a correspondence between its end and its beginning; for each is about the afflictions that beset the Writer. There is, however, a profound difference. Stanzas 1-5 move towards the Yahweh of their hinge stanza (vv. 16-18) without ever calling Him by that name; nonetheless it is 'He', it is this God, who by 'the rod of his wrath' is causing all 'my' sufferings. In contrast, as stanzas 18-22 move on from the Yahweh of *their* hinge stanza (vv. 49-51) the name is repeatedly appealed to; it is not He who is the enemy here.

Could the Writer be Jeremiah? The prophet's book does not specifically mention the stone or the waters of verses 53-54, but such words could certainly stand for the kinds of

---

21 William Cowper, 'O for a closer walk with God.'

persecution that he did suffer in the last days of Jerusalem. He would in that case be speaking in the opening verses on behalf of the City, weeping with those who weep, in distress as the Babylonians punish her; and then speaking on his own account in the closing verses, in distress as the Israelite establishment torments him. She is being punished for her sins, he is being tormented for his faithfulness. Yahweh is both causing the first and allowing the second. But the 'soul-refreshing view' which actually is there, beyond all this affliction, the future and the hope that we shall find in due course at the heart of the prophet's book,[22] is for Jeremiah in his pit, not for Zedekiah in his palace.[23]

A lamentable loss of privileges (4:1-22)

The Writer of the fourth song may or may not have written the first three, for though we have here another acrostic on the same subject, this one is much simpler. Each verse has only two lines, each letter of the alphabet begins only one of them, and there is little sign of anything palindromic, unless we are meant to see it in the naming of the City, which (almost) brackets each half of the song: verses 2 and 11, verses 12 and 22. That seems to be the limit of its sophistication; except that when so divided, the two halves do give a stereoscopic view, as it were, of the downfall of the City. The first half pictures the misery of the citizens, and the second half the failure of their leaders. And the events to which they refer seem to be those of one particular day, or at most one particular week; for King Zedekiah has been captured trying to escape as the City falls to her besiegers (vv. 19-20), but no aid has yet come to the children starving in her streets (v. 4).

The children 'beg for food', and beg in vain, in the City that once 'feasted on delicacies' (v. 5). Verses 1-11 are all about that kind of sharp decline from prosperity to penury. Where once there was feasting, now there is begging; once gold, now earthenware; once finery, now ashes; once beauty, now disfigurement. This is more than simply a catastrophic downturn in the kingdom's fortunes. This is Yahweh

---

22 Jeremiah 29:11.

23 'Pit' in Psalm 28:1 and several later psalms (most notably 88:3-7) is the same word as 'cistern' in Jeremiah 38:6ff.

depriving it of precisely the gifts that went with the land He had promised to His people if they would believe and obey Him.[24] They have not done so, and now they have to learn that sin has consequences. The City deserves to die. Death in the sudden overthrow of Sodom (v. 6) or by an enemy's sword in battle (v. 9) would have been a great deal easier and quicker than this protracted agony, but a great deal less educational. It was the privileges of Yahweh's chosen people that were being taken away, and they must ask themselves why.

This lesson should have been painfully obvious. But something else lay beyond it, which emerges in the second half of the song. Everyone, even 'the kings of the earth' (v. 12), knew of Yahweh's guarantee to preserve Jerusalem against all comers; why then had He broken His word? Undoubtedly the primary reason was that the City, representing the nation of Israel, had broken her side of the agreement, as we have just seen. But against this accusation she now makes a defence of sorts. Even if she cannot shift the blame entirely, she aims at least to share it. Her prophets and priests have been greatly at fault, failing her in their duty of leadership, and she repudiates them (vv. 13-16). Her friends in Egypt are berated because they did not come as she hoped they would (v. 17), her enemies from Babylon are berated because they *did* come, as she hoped they would not (v. 18), and I think it is still she who finally rounds on her neighbours and kinsmen in Edom (v. 21): 'You may laugh' (she is angry at Edom's gloating over the fall of Jerusalem, which is the theme of the book of Obadiah), 'but before long you will be suffering as we are now.'

Such a tirade, reeking of impudence, is no doubt very reprehensible (though also very understandable). But though as the Writer presents her she may be trying to justify herself by blaming everybody else, what she says is nothing but the truth, and top of her hit list are the self-seeking religious leaders of verse 13. The people of Israel had long enjoyed the privilege of living in security in a land of plenty, 'a good land ... flowing with milk and honey,'[25] and that had now been taken from them; but so had the greater privilege of being watched over and guided by leaders through whom the

---

24 Deuteronomy 8:6-18; 2 Chronicles 1:11f., 7:19-22.
25 Exodus 3:8.

ever-relevant word of Yahweh their God was regularly made known to them. Of all these, prophet, priest, and king, they had now been deprived. The people's indignation with their leaders, cursing them like lepers ('Away! Unclean!', v. 15), rings hollow; the pot is calling the kettle black. The leaders have misled the people, but the people have been more than willing to be misled.

If much of this second half of the song is a bitter and anguished cry put into the mouth of the City, the 'daughter of Zion', its final verse takes us back behind the scenes, where the Writer foresees an end to her suffering, and a brighter future than she either imagines or deserves.

A lamentable lack of prospects (5:1-22)

For most who have survived both the siege and the sack of Jerusalem, however, the future seems far from bright. The last chapter of Lamentations belongs to them, and to the days and months that follow those terrible events. Again there are 22 verses of poetry, but that is practically the only similarity between this song and its predecessors. Here we have no acrostic, no palindrome, shorter verses, fewer metaphors; no frills. It is as though the Writers of these songs have led us along a series of gloomy but ornate thoroughfares, to bring us finally into a dreary, unlovely street, unadorned by any poetic tricks, that stretches ahead into even deeper gloom.

For all its artlessness, this fifth song may, however inexactly, fall of its own accord into the now-familiar palindromic pattern, and in doing so it points the way towards the hope of which we caught a glimpse in 4:22. Notice the pronouns strung out along these twenty-two verses. A paragraph at its midpoint (vv. 11-14) is about 'them', that is, the remnant left 'in the cities of Judah', disrespected and abused by the invaders and their allies. Before that (vv. 2-10) and after it (vv. 15-18), it is 'we' who are equally the objects of this oppression. And the song begins (v. 1) and ends (vv. 19-22) with 'you', namely Yahweh. You, we, they, we, you.

There is no denying that this is the bleakest chapter of a bleak little book. It may recall the frame of mind in which 'the words of Job are ended', before Yahweh finally responds to the prolonged and bitter complaints of His suffering

servant.[26] Among the Psalms we may be reminded, not so much of Psalm 22 ('My God, my God, why have you forsaken me?'), since that ends with praise, as of Psalm 88, which literally ends in darkness.

However, the Writer of the fourth song took up the mention of Edom in 4:21 to comfort the City with the promise of 4:22: there was a punishment still in store for Edom, because of her hatred of Zion, but Zion's punishment had, for that time at any rate, been 'accomplished'. Its effects would rumble on, certainly; but a new chapter was opening in the story of God's people. They should bear that in mind, says Lamentations, as the limited view of the fifth song can see only their present afflictions. For Yahweh is there, and they know it; there in its first and last verses, hemming them in behind and before, says Psalm 139:5, the Alpha and the Omega, says Revelation 1:8. And they do at any rate believe in him sufficiently to talk to Him, even if His answers are a long time coming. Out of this present death will come a resurrection. The Book of Jeremiah is about to take us in painful detail through the necessary process of dying, to help us understand and appreciate something of the promise of new life.

---

26 Job 31:23, 40.

2

The View from Anathoth
(Jeremiah 1)

A very long book

However eager the Christian convert might be to explore the holy book of his new-found faith, he would be unlikely to find the various individual books within it to be uniformly engaging. All Scripture is profitable, certainly[1] (that conviction increases with experience), but one still has one's preferences; I personally feel more at home with Scriptures that have a plot-line, like the Gospels, or a poetic shape, like the Psalms, than with a 'miscellaneous' book like Proverbs, where plot and shape are not to be expected.

It is I think for this reason that only now, after a good many years in the preaching ministry, am I at last getting to grips with Jeremiah. The man, of course, is hugely impressive; and you could say the same about his book, except that though you may be lost in admiration as you approach this massive edifice, you find yourself lost in a more obvious sense when you get into it and start trying to find your way around. The trouble is, there is just so much of it: not only in quantity, but also in variety and complexity. There are chapters about Jeremiah, and chapters by Jeremiah; prophecies sometimes spoken, sometimes written; warnings before the event, laments during it, reflections after it; prose and poetry, biography and history; and all in a very peculiar sort of order. Not surprisingly, the book has given rise to years of debate

---

1 2 Timothy 3:16.

about plot and shape – who wrote what, and when, and why
it was put together as it was, and how (as some think) it might
with advantage be rearranged.

My hope is that in approaching these fifty-two chapters as
they lie before us in their present form, I and readers like me,
for whom they are to some extent 'fresh woods and pastures
new', may grasp something of their geography, not just
of their flora and fauna. I notice, for example, the very first
statement from the mouth of God about what Jeremiah is to
be: a prophet to the nations (1:5). Imagine you have already
worked your way through the whole book, and are now
starting again; you will be aware that in the middle of it, in
chapter 25, that verse is taken up and amplified, and that at
the end of it, no fewer than six chapters (46–51) are given over
to the same theme, Jeremiah as a prophet to the nations. Might
these be three hooks on which the whole vast tapestry hangs?
I hope you are as eager as I am to see how such possibilities
work out.

Many nations
The Book of Lamentations, and the horrors that will give
rise to it, are still forty years in the future when the Book of
Jeremiah opens. It is not they that dismay the young man here
at the outset, since he has no notion that they are on their way;
it is the alarming call that has come to him in the days of King
Josiah, 'in the thirteenth year of his reign,' 627 b.c. – this word
from God, that he is to be 'a prophet to the nations'.

Everyone in that ancient world knows what a prophet is.
Every nation has its gods, and every god has his prophets,
human voices that speak on his behalf. Josiah's people are no
exception. They look back to the towering figure of Moses,
through whom 800 years ago the tribes of Israel were forged
into a nation, and more recently to the scarcely less imposing
figure of Samuel, through whom the nation became a kingdom.
Each was a mouthpiece for Yahweh, the God of Israel, and
so have been their successors, a line of prophets throughout
the kingdom years whose words have been Yahweh's words,
guiding or rebuking or encouraging the line of kings who
have ruled Israel in His name from His city Jerusalem.

Jeremiah is well aware how the role of Yahweh's prophets has expanded over the years. When the kingdom split in two in 930 B.C., its northern half abandoned the rulers of Yahweh's choice and the worship of Yahweh's temple, but could not escape the words of Yahweh's prophets. There have always been regular prophetic messages for the royal line of David in the south, but also, since the partition, Amos has been sent with his message from the south to the north, and Hosea actually belongs in the north, as do Elijah and Elisha. Obadiah's message will be for Edom, which is outside both the Israelite kingdoms, Jonah's has been for the capital city of Assyria, Daniel's will be for the kings of Babylon. But God intends to speak to a wider audience yet, for Jeremiah is to prophesy not to this or that particular nation, but to 'nations' in the plural (1:5), indeed to 'all the nations' (25:15).

The challenge becomes all the more daunting when you consider where, and to whom, it is being presented – the place and the person. Anathoth is an insignificant village, an hour's walk over the hills northwards from Jerusalem, hardly mentioned in the Bible except in connection with Jeremiah. What another prophet, Micah, has said about another village, Bethlehem, not far beyond the city on its opposite side, applies here too: that one 'little … among the clans of Judah,'[2] this one little among the clans of Benjamin. Yet 'from you', says God to that other little place, 'shall come … one who is to be ruler in Israel.' Such is His regular practice: He chooses 'the lowly things of this world and the despised things … so that no one may boast before him.'[3]

And the same applies also, of course, to His choice of person. Others before Jeremiah have reacted to a similar call in a similar way, with dismay, if not horror. Here is Gideon: 'What, me? The most unimportant person in the weakest clan in the tribe?' Here is Moses: 'No, no, Lord – *please* send somebody else.'[4] So now Jeremiah: 'I do not know how to speak, for I am only a youth' (1:6). The word for 'youth' is not at all specific – it need mean nothing more than a younger man rather than an older one – but clearly Jeremiah, at eighteen or

2 Micah 5:2.
3 1 Corinthians 1:28f. (NIV).
4 Judges 6:15; Exodus 4:13. (GNT)

thereabouts, feels he lacks the maturity, or the experience, or the standing in the community, that must surely be required for such a task. Again, not so. The more unpromising the human tool, the more we admire the divine Workman. God will give this diffident youngster the words to speak: he has simply to speak them.

Three kings

My friend David leads a dedicated team of 'prophets', who having received the Word of God now proclaim it to the nations. They don't have to travel in order to do so (though David has in fact travelled widely, following up their ministry), because they are the staff of a Christian radio station, and modern technology reaches the parts that Jeremiah's preaching could not possibly have reached in the seventh century b.c. For much of his ministry it must have seemed that a message intended for 'all nations' was being heard by only one nation, and indeed by only half of that: the people of Israel as represented now by the kingdom of Judah, during the reigns of Josiah, Jehoiakim and Zedekiah (1:1-3).

If, as is likely, he was born in the last days of King Manasseh (who died in 642 b.c.), his life actually spanned the reigns of seven kings, not three – more, so far as we know, than that of any other prophet.[5] Manasseh's long reign of wickedness had sealed the fate of the kingdom. A royal change of heart towards the end of it could not mend matters, and must have alienated Amon, his son and heir, who had seen eye to eye with the old unregenerate Manasseh, and who as soon as he had the chance set Judah on the downward slope again. Fortunately, after only two years Amon's reign was brought to a sudden end by an assassin, and his little son Josiah found himself on the throne at the age of eight. Arguably the best and the greatest of all David's successors, Josiah would share the ideals of Jeremiah, who was only a few years his junior; though each ploughed his own furrow in pursuing those ideals, as we shall see.

---

5 The main biblical sources for the period are 2 Kings 21–25 and 2 Chronicles 33–36. For a narrative account of these seven reigns as part of the history of the Hebrew monarchies, see my *In the Days of the Kings* (Tain: Christian Focus, 2010).

His death in battle in 609 marks the point at which Judah was finally and fatally ensnared in the power politics of the Middle East. Assyria, which had destroyed the northern kingdom of Israel a hundred years before, was now in decline, and was threatened by Babylon, the 'new kid on the block'; an Egyptian army went to Assyria's aid; Josiah, keen to see the power of the Assyrians broken, tried to stop it, and perished in the attempt. Jehoahaz, one of his sons, was enthroned in his place. But as Judah had interfered with the Egyptian pharaoh's march north, the pharaoh had good reason to interfere in Judah's affairs on his way home; he removed Jehoahaz, taking him into exile in Egypt, and replaced him by his more pro-Egyptian brother Jehoiakim. After an eleven-year reign the latter died, and the crown passed to his young son Jehoiachin. By now the Babylonians were in the ascendant, and it was their turn to interfere. Led by their king Nebuchadnezzar, they invaded Judah, capturing Jerusalem, taking young Jehoiachin into exile, and replacing him with his uncle, Josiah's remaining son Zedekiah. This last king of the line of David made the ill-advised decision, a few years later, to change sides and throw in his lot with Egypt again, which brought Nebuchadnezzar back from Babylon to deal with the troublesome little kingdom once and for all.

This brief overview of a sequence of seven kings serves a double purpose. First, it provides us with an outline 'map' of those sixty years, and some notion of who was who and what happened when. Beyond that, much more importantly, it helps us to see what it meant for Jeremiah to be a prophet in those times, and what we can learn from him in our own times. For we have to get right away from the idea that he (or any other of Yahweh's prophets) was a kind of astrologer producing horoscopes for a regular column in the *Jerusalem Times*, for readers eager to know what was going to happen in the week to come. Certainly he foretold the future; but he did not do it to order, or in detail, or with much concern for the how or the when of the events that lay ahead. His prophecies were many and frequent, but even so there would have been times when the prophetic voice was silent.[6] Sometimes I travel in my brother-in-law's car along a route known to me but not

---

6 The persistence noted in 25:3 does not imply non-stop talk.

to him. He has no need for a running commentary on what
we shall see round every next bend; my navigating should
consist of little more than 'Carry on to the next roundabout,
then take the third exit,' or even simply 'Follow this road until
I say otherwise.' Apart from that sort of guidance, all that
Judah needed to know were the rules of the road and the lie of
the land – how to drive, and where to aim for – and Yahweh's
prophets had been telling His people those things ever since
the days of Moses.

So we may picture Jeremiah – feeling so inadequate (1:6),
but the word, when it came, was a fire in his bones that he
could not hold in (20:9) – constrained to speak on a variety
of occasions, but particularly in 627, in the middle of Josiah's
reign; in the winter of 604, to Jehoiakim; and in the countdown
to the final disaster of 586, to the wretched Zedekiah. These
were the three kings of 1:1-3, leaders of the nation to which
the prophet's message would come first, on its way to the
nations, all the nations, that lay beyond their frontiers. Good
King Josiah, who had already been on the throne for thirteen
years when the prophet began his ministry, had eighteen more
to go; it was not he, but his people, who needed the message,
for without their heartfelt repentance all his zealous reforms
would count for nothing. Bad King Jehoiakim, through eleven
years of misrule, cared not at all for his father's principles,
or for Yahweh, or Yahweh's word, or Yahweh's people, and
loathed Jeremiah and all he stood for. Weak King Zedekiah
could never quite bring himself to do what he knew was
right, and was pulled in different directions by advisers more
strong-minded than he was, through another eleven years that
brought the kingdom finally to ruin. Jeremiah was a prophet
of warning for Josiah (or rather for Josiah's people – the king
knew very well what the score was); a prophet of doom
for Jehoiakim, who would heed no warnings; and, perhaps
surprisingly, a prophet of hope for Zedekiah, except that it
was a forlorn hope, because Zedekiah could not make up his
mind to close with the offer. So, it seemed, the dream of an
everlasting Davidic kingdom centred on Zion, the eternal city
of the Great King, was after all only a dream, and on August 17
in year 586 B.C., as Jerusalem went up in flames, it died.[7]

---

7 See footnote 6, p. 230.

All that, however, we know from hindsight. During those forty years, Jeremiah, like everyone else, had to live a day at a time, and we have to learn to live, as he did, holding in tension what we know of the overall plan of God, the big picture, and what we experience in the actual events of everyday life, where His methods and His timing are so often different from what we expect.

Two visions
Almond trees would have been a familiar sight around Anathoth, and perhaps Yahweh drew young Jeremiah's attention to a particular almond branch, as a picture of one aspect of the message he was to pass on first to Israel and then to 'all the nations'; and perhaps Yahweh in the same way caused the young man to notice something else equally unremarkable, a cooking pot bubbling over a fire, and invested that too with prophetic meaning. On the other hand, He was just as likely to have given Jeremiah the kind of visions with which Zechariah's prophecy abounds, or the kind of dreams which Daniel was called to interpret. How the newly appointed prophet 'saw' the two signs is neither here nor there. They were imprinted on his mind, together with the meanings that Yahweh gave them; for a God-given sign will always have a God-given word to explain it.

Unlike Peter Bell in the poem ('A primrose by a river's brim A yellow primrose was to him, And it was nothing more'),[8] every Israelite knew that the almond was more than a nut tree; in Hebrew it was called a 'wake-tree', because its blossoms were the first to awaken after the winter's sleep. And a boiling pot beginning to tip, as the fire on which it is perched begins to settle, obviously threatens danger.

Whether or not the two visions came to Jeremiah in quick succession, they are together here at the beginning of the book, and together they set the tone for all that follows. Here in chapter 1 Yahweh explains their immediate meaning for the prophet. First the almond: if Manasseh's sins had sealed Judah's fate, why was the kingdom not only surviving, but even being blessed by the rule of the godly Josiah? Or conversely, if it had after all been reprieved, why the threat

---

8 William Wordsworth, *Peter Bell*.

of the boiling pot? Does God really know what He's doing? Yes, says Yahweh; I am awake, and aware, and overseeing all these events, bad and good, to bring about my own purposes. And secondly, the pot: before very long it *would* tip, and tip from the north, to flood the land with its scalding contents. Egyptian armies had occasionally attacked the Israelites from the south, but the days when Egypt was their first great enemy were long gone; their nation had since become a kingdom, and the kingdom's last enemy would come from the north, Babylonians completing what Assyrians and Arameans (and even Philistines, going the long way round and swooping southwards to destroy King Saul)[9] had begun.

But the 'blossoming twig and the boiling caldron' will be a picture of Jeremiah's entire ministry and of its ongoing relevance. In the words of George Adam Smith a century ago, it was, and is, 'all blossom and storm, beauty and terror, tender yearning and thunders of doom … While the caldron of the North never ceased boiling out over his world … he never, for himself or for Israel, lost the clear note of his first Vision, that all was watched and controlled … Be the times dark and confused as they may, and the world's movements ruthless, ruinous and inevitable, God yet watches and rules all to the fulfilment of His Will – though how, we see not.'[10]

One God

It is the pot whose meaning is spelt out at once (vv. 13-16). Jerusalem in particular is threatened by it, besieged and assaulted more than once in the past but never yet conquered, let alone destroyed. Jeremiah has only to walk up the road from his village to come within sight of the city's skyline, still intact, still a heart-stirring spectacle. But now his eyes are opened to the unthinkable prospect of holy Zion becoming a smoking ruin. When the pot pours out its contents, that will be the view from the hill above Anathoth. The village itself will surely have no more chance of survival than a sandcastle in a tsunami. Yahweh's words hammer home the totality, the finality, of the coming destruction: all the kingdoms, all the

---

9 1 Samuel 29–31.

10 George Adam Smith (1924), *Jeremiah*, 3rd ed. (London: Hodder & Stoughton), p. 87.

kings, in an assault on all Jerusalem's walls, all Judah's towns, all the land's inhabitants (vv. 14-15). Make no mistake, this is His doing; and the cause is not far to seek – the people He made his own by a covenant of love and mercy and power have broken that covenant, and forsaken Him for other gods (v. 16).

Before and after the prophecy of the boiling pot, this mind-stretching first chapter of Jeremiah's book makes two other predictions of tremendous moment. Already the young man has been appointed 'a prophet to the nations', with a commission that shows clearly how Yahweh is just as much in control of peoples who are not in covenant relationship with Him, and of their rise and fall, as He is in control of His own people Israel (vv. 5, 9-10). In our modern world, we may be sure that He calls the tune not only in the so-called 'Christian West' but also in the Moslem world of the '10-40 window', and in lands where other religions and ideologies seem to dominate; and closer to home, not only in the increasingly beleaguered Christian community of our own country, but throughout our increasingly secular society. As a rank outsider came to recognize, two centuries before the time of Jeremiah, 'there is no God in all the earth but in Israel.'[11] The man who confessed that truth was Naaman the Syrian, healed by one in whom he used not to believe, and the God was He who is now known, not only in Israel but all over the world, as the triune God of the Christian faith, Father, Son and Holy Spirit.

Finally, as the nations move against Judah and Jerusalem, and as Yahweh then moves against the nations, so in verses 17-19 Judah moves against Jeremiah. But unlike the others, this last is a move that will not succeed. Can the diffident young man grasp what he is hearing? Does his heart sink, or will he catch the vision? 'I make you this day a fortified city, an iron pillar, and bronze walls, against the whole land, against the kings of Judah, its officials, its priests, and the people of the land. They will fight against you, but they shall not prevail against you, for I am with you, declares the LORD, to deliver you.'

_____

11 2 Kings 5:15.

3

Judgments
(Jeremiah 2–6)

Arraignment: God puts His people on trial (2:1-37)

Discernment, criticism, trial, verdict, condemnation, sentence, punishment: all are to be found among the dictionary definitions of 'judgment'. Picture a modern courtroom, and you can readily see how these various facets of the meaning of the word apply when someone is put on trial. Many of those involved are concerned with judgment in one sense or another, whether on the bench, or in the witness box, or in the jury box, or in the well of the court, or behind the scenes.

A trial in a court of law is the background to the first of the five chapters before us, though the legal language is spelt out only in verses 9, 29 and 35 (the bringing of charges – 'contending' in the ESV – and the passing of judgment). We are shown Israel brought to trial, arraigned before the supreme court. She stands in the dock, facing Yahweh, her judge. But in this courtroom she sees His face on all sides, wherever she looks. There is a bizarre and frightening aptness in Lewis Carroll's words: 'I'll be judge, I'll be jury' (and, says Yahweh, I'll be plaintiff and I'll be prosecuting counsel as well), 'I'll try the whole cause, and condemn you to death.'[1] The words of Psalm 139:5, comforting in the context of Lamentations 5,[2] are terrifying here: He hems her in, behind and before.

---

1 Lewis Carroll, *Alice's Adventures in Wonderland*, ch. 3.
2 See p. 29

When Yahweh speaks in His role as counsel for the pros-
ecution, we must prepare to be blown away by the vehemence
of His exposure of the defendant's misdeeds. Detached and
impersonal it certainly is not. And while the picture of a law
court may be the background to what He is saying, He would
at the same time have His people confront a whole gallery
of other pictures. John Mackay[3] sees the chapter as a kaleidoscope repeatedly twisting to display new patterns, new metaphors; and first to view, in verse 2, is a wedding scene.

This is Yahweh taking Israel as His bride at the time of
the exodus. True, there was disaffection in the ranks from
the word go, but the people had at any rate been willing to
follow Moses as he led them out of their Egyptian captivity.
Having crossed the frontier into 'a land not sown', they
were rid of the discredited nature-gods of Egypt and not yet
tempted by those of Canaan; instead, sustaining them with
bread from heaven, Yahweh there showed Himself to be their
all-providing husband. Then, in the blink of an eye, where
we have just seen a wedding celebration we now see (2:3)
a harvest festival – in the wilderness! – with Israel herself as
its firstfruits, another symbol of His love and care.

Next we find God's people settled in the land of promise,
but regrettably only too ready to follow leaders who do not
appreciate that love and care (2:4-8). After that there suddenly
appears an eagle's-eye view of all the surrounding lands, from
western sea to eastern desert (vv. 9-11). No nation in any of
those lands has seen any point in changing its gods, being
well aware that all these deities are much of a muchness; only
Israel, who alone among them has had a God worth having,
has unaccountably elected to 'switch suppliers'. But in doing
so she has made a ludicrously bad bargain, in opting (2:12-
13, where the picture changes again) for a leaky cistern of her
own in place of Yahweh's unfailing spring water.

For a fleeting moment we see lions from the north and
'skull-breakers' (?) from the south attacking Israel. Such
things might happen to a slave, says 2:14, but not to Yahweh's
firstborn, surely? (for the nation which from one point of view
is His bride is also, in another metaphor, His son). Then the
water image returns to dominate 2:17-19. Egypt's Nile and

---

3 Mackay, *Jeremiah*, vol. i, p. 156.

Assyria's Euphrates are great rivers, a far cry from Israel's choice of a leaking tank, but still 'evil and bitter' compared with the living water that Yahweh would guarantee.

The kaleidoscope turns ever faster through 2:20-25: a bride becomes a prostitute, a choice vine produces useless grapes, soap fails to wash away sin, a camel runs amok, a wild she-ass's one passion is to indulge her lust, an addict denies the possibility of reforming. And a thief is caught red-handed (2:26); whereupon for three verses the masks are off, and the nation of Israel from top to bottom is seen, not now in picture-language but in actuality, abandoning Yahweh for the worship of false gods. A stick and a stone, Jeremiah rudely calls those gods; and even there Israel has no discernment, addressing the female deity as 'father' and the male one as 'mother'. One of the purposes of the coming 'time of trouble' (2:28) will be to show up these gods for the nonentities they are.

By the time we reach 2:29 we may be aware of a subtle shift in the picture language of Israel's arraignment before Yahweh. We seem to be moving out of modern Western courts of law and into courts of a different kind, the courts of kings in the ancient Middle East. In that place and time we find big empires and little nations, and every great king is likely to be overlord of many small kings; and since an overlord recognizes no authority greater than his own, there will be no impartial third party to arbitrate in disputes between him and his vassals – no judge, no jury. 'Contending' is the word in 2:29, that is, the bringing of charges, and we remember that Yahweh used the same phrase in 2:9 to describe what He would be doing throughout the chapter; but He is not now a barrister presenting a case before a judge. Instead, we should visualize the great king, the overlord, displeased with some vassal nation, sending 'a royal envoy with a statement presenting his grievances against the errant people and urging them to mend their ways... If they were open to verbal persuasion to see things their emperor's way, then this would spare him the expense and trouble of sending an army to coerce them back into line.' That is what is happening in Jeremiah 2; except that in 2:35 Yahweh already hears Israel claiming to be innocent, and responds, 'I will bring you to judgement for saying "I have not sinned."' As the quotation from Mackay continues, 'there

was no escaping the threat that punitive measures would be taken if persuasion was unavailing.'[4]

Since this chapter is the first prophecy in Jeremiah's book, it is natural to assume that it dates from the beginning of his ministry, in the middle of the reign of Josiah.[5] If this is so, it will colour the way we understand some of the things he says. As far as the great empires are concerned, Assyria's day is past, Babylon's is only just dawning, and Josiah recognizes no overlord but Yahweh. From Yahweh, therefore, comes this message, setting out His displeasure at what is going on in Israel (meaning not the northern kingdom, long since defunct, nor the remnants of its population that still live in those parts, but Josiah's kingdom of Judah, all that is now left of the original Israelite kingdom of earlier days). He hears His people protesting their innocence, but wants them instead to confess their guilt. He has no fault to find with Josiah, who is doing all that a king can do by way of reform and the changing of structures; but to the prophet's task, the preaching of repentance and the changing of hearts, he has appointed Jeremiah. The way is still open for the nation to turn from its sins. The die is not yet cast, punishment is not yet inevitable. It is prophecies of warning rather than doom that Jeremiah has to convey to Josiah's generation.

Appeal: God pleads with His people (3:1–4:4)
There has already been one kind of judgment upon Israel, in the sense of Yahweh's judging that something is very wrong in the nation, and that it has to be dealt with. If the action he takes in chapter 2 is the sending of the type of warning message just described, designed to bring Israel to her senses, it has elicited not the required confession and apology, but a profession of injured innocence, and even an impudent tit-for-tat in the bringing of counter-charges against Yahweh (2:9, 29, NIV). How unwise! Both the sister kingdoms have been here before, confronted with the might of a human overlord, and each found that an unwillingness to confess and grovel before the Assyrians brought their war-machine rolling across her frontier to the gates of her capital city, to Samaria in 722

---

4 Mackay, op. cit., vol. i, pp. 124, 141.

5 Jeremiah 25:3.

and to Jerusalem in 701. How foolish to imagine that their divine Overlord might be a softer touch.

And yet they might be excused for thinking so, for He still holds back from the kind of 'judgment' that means punishment. The reason is the relationship with which chapter 2 began; here it is again, underlying this whole passage from 3:1 to 4:4. Other Scriptures speak of God as Judge and King, and under each title in turn He addressed Israel in chapter 2; but older than her experience of Yahweh as her Judge or her King was that of Yahweh as her Husband, and here in chapter 3 He speaks as the Husband wronged.

We cannot help but notice a word that figures in some shape or form no fewer than eighteen times in these twenty-nine verses. Basically the verb 'to turn', it means sometimes 'to turn away' (English versions may translate this as 'backsliding' or 'faithlessness'), and sometimes 'to turn back' (to return, or repent). It is this second meaning that figures first in 3:1-5. Yahweh's people have repeatedly broken their marriage vows, and could scarcely expect Him to take them back as if nothing had happened, for all their impertinence in suggesting that He might (3:4-5a). But in fact Old Testament law itself forbids such a thing; once a husband and wife are divorced they may not at some later date remarry each other; divorce is permanent.

Although all these early chapters probably belong to the reign of Josiah, he may be mentioned here by name because of his efforts to reform not only his own kingdom, but also what was left of the Israelite community to its north. So Yahweh speaks in 3:6-11 as if there were still two sister-kingdoms, 'Israel' meaning the northern one. She had long since 'turned away' (that word again, seven times between verses 6 and 22), so in the end Yahweh had actually 'sent her away with a decree of divorce' (v. 8) into exile in Assyria. In other words, with the law saying that once the marriage vow was broken there could be 'No return', Israel, in no way abashed, agreed that there should be 'No return'; and even Judah, more privileged but therefore more guilty, was also saying that there would be 'No return' (v. 10).

All the more remarkable then is the passage that follows, 3:12-18. Jeremiah is given a message for the north (where

surely there is no one left to listen?), and it is a plea for the remaking of the marriage (which surely cannot happen?). Yet Yahweh says that His appeal *will* be heard, and it *will* come true, and He affirms the fact in a prophecy so awesome that even Jeremiah must have been shaken to the core as it was put into his heart and mind. A nation restored, reunited, reinvigorated, with godly leadership, and the heathen brought in (!), and the ark of God thrown out (!!), and a total change of heart? It seems Yahweh is in some unimaginable way going to overrule all the impossibilities.

Thereupon, as if to say that all this is not so far-fetched as its hearers might imagine, Yahweh goes back to the beginning, as it were, and gives a different account of Israel's turning away (3:19-20) and of the appeal that she should turn back (3:22). This now, the whole passage from 3:19 to 4:4, is the way things ought to happen. It is addressed to Israel (3:20, 23; 4:1), which now means the actual surviving Israelite nation of Josiah's time, namely the men of Judah and Jerusalem (4:3-4). To them Yahweh sets forth His past goodness (3:19a), His hope (3:19b), and His disappointment (3:20); and in this scenario they do repent and return (3:21-25), as He makes clear to them what real repentance means (4:1-4). For when the appeal of the wronged Husband finally breaks through to the conscience of His errant wife, there is no wrong that cannot be righted.

Assault: God brings punishment on His people (4:5-31)

In this next prophecy, the meaning of 'judgment' has passed beyond the weighing of evidence, beyond the pronouncing of a verdict, even beyond the passing of a sentence. When in 4:12 Jeremiah is told that God is speaking 'in judgment', he knows that this time the word means the inflicting of the penalty, the 'disaster from the north' signalled in 4:6.

Yahweh spells out the impending fate of Judah in terms that could not be plainer. The 'lion gone up from his thicket' and the 'hot wind from the desert' are the only metaphors in this prophecy. The rest of it is unvarnished, terrifying fact: the country is to be invaded, the city is to be besieged, and punishment, bitter but richly deserved, will strike the nation to its heart (4:18).

A schizophrenic experience for Jeremiah! For he is told to proclaim words of doom that come from the mouth of God, and part way through the fourteen verses of this proclamation (4:5-18), cannot help but cry out his own appalled reaction to what he himself is having to say: 'Ah, Lord GOD, … you have utterly deceived this people.' The very first thing God had said to Him, back in 1:4-6, had provoked a similar protest, and there would be many more in the years that followed.

For the modern reader, this protest (Jeremiah's interjection at 4:10) illuminates his book in two ways. It helps us to see in our mind's eye both the receiving and the recording of these prophecies. With regard to the latter, we know of Baruch's invaluable role as Jeremiah's colleague in transcribing and editing them, and we have the vivid picture of him writing down at Jeremiah's dictation, whether in Jerusalem before 586 or in Egypt afterwards, passages like this one: 'Yahweh had me say "such-and-such", and I said, "Ah, Lord, surely not?"' It brings to life the excruciating demands – for in New Testament terms this is the taking up of one's cross, to follow Christ – that may be made of any faithful servant of God.[6]

As for the original receiving of such prophecies, 4:10 seems to set this one in Josiah's reign, almost as clearly as 3:6 sets the previous one there. For Jeremiah's protest (Yahweh has promised His people that all will be well, and is now going back on that promise) looks like a reference to the message sent to the young king through Huldah the prophetess in 622: 'Because … you humbled yourself before God when you heard his words against this place and its inhabitants, … you shall be gathered to your grave in peace, and your eyes shall not see all the disaster that I will bring upon this place and its inhabitants.'[7] So God's promise in 4:10 ('It shall be well with you') would be kept, but only until Josiah's reign came to an end; then 'in *that* day' (4:9), 'at *that* time' (4:11), the disaster represented by the lion and the desert wind might be expected at any moment.

Yet still, in the event, it was delayed. Jeremiah, like so many of us, had to learn the hard way how often God tells us the 'what' of His plans, but not the 'when'. With the death

6 Luke 9:23-25, 14:25-27.
7 2 Chronicles 34:27-28.

of Josiah in 609, the picture of the final assault on Judah and Jerusalem comes to the forefront in the prophet's mind – and hangs there, menacing but unfulfilled, for the next twenty-three years!

But it is, all the same, dramatic in the extreme. The first half of the prophecy, 4:5-18, is Yahweh speaking, with the one protest by Jeremiah slotted in as 4:10, and we can read the second half similarly, but with the pattern reversed: Jeremiah speaking (4:19-31) with one interruption by Yahweh at 4:27-28. It is of a piece with so much of Lamentations: carefully constructed poetry that nevertheless pulsates with agony. Yahweh's words are powerful enough, but Jeremiah's are given an extra edge by his 'anguish' at what he hears (4:19-21) and sees (4:23-26) of the enemy's assault – the latter surely a pointer towards John's visions in Revelation.[8] Even so, we see as before a shaft of light in the gloom: 'Thus says the LORD, "The whole land shall be a desolation; yet I will not make a full end"' (4:27).

Accusation: God specifies His people's sins (5:1-31)
We shall find two more such gleams of hope in this fourth prophecy, a chapter which is otherwise dark from start to finish.

Working your way through it, you could indicate in the margin who says what, just as you can in Lamentations. Yahweh's words alternate with Jeremiah's words, with an occasional quoting of what the people of Israel are saying. More to the point is the state of affairs revealed by what is being said. 'Run to and fro through the streets of Jerusalem,' is Yahweh's command to Jeremiah, and everything the prophet sees when he does so is uniformly bad. Before the disaster of chapter 4 actually arrives, he is shown here in chapter 5 the kind of thing that is going to precipitate it.

He finds a nation that cares little for truth and right, however much it may parrot the words of those who do love such things ('As the LORD lives' is not unlike the meaningless and profane modern exclamation 'Oh my God!'); he finds the same thing among its leaders, which is even worse, because they ought to know better (5:1-5). He finds people to whom

---

8 'I looked, and behold,' as at Revelation 4:1 and then frequently.

God has given 'all things richly to enjoy'[9] despising those gifts, and instead panting after forbidden pleasures (5:7-8). He finds the traditional understanding of the words of God and His prophets contradicted (5:11-13). He finds the obvious evidences of God's power and love in the created world around us simply denied (5:20-24). He finds the powerful enriching themselves, with cruelty and injustice, at the expense of the powerless (5:25-28). He finds a society riddled from top to bottom with false beliefs about God (5:30-31).

This volley of accusations is punctuated by threat after threat of the divine anger against all such wickedness. Lion and wolf and leopard will rend the nation (5:6). The vineyard will be stripped (5:9-10). More literally, the fiery words of the prophet and then the destructive power of an invader will be deployed against Judah (5:14-19). Yahweh Himself will come with punishment and vengeance (5:29).

Many a time in the course of Christian history God's people must have felt they could read off from Scriptures like Jeremiah parallels to situations in their own world, seeing in the life of their own nation exactly the kind of thing the prophet is here describing. Many a Scripture told them not only to recognize and repent of such things in their own lives, but also to expose and combat them in the world around them. As well as being the light of that world, the church has been called to be the salt that will inhibit its decay and preserve what is good in it – to confront its evils and to engage with them.

But even so that is not the main thrust of this chapter. Here it is the church, not the world, which is under scrutiny. It is among God's people, in God's city, that Jeremiah is discovering these evils. 'It is time for judgment to begin at the household of God,' says the New Testament.[10] Since it is also true, if not explicitly biblical, that 'what the eye don't see the heart don't grieve over', Christians may well not recognize themselves as the untruthful, lustful, wilful, unjust, greedy, foolish people that Jeremiah finds in the 'streets of Jerusalem'. But it is only a matter of degree. The more devout you are, the more aware you will be of your sinfulness, and the more readily you will confess, in the words of the Prayer Book, that you

---

9 1 Timothy 6:17, (KJV).

10 1 Peter 4:17.

have erred and strayed from God's ways like lost sheep; you
have followed too much the devices and desires of your own
heart; you have offended against God's holy laws; you have
left undone those things which you ought to have done, and
have done those things which you ought not to have done,
and there is no health in you. Let today's 'Jerusalem' take note!

For the Jerusalem of Josiah's time, however, the judgment
was inevitable. In a moment, we shall look at the glimmer
of hope that we have noticed more than once, but if the city
believed that even then the threatened assault by invading
armies might be averted, it was going to be disappointed.
Yahweh had simply said, 'I will not make a full end'. That,
however, he had said – twice in this chapter, in 5:10 and 5:18,
and before that in 4:27; and even before that had come the
extraordinary promise of 3:14-18.

Assay: God puts His people through the fire (6:1-30)

Chapter 6 completes this group of five prophecies about
Yahweh's judgment on the Israel of Josiah's day. Once more
Jeremiah is given a series of vivid word-pictures, which this
time end with a new and particular kind of judging.

Prospectors in their thousands trekked westwards across
North America in the 1860s, lured by the cry 'There's gold in
them thar hills.' There was; but a man had to be sure that the
product of his digging or panning really was gold, so would
take it to the nearest assay office to have it officially tested and
certified. Of judgment in this sense Yahweh is going to speak
in 6:27-30. Along with the process of assaying goes the related
process of refining from the ore, if possible, such traces of
precious metal as might be hidden among the dross. Hence
the double picture, testing and refining, that is presented at
the end of the chapter.

The other pictures that lead up to it all have to do with
the threatened sack of Jerusalem. First a trumpet, warning
the towns of Judah of an imminent invasion from the north
(6:1). Then shepherds: not here the 'gentle shepherd' of the
New Testament,[11] but the frequent Old Testament use of
the word to mean a king, and in this case aggressive kings
coming against Zion (6:2-3). Next these invaders are heard

11 John 10:11-16.

planning their final assault: 'Straight away', says one; 'There's not enough daylight left,' objects another; 'Even better,' retorts a third, 'we'll catch them off guard with a night attack' (6:4-5).

A more thorough and certain strategy is demanded by the next voice, in 6:6-8: 'Clear the ground for the building of a siege ramp, to rise to the height of the city walls, and you can simply march in.' But which enemy is proposing this? Shockingly, the speaker is Yahweh. He who is warning His people to flee from the coming disaster is Himself telling their enemies how to bring it about.

In 6:9-12 the picture of a stripped vineyard is repeated from 5:10-11. Still Jerusalem won't listen, but still Jeremiah ('full of the wrath of the Lord,' and 'weary of holding it in') has to speak. And his message is for everyone. For the extended picture that spans the next nine verses is that of an entire people, 'from the least to the greatest' (6:13), 'parents and children together' (6:21), in dire peril. It includes some of Jeremiah's most memorable images: the empty reassurance of 'Peace, peace, when there is no peace'; the crossroads, with 'the ancient paths, where the good way lies,' clearly marked yet ignored. So the God who smoothed the way for the invader (6:6) is at the same time laying stumbling blocks before His own people (6:21).

This, says Yahweh, is what lies ahead. And in the meantime – it is to Jeremiah that He is now speaking – 'I have made you a tester and a refiner among my people' (6:27, nrsv). Gold refined in the fire is a familiar biblical metaphor,[12] and since Jerusalem was destined to go up in flames, quite literally, a quarter-century after Josiah's death, it might seem at first glance that that event, with all the attendant suffering, would be the testing and refining that are foretold here. But no. Yahweh makes it plain that the assay has begun already, and that Jeremiah is the assayer. Through the whole forty years of his ministry the word of Yahweh through him will be putting Israel to the test, judging what she is made of. Bronze (that is, copper and tin), iron and lead, all figure in the process; of gold there is no sign; the best you can hope for is silver, and even that hope will be disappointed.

---

12 Proverbs 17:3, 27:21; Isaiah 48:10; 1 Peter 1:6-7; Revelation 3:18.

4

Delusions

(Jeremiah 7–10)

The nature of the delusions (7:1–8:3)

The book's opening verses told us that the word of the Lord came to Jeremiah in the reigns of Josiah, Jehoiakim, and Zedekiah, and we shall in due course find the middle one of these three kings appearing, right on cue, in the middle of the book (26:1). But what we have before us is not a simple story, told in straightforward chronological order. It should be no surprise to find that the prophecy given there in chapter 26 figures here in chapter 7 also; there we shall see the consequences, here we see the content, of what is commonly called Jeremiah's 'temple sermon'. The later passage will tell us that Jehoiakim was king at the time, and we may take chapters 7 to 10 as belonging to his reign, with chapters 2 to 6 having been directed to the Judah of Josiah's day (3:6).

I suggested earlier that to the three kings came respectively messages of warning, doom, and hope. In a sense Judah was doomed even before Josiah came to the throne; the wickedness of Manasseh had already sealed the kingdom's fate.[1] But Josiah, with the promise that the doom would not fall in his lifetime,[2] did his kingly best to bring his people back to God before it was too late. He set up the structures so that anyone with the slightest inclination to heed the warning and repent had every opportunity to do so, while Jeremiah had

---

1 2 Kings 21:10ff., 23:26f., 24:3; Jeremiah 15:4.
2 2 Kings 22:14ff.

the prophet's task of setting before the nation the ways God's judgments worked; hence our heading for chapters 2 to 6.

Within the space of three months in the year 609, Josiah had been killed in battle, his successor Jehoahaz deported by the Egyptians, and their nominee Jehoiakim made king. The prophet was given a solemn message for the kingdom and its new ruler, which at first seemed to say nothing they had not heard before: 'Amend your ways and your deeds, and I will let you dwell in this place' (7:3). It was the old warning repeated. But two sentences in chapter 7 strike a new note as the new reign begins. In telling Jeremiah what he is to say to the nation, Yahweh has a strange further instruction for him: 'Do not pray for this people ... for I will not hear you' (7:16). The warning is to be given, but the prophet is to understand that it will not be heeded, and that Yahweh has other tasks for him than pointless praying for a kingdom which is now in fact doomed.

The other significant sentence is the key to this present section. Immediately after the warning with which He begins in 7:3, Yahweh says, 'Do not trust in *these deceptive words*: "This is the temple of the LORD"' (7:4). Note the phrase in italics. We shall feel the force of these chapters, and incidentally get closer to the original text, if we understand Him to be saying, 'Listen to the word of the Lord, and not to *the words of the Lie*.' To assume that Yahweh is bound to protect His people as long as they maintain His temple and its activities, regardless of their conspicuous lack of personal devotion to Him, is to believe a lie. It is just one aspect of *the* Lie, the great Delusion. And a range of 'these deceptive words', delusions that bedevil the life of the nation, and are sprouting everywhere now that its last godly king is no longer there to weed them out, is the theme of these four chapters.

So what exactly is the nature of these delusions?

Jeremiah is driven to speak first of what he and his hearers can see around them, then and there, in the temple (7:8-15); next, of what they would see out in the streets of the city (7:17-26); and after that, of what they would see beyond the city walls (7:30-31). They may be sure that Yahweh too has seen it; verse 11 reminds us of the almond branch, the 'wake-tree', of 1:11-12 ('I am watching'). And Yahweh begins by

bringing against those who 'stand before me in this house' – against church people, as they would be called today – the evidences of lives lived without the slightest concern for His law (7:8-10). 'You trust in deceptive words,' says the prophet, and the first such lie is that mere lip service, mere church attendance, merely going through the motions, will guarantee you God's protection, in spite of your manifold sins and your unrepentant hearts. They won't. The abandoned sanctuary at Shiloh, where Yahweh used to meet His people in the days of Samuel, and indeed the much more recent demise of 'Ephraim', that is, the northern kingdom of Israel, are evidence that He is quite prepared to pull the rug from under such presumption.

After the warning we have already noted in 7:16 (that there is no point in praying for these people), Yahweh, through Jeremiah, exposes another lie (7:17-26). Having first focused on the man in the pew, the prophet now focuses on the man in the street. On the family, in fact: Dad, Mum and the kids. Every age knows something like this group and its way of thinking. Although the ordinary citizen in those days was much more likely to be 'religious' than his modern counterpart, on this they would agree: they were not too keen on religion that was either official and formal or embarrassingly earnest. But such people would say that, of course, there are, even so, occasions when a few hazy religious notions will not seem altogether out of place. A Deity up there who might hear a prayer in an emergency, a Providence that (sometimes) looks after us, a Nemesis that finally catches up with villains, some kind of afterlife among the stars or the angels for those we have loved and lost. Such things may be brought to mind on particular occasions (Harvest, Remembrance) or by particular things (hot cross buns, Christmas trees); and in Jehoiakim's Judah there is once again a call for 'Queen of Heaven' cakes, banned under the puritanical regime of Josiah. You never know, she might grant your wishes.

It is a lie. 'Every good gift … is from above, coming down from the Father of lights,'[3] not from some trumpery pagan goddess, as is well known to every Israelite who is not wilfully deaf to the repeated message of Yahweh's prophets.

---

3 James 1:17.

Having yet again warned Jeremiah that 'You shall speak all these words to them, but they will not listen' (7:27f), Yahweh then makes the prophet's hearers face up to what they would see if they went outside the city. After the man in the pew and the man in the street, the man in the Valley of the Son of Hinnom (7:29–8:3), engaged in an unspeakably evil ceremony, claiming divine favours in return for burning his own children alive. How could anyone possibly believe that such a thing was the will of God? It was yet another lie; 'that was no command of mine, nor did it ever enter my thought,' says Yahweh.[4] The human sacrifices in the valley, and the superstitions in the city, and the hypocrisies in the temple, were all equally misrepresentations of what the God of Israel looked for from His people. Lies, all lies. And labouring under such delusions 'this evil family' (8:3) was on its way to destruction.

The cause of the delusions (8:4-17)

The message Jeremiah has brought to King Jehoiakim has thus far been an exposure of the word of the Lie, which in so many ways is corroding his nation's life. In contrast, what follows now in 8:4-17, whether these verses were part of the temple sermon at the time or were linked with it later, is very much the word of the Lord, with His name proclaimed eight times over in the course of the passage. It is bracketed between His probing of the cause of Israel's delusions (8:4-5) and His declaring of the consequence of them (8:17).

First, the Lie leads His people to make such idiotic choices (8:4-7)! Common sense dictates that when you fall down you get up again, and when you miss your turning you retrace your steps. Instinct dictates that when the season is right the birds migrate. Should not wisdom dictate that it is when the Maker's instructions are followed that the machine works properly? Should that not be the natural, the obvious, thing to do? Why then do 'all go astray as they pursue their course'?[5]

'But my people know not the rules of the LORD,' and it is precisely the leaders who are supposed both to know and to teach those rules (8:8-11) who are guilty of failing to do so: the 'scribes' appointed to that very task, and the wise, and

4 Jeremiah 7:31, (NEB).
5 Jeremiah 8:6, (JB).

the prophets, and the priests. 'They have rejected the word of the LORD, so what wisdom is in them?' With their privileged position, they are more concerned with what they can make for themselves than with what they should be doing for others, particularly in their role as teachers of truth.

So the reason why the Lie has taken such a hold is that the nation's leadership has culpably failed to guide its people according to Yahweh's word. Shameless, fruitless, hopeless, is His verdict on this kingdom of Jehoiakim's, because the truth is not being taught there; and the horses of enemy armies are snorting at its frontiers, like the hissing of a plague of venomous snakes (8:12-17).

We should remind ourselves that here, as everywhere in this complex book, we have words of Yahweh directed in the first instance to the kingdom of Judah in the final forty years of its existence, but intended also for those who for seventy years after that would endure the Babylonian exile, *and* for those of the following generation who would return to their homeland, *and* (in God's providence) for all succeeding generations down to and including those of the Christian era, to this very day. The word of the Lord, now amplified and underlined, is still the Maker's handbook. The word of the Lie, adapting itself always to suit the current situation, is as plausible as ever, and as ever offers more gratifying results by quicker and easier methods. The gurus, the opinion-shapers, those who (as a memorable prayer puts it) 'speak where many listen and write what many read', are as likely now as they were then to have unacknowledged prejudices, or faulty reasoning, or hidden agendas, for which God's people need to be constantly on the alert.

But even as in each part of this book we look for timely applications of it to the present day, we must also be aware of what it was saying to its own place and time, namely Jerusalem in the days of Jehoiakim, and of how the events of that sordid eleven-year reign have their own unique, pivotal, place in the long story of God's dealings with the human race.

The effect of the delusions (8:18–9:11)
By regarding Lamentations as an introduction, not an appendix, to Jeremiah, we already have some clue about the

kind of poetry that makes up a large part of the longer book. That will help us to grasp the rather tricky construction of this next passage, on which there is some disagreement. Of two features in particular, the more obvious one is the sharing of the lines between two or more voices, like a dialogue between actors. As in Lamentations, so here, the speaker of any particular section may be the Lord, or the writer or speaker, or the city or nation, and the question is who says what. The other feature is what we might call the 'rhyme scheme'; not in this case acrostics, let alone the modern technique of rhymed line-endings, but the chiasmus/palindrome technique of a there-and-back, ABCBA, pattern.[6]

It is surely the prophet who grieves in 8:18, and the 'daughter' in 8:19 means the people of Judah and Jerusalem. At the end of the same verse it is Yahweh who is 'provoked … to anger', while in 8:21 first the 'daughter' and then the prophet are wounded. Within the space of four verses we have both the trio of voices and the chiastic pattern: the prophet, the people, the Lord, the people, the prophet.

Though brief, this dialogue is not simple. For example: the question about the Lord being in Zion and the statement about the harvest being past – who is speaking in each case? (since the punctuation in our Bibles is a modern insertion and may change the sense intended by the original writer). And in what tone of voice? (since both 8:19b and 8:20 will sound either distraught or indignant, depending on who is supposed to be saying them).

The commentators differ, and the following suggestion is tentative, but it assumes that 8:19 is following a formula often found in Jeremiah – indeed, in two other places in this very chapter (8:4-5 and 8:22): 'Is Fact A true? Is Fact B true? Then why not Fact C?' On this showing, the little palindrome in these verses would combine 19b and 19c, as follows:

18, the prophet grieves;
    19a, the people cry;
        19bc, the LORD asks, Am I not still here? Am
        I not still King? Why then do they need all these
        other gods?
    20, the people continue to cry;
21, the prophet continues to grieve. (vv. 18-21)

6 See p. 17, footnote 6

The next triple question follows immediately, the famous 'balm in Gilead' passage. It is the last verse of chapter 8 ('Is there no balm? Is there no physician? Why then no healing?'), and it leads into chapter 9 and another heart-rending cry of distress from Jeremiah. But at 9:3 Yahweh takes over, and begins a magisterial exposé of the effects of the great Delusion. This verse is His first declaration: because these people refuse to recognize Him (though He is still as real and as present as ever), the Lie spreads its contagion throughout the land.

The second declaration (9:4-6) opens up the first. As a result of those original delusions about Judah's relationship with her God, no human relationship can be relied on either; every lie breeds another; everyone is busy building a whole culture of deceit, till they themselves are sick of it and yet refuse the only one who can save them from it. They find the world is vain, yet from the world they break not free, as the old hymn says.[7]

It will not have escaped the careful reader that to Yahweh's eye the attitude of His people is thoroughly ambivalent. They are crying out in distress, the victims of misfortune and of the sins of others. Yet at the same time they wilfully persist in ignoring Him and flouting His wishes, richly deserving punishment and vengeance at His hands. The distress will become more evident as the doom of the kingdom draws nearer and is finally seen to be inescapable, but the sin has been there from the start, never repented of. Such is His third declaration (9:7-11), as He speaks again of the assaying and refining process that He decreed for the nation at the end of chapter 6; and He gives Jeremiah advance warning of what in less than twenty years' time will be the view from Anathoth: 'Jerusalem a heap of ruins.'

The delusions blown away (9:12-26)

At 9:12 we find another of those triple questions ('Who …? Who …? Then why …?'). This time there is a new twist. Here the questions are not rhetorical; they expect answers. 'Who has been given a mind to grasp this message of doom?' Answer: Jeremiah the prophet. 'Who has been given ears to hear, and a voice to declare, what Yahweh has said?' Answer: again, Jeremiah the prophet. 'So tell us then, Jeremiah, why

---

7 Henry Twells, 'At even, when the sun was set.'

the devastation of the land?' And the answer to that is the one given now by Yahweh through the mouth of His servant, and set out forthwith in seven powerful declarations.

Yahweh says first that this nation has made a choice, a fateful choice, between two kinds of God (9:13-14). The first kind has been there through her whole history, setting His law before her daily as an ever-fresh guide to holy, happy living. Note that there is only one of Him, and in English we spell Him with a capital G. Of the other kind there are many. In some times and places they are the gods Jeremiah is going to ridicule in chapter 10; increasingly in our times they are also impersonal ideologies and philosophies. Their devotees betray either a lazy mind, swallowing uncritically 'what their fathers taught them', or an arrogant spirit, 'following their own hearts'. Such has been the choice of these who – what irony! – were chosen so long ago, and blessed over so many years, by the God they now reject.

Yahweh says secondly that such people will find life increasingly bleak, their souls envenomed and their communities fragmented (9:15-16). Both inwardly and outwardly, in spirit and in circumstance, they will experience what Yahweh calls the poison and the sword. And it is from Him that these afflictions will come, so that to be rescued from such things they would need to beg mercy – again, the same irony – from the very God they do not acknowledge.

Yahweh says thirdly that as such afflictions increase it should become obvious that Judah is dying (9:17-19), for when the professional mourners are called in, a funeral is in the offing. What is meant by this imminent 'death' is the downfall of the kingdom, the devastation of the country and the deportation of the people.

Yahweh's fourth word (9:20-21) gives the mourners the text of their laments, spelling out that this will indeed be the 'last enemy',[8] death now in the literal sense, no longer lurking out of sight in discreet cemeteries, but invading their streets and rising like a flood to burst into their homes. And as his fifth word says (9:22), slaughter in the towns will be matched by slaughter in the countryside; so the coming 'death' of Judah

---

8 1 Corinthians 15:26.

means the actual killing of thousands in her own land as well as the exile of thousands more in another.

The next paragraph is both topped and tailed by the 'Yahweh's word' formula (9:23-24), and there is something else distinctive about it to which we shall have to return in a moment. First, we have here a *verb. sap.*, a word to the wise, which should remind us of the two previous references to wise people in these chapters. We saw in 8:8-10 that those with a reputation for wisdom were precisely those who had been disseminating the word of the Lie, the 'deceptive words' of 7:4. But 9:12 has reminded us that there is at least one man in Jerusalem 'so wise that he *can* understand' what is going on, namely Jeremiah. He it is who is now, for the sixth time in this chapter, speaking truth over against all the lies. The wisdom given to him is no grounds for conceit, any more than power or riches would be (further delusions under which so many of his contemporaries are labouring); in fact it often places on him a burden that is grievous to bear. Yet at the same time what a privilege to know this Lord, the source of all 'steadfast love, justice, and righteousness'! These things belong to His unchangeable character, and they, it goes without saying, will survive the disasters Jeremiah has had to foretell.

And so will the prophet himself. He will not have forgotten what Yahweh said to him at the time of his call: that as the kingdoms of the north attack Judah, and as the powers-that-be in Judah attack him, it is he, of all Yahweh's servants the most diffident and self-effacing, who will stand firm, 'a fortified city, an iron pillar … They shall not prevail against you, for I am with you, declares the LORD' (1:13-19).

Not all, then, will perish in the doom that awaits the kingdom of the Lord in its political Old Testament form. Yahweh's sixth word has specified who will survive that judgment, namely the one who with true heart-commitment 'understands and knows' him (9:24).[9] And his seventh and last word (9:25-26) is the other side of the same coin, specifying who will *not* survive. Its focus on circumcision may seem

---

9 Derek Kidner in *The Message of Jeremiah* (Leicester: IVP, 1987) quotes on p. 55 the rendering of C. F. Keil in his 1872 commentary: '"Having understanding, and knowing me" … brings out the distinction between the two verbs, and avoids the impression that we can "understand" God.'

a little peculiar; but that rite, which would come to be regarded as the proud distinguishing mark of a Jew, was in fact shared by some of Israel's pagan neighbours in Old Testament times, showing that the physical sign was not in itself a guarantee of God's favour. As Paul would later say, true circumcision is not 'merely outward and physical'; it must be 'circumcision of the heart'.[10] Lacking any true commitment to Yahweh, the Judah of Jehoiakim's day was as 'uncircumcised in heart' as Egypt or Moab; and that was why it was doomed.

Reverting now to the sixth word (9:23-24), something about it may seem rather more significant than the fact that it is framed between a brace of 'Yahweh says' markers. For George Adam Smith, writing in the early twentieth century, this passage is one of those whose subjects 'are irrelevant to their context';[11] passages, that is, which some editorial process has shifted from where they were originally to a place where they do not seem to fit. And John Thompson spells out what he takes to be the implications, and how they apply here in the chapter before us: 'At this point in the book' (that is, at 9:23) 'the theme changes completely. The dirge gives place to some reflections on wisdom … We are dealing with an anthology of Jeremiah's utterances which an editor has brought together according to his own scheme, and it is not always possible for us now to discern his thought processes or the logic of his arrangements.'[12]

Such comments have given up too readily the attempt to make sense of the book as it stands. Jeremiah is Jeremiah – that is, in respect of both the prophet and his book, what we have is what we have, and what the God of Old Testament and New intends us to have. Yahweh, overseeing His people's progress throughout history, appointed Jeremiah to say what had to be said to them at that point in time (1:1-3), appointed Jeremiah's friend Baruch to write it down (36:4, 17-18, 32), and preserved both of them (we may bracket 1:19 with 45:5) through the last tumultuous years of the kingdom into the years of exile in Egypt, thus giving them the opportunity to complete their book. Whether or not others in later times

---

10 Romans 2:28f. (NIV); see Galatians 6:15; Philippians 3:3.

11 Smith, p. 18.

12 J. A. Thompson, *The Book of Jeremiah* (Grand Rapids: Eerdmans 1980), pp. 317f.

had a hand in editing or rearranging its contents, the Book
of Jeremiah as it finally figured in the Hebrew Bible in the
time of Christ, and as it figures today in our Christian Bible,
was vouched for by Him as 'Scripture [which] cannot be
broken'.[13] So, if I may dare to take issue with both Smith and
Thompson, nothing in this book is irrelevant to its context,
and it should be possible to discern at least something of the
thought processes, not perhaps of those who put it together,
but of the Spirit who moved them to edit the material in the
way they did. Some may think they hear a grinding of gears
as the text shifts from 'lament' mode to 'wisdom' mode at 9:23;
but should we not rather hear the voice of Yahweh integrating
the whole passage by His sevenfold declarations, a sequence
of undeniable truths that blow away all the delusions?

The gods of delusion and the God of fact (10:1-25)
'The word that came to Jeremiah from the LORD' is the phrase
with which our present section began, at 7:1. It will be repeated
at 11:1, and we may take that to be the start of the following
section; meanwhile we are finding chapters 7 to 10 bound
together by the 'delusion' theme, with the word *seqer* figuring
in each of these chapters, seven times in all.[14]

It is Yahweh's intention, through Jeremiah, to blow away
the fog of delusion, and to exhort His people to turn back
from the word of the Lie and listen instead to the word of
the Lord (not that that is likely to happen while Jehoiakim
rules Judah; remember 7:27). So He now presents Himself
as 'the true God' (10:10). A cluster of related ideas presents
itself: Israel needs to grasp that He is the God of truth, of
integrity, of reality. Perhaps best of all such near-synonyms,
in the circumstances, is that over against the gods of delusion
He should be recognized as the God of *fact*. He is, implacably
and undeniably, *there*. And as the God who, in fact, is and has
been and always will be there, He presents Himself to His
people in ways they will not be able to gainsay: as the God
of life (10:1-10), the God of creation (10:11-16) and the God of
judgment (10:17-25).

---

13 John 10:35.

14 The ESV translates it 'deceptive' (7:4, 8), 'false/falsehood/falsely' (7:9; 8:10;
9:3; 10:14), 'lies' (9:5). 'Delusion' (10:15) represents a different Hebrew word.

We notice the neat chiasmus which in chapter 10 follows the introductory verse 1: the nations (vv. 2 and 10), the making of their idols (vv. 3-4 and 9), the idols lifeless and useless (vv. 5 and 8), and at the centre Yahweh incomparable (vv. 6-7). This surely is intended to be the first section of the chapter. What would the nations mean by 'the fear of God'? They might well have a superstitious fear of what is written in the stars (10:2), and one day they will be truly terrified by what will be spoken by the Maker of the stars (10:10). But in practical terms the phrase is likely to amount to little more than a perfunctory nod, with the usual offerings, in the direction of these idols: impressive figures, no doubt, but still mere artefacts which they themselves have made. Ask what such gods can actually *do,* and you ask in vain.

Nowadays, it is only in the remotest corners of the earth that 'the heathen in his blindness bows down to wood and stone'[15]. But for millions of more sophisticated people the notion of 'God' is still a reality, even if they are neither Jews nor Christians. They believe in him, these adherents of other religions, whether or not they give him the capital G, whether he is singular or plural, and whether they call him by that name or another, or assume him as the unknown authority behind the teaching of some sage in the ancient East. The great question for all such people is, is their God *alive?* Can he speak? Can he get around? Can he *do* things – not just destructive things (as when his devotees imagine that he requires violence and cruelty from them), but positive, loving, long-term, deeply effective, miraculously good things?

The answer has to be No. In contrast, say the people of Yahweh, here is our Lord, 'the true God'; and the first big fact about Him is that 'he is the *living* God' (10:10). Unlike the idols, He has life; in fact He is life, and He gives life.

The idea of Yahweh as the giver of life moves us on towards the second part of the chapter, across the bridge provided by verse 11. A real curiosity, this: out of the 1,300-plus verses that make up Jeremiah's book, just one which is not in Hebrew but in Aramaic. No one seems to know where it came from, but it fits well enough in the context. As the chiasmus we have just been studying ends right on cue at 10:10, we may suppose this

---

15 Reginald Heber, 'From Greenland's icy mountains.'

to be perhaps a familiar Aramaic saying quoted as a lead in to the five-verse section that follows.

'Yahweh the giver of life' also prompts the thought that that is not a line of business which He has only recently taken up. 'Life from nothing began through him,' says J. B. Phillips's magnificent translation of Colossians 1:15-18, verses which apply Old Testament Scriptures like this one to our Lord Jesus Christ, and 'he is both the first principle and the upholding principle of the whole scheme of creation.' The majestic threefold statement of 10:12 places Yahweh at the beginning of all things, and it is the power that brought earth and sky into being in the first place that is in operation still, so that wind and storm sweep across our skies today because He summons them now just as He did then (10:13).

Thus the picture of Yahweh as the God of life is now expanded, with His word opening up the past for us and showing Him as that kind of God right from the start. He is, to coin a phrase, the great Initiator, the God of creation; that is the second big fact about him.

And in this respect also He speaks to our times. Increasingly the developed world is a secularized world, in which religion – religion generally, but especially the Christianity which shaped so many of its values and liberties – is first patronized, then sidelined, then in due course ridiculed and persecuted. In our society, which like an omniscient teenager knows so much better than its elders, every kind of god, including God Himself, has been dethroned. Nowadays the ultimate power is Nature (isn't she amazing?), or the Market (what unpleasant surprises will he spring on us next year?), or Sexual Fulfilment (get this right, and all your wishes will come true), or Science (the great deity, who knows everything). Obviously none of these is a person, but surely anyone with half a brain can also see that none of them is an ultimate reality! Who created 'Nature' and the rest of them? Who initiated the processes that brought them into existence? Modern man, as we are well aware, deifies them. As at Sinai, he acclaims the golden calf: 'These are your gods,' he cries, 'who brought you up out of the land of Egypt!'[16] No, they aren't. No, they didn't. The replacement 'gods' are not gods at all; they initiate nothing.

16 Exodus 32:4.

The 'images are false, and there is no breath in them. They are worthless, a work of delusion; at the time of their punishment they shall perish' (10:14-15).

So Jeremiah speaks across the centuries to our day, to tell the secular world that God is behind everything in it, and to offend half the religious world by identifying this creator God with the God of Israel, and no other (10:16).

He whom any generation may know in its own time as the living God, and who was at the beginning the creator God, will eventually also be revealed as the God of judgment; He maintains the world today by the power with which He made it on the first day and will unmake it on the last day. Of course, the final universal judgment still lies ahead, but a foretaste of it awaited Judah as the seventh century B.C. drew to a close; and on that the third and last part of chapter 10 is focused.

There should be no mystery about Yahweh's doings in the present and in the past, so Jeremiah's audience has been given only a very broad-brush picture of them. The picture of Judah's future is quite different. The sweeping overviews of 10:1-10 and 10:11-16 suddenly give place to a preview, concrete and immediate, of what lies ahead (10:17-25). The rapid series of harrowing images in its first six verses, facets of the looming disaster, is only too detailed: armies on the march, a besieged city, refugees who have lost everything except what they can carry, a grievous wound, homes destroyed, children lost; sheep scattered across the countryside, jackals roaming the ruined towns. The breathless catalogue of woes recalls the 'kaleidoscope' of chapter 2. Some of its pictures are to be taken literally, while others are metaphors. The tent in verse 20, for example, stands for the dwellings of God's people (perhaps here the whole city of Jerusalem), though for generations past they have, of course, been living in houses; the picture of nomadic life takes us back to Israel's beginnings, to the days of Moses and the exodus, or even of Abraham travelling from Ur – it is the entire history of Israel that seems to be coming to an end. As for verse 21, no doubt actual sheep, as literal as the jackals of verse 22, would be scattered when the invasion came; but the flock here means God's people, and the shepherds are the nation's leaders, failing at what has always

been the crucial point, the touchstone of Israelite leadership: will they or will they not 'enquire of the LORD'?[17]

Although what Jeremiah foresees is so sharply defined, it is in one respect curiously vague. God is telling His people the What, but not the How or the When. The scaremongers will no doubt be out on the streets crying 'The End is Nigh' when in the year 605 they hear 'commotion out of the north country' (10:22), and see Nebuchadnezzar's armies marching towards Jerusalem, demanding tribute and hostages; but things will simmer down again. The Babylonians will be back, and in 597 will remove Jehoiakim's young son from the throne; will that be the disaster Jeremiah has been predicting? No, apparently not that either. As Jesus would one day say concerning this very topic, there will be no mistaking the End when it does arrive.[18] Don't try to work out God's methods and timing; just be constantly alert and always ready. The king of Babylon will be here yet again in 589, and when that happens Jerusalem will assume that this is just one more predicament from which her God will deliver her, echoing in effect the words of Samson, 'I will go out as at other times and shake myself free.'[19] One final delusion! For in the event the siege of 589-586 actually will herald the End – the end, that is, of the kingdom in its Old Testament form, and the end of the dream of a political, territorial Israel, ruled from Jerusalem for the rest of time by kings of the line of David.

Just as Jeremiah's vision of coming judgment is set before his hearers in a series of word-pictures, and just as there will be a series of occasions on which it will seem to be coming true, so it is put across (as in Lamentations) by a series of voices, raising again for us the question of who says what. Of these nine verses, 10:17-25, the first is spoken by the prophet, and the second by the Lord, but who says the next two? It must be the city, if Lamentations 1 is anything to go by; on the other hand, might it be Jeremiah again? Granted, this is a bereaved parent speaking, whereas he never marries, and

17 One or other of the two Hebrew words for 'enquire' (*daras* and *sa'al*) is used of several Israelite kings, especially David, who regularly did, thereby showing himself to be a man after God's own heart (1 Sam. 13:14; Acts 13:22). Saul did not, and it was the cause of his rejection (1 Chron. 10:14; 13:3).

18 Matthew 24:6, 27.

19 Judges 16:20.

has no children; this could nonetheless be his voice, bewailing the fate of the city, and identifying himself with its suffering. We must keep that thought in mind; there will be more to it than we may at present realize.

Stupid shepherds (10:21) and noise from the north (10:22) must be Jeremiah's words. So must the final three verses of the chapter, one would think; but they set before us one more series, this time a series of questions to which the answers are far from obvious. Is the prophet speaking on his own account, or is he identifying with the city and voicing her prayers to Yahweh, or are these verses after all a note added (for reasons best known to himself) by a later editor? Does 10:23 mean that man is only human, and so cannot determine his own destiny, or that he is sinful, and so cannot go the way he knows he should? Why does 10:24, fearing Yahweh's anger, appeal to his justice, as if that were a softer option? And why does 10:25 call down wrath on the nations, for having done simply what Yahweh ordained and Israel deserved? And is not this last verse in any case simply a quotation of Psalm 79:6-7, inserted perhaps by our supposed editor? Or is it maybe Jeremiah who is voicing the city's reaction to the coming disaster, with her typical half-baked theology, partly but still not fully grasping the way things actually are?

This last possibility may come closest to the truth. We have to bear in mind, first, that the book has been put together in such a way that the four chapters 7–10 follow on from the prophet's call to preach his 'temple sermon' in 7:1-2; secondly, that Jeremiah and Baruch had repeated opportunities in the years that followed to edit that and everything else God had given His servant to proclaim; and thirdly, that in doing so they had an eye to the book's relevance both to the final years of the kingdom and to the years that followed, both to the city while it lasted and to its people in exile, and even beyond that, both to other nations (1:5) and to later generations.

These nine verses can be read as a coherent prophecy about the God of judgment and His people's future, if we understand the last three of them something like this. There is no first-person pronoun between 10:19 and 10:23, and therefore no reason why the voice in the earlier verse should not still be speaking in the later one. That is, if 10:19-20 is the city's

lament, beginning with 'I said, "Truly,"' then 10:23-25 can be the city's prayer, continuing with 'I know, O LORD'. As the prophet identifies himself with the city's sufferings, he hopes that she may begin to talk his language; that as increasingly he feels as she feels, so she gradually will come to see as he sees. For the theology of the prayer is in fact not at all half-baked. We might adapt an ancient scenario to this occasion: the hands are the hands of Jerusalem, meaning the evidence of one's senses, the desolation, the bereavement; but the voice is the voice of Jeremiah, meaning the prayer that he longs for her to utter, the work of God in the heart.[20] He wants her to recognize that it is not within her power either to decide her own destiny or to walk righteously on the way to it (v. 23). He wants her to accept that she needs correcting, that God's anger would destroy her, but that His justice in some unimaginable way will include mercy (v. 24). And he wants her to look with confidence for the ultimate defeat of every power that would presume to lift up its head against Yahweh and His people (v. 25). Perhaps as she is made to confront reality in the shape of Yahweh's judgment on Israel, the last shreds of delusion will be blown away.

Alas, it is not going to happen. The ominous words of 7:27 are still audible, like an unresolved discord hanging in the air: 'You shall speak all these words to them, but they will not listen to you.' The people of Jerusalem and Judah will not identify with Jeremiah in the prayer of 10:23-25; he has to go down a great deal further yet in order to identify with them in the pit they are digging for themselves.

---

20 Genesis 27:22.

5

Protests: The First Group
(Jeremiah 11–15)[1]

Jeremiah's 'confessions'

A new thing begins with chapter 11. Up to now, the book has consisted almost entirely of what Yahweh says to Jeremiah, messages to be passed on by him to the people of Judah. But for the next ten chapters such messages alternate with what Jeremiah wants to say to Yahweh. Traditionally these words of the prophet have been labelled his 'confessions' – an unhelpful tradition, to my mind. To 'confess' means to 'say with'; we confess our sins when we go along with what God says about them; we confess our faith when we go along with what God says about Himself. But going along with what God says is precisely not what Jeremiah is doing here. On the contrary, he is objecting, he is protesting. These so-called 'confessions' are better termed his 'protests', and that is how we shall consider them.

But first, this is an appropriate point to raise some of the basic questions, long debated, as to how Jeremiah's book came to take the form in which we now find it. Did he himself put this complicated piece of work into its present shape? No, is the general consensus in the world of biblical scholarship. Beyond the many persons named in the story as his contemporaries, it holds that there were many more, unnamed, in the years that

---

1 In what follows, the 'protests' are divided into two groups of three simply to make our chapter length manageable, in this case (and likewise in the next) covering five of Jeremiah's chapters rather than ten.

followed, who had a hand in assembling and shaping and editing the various prophecies and narratives. Certainly when this part of the Hebrew scriptures was translated into Greek (the Septuagint version, from the end of the Old Testament era), a good deal was omitted, a little was added, and six chapters were moved from the end to the middle of the book. But critics in modern times have gone much further than that in proposing various kinds of editorial work (each with its own motives and methods and presumed editors) which they think must have taken place between Jeremiah's original uttering of his prophecies and the completion of the book that we have today.

Such critics also are many! And while their object is, of course, to make a difficult book more comprehensible, their varied and often contradictory efforts to explain how it came to be the way it is are themselves pretty bewildering. I wonder whether Jeremiah would shake hands across two millennia with the medieval philosopher William of Ockham, with his doctrine of 'ontological economy'? Not a phrase we use every day, I suspect, but it means something like 'The simpler the better' or, in the case of Jeremiah and the question of how his book was put together, 'The simpler, the more likely'. The dictum became known as 'Ockham's razor', designed to cut through just such tangled complications.[2]

So while recognizing the diligent work of many critics over the years, it is still quite proper for us to cut to the book as it now stands. It is, after all, in this form that Christ and His apostles knew it and vouched for it as divine Scripture.[3] And if we read it both with close attention to the text (huge though the task may seem) and with an imaginative overview of the context (not the kind of imagination that fills in what is not said, but the kind that fills out what is said), a consistent picture does begin to emerge. Here is a diffident man faced with a daunting, almost overwhelming, task, but made equal to it by the will of the God who has called him. He has a single

---

2 The principle that 'entities are not to be multiplied beyond necessity'. For example, Mackay notes the various views of five earlier commentators on a 'problem' in 11:2-3, then points out a simple way of understanding the text which 'makes involved hypotheses unnecessary'. See below, n.4.

3 Matthew 5:17-18, John 10:35, 2 Timothy 3:16.

message that will nonetheless be adapted to each of the five successive audiences to which it is addressed: the people of God first in the reigns of Josiah, Jehoiakim, and Zedekiah, and then in exile, and finally the rest of the nations and the rest of history. Here alongside this man is a succession of friends, few but faithful, to support him through the dark days. Baruch, whose friendship is to be the most enduring and surely the closest of them all, will be privileged with the task of noting all that the prophet says and converting the spoken word into the written word. I have yet to find any compelling reason why what was then dictated should since have been altered, and I like to imagine Jeremiah himself going over a modern reprint of the Hebrew version of the book that now bears his name, with blue pencil in hand and never once having to use it.

More than any other of the prophets, he teaches us not only by what we hear of his words, but also by what we see of him himself. In the section of the book at which we now arrive, chapters 11 to 20, his personality begins to take fuller shape before us. Set into the pattern of these chapters are a number of confrontations between him and his God. He repeatedly argues the toss with Yahweh, and we should find it encouraging that there is no timidity about this, no sense that it is not quite proper, no foolish reluctance to lay bare his hurt and doubt and perplexity. We have already begun to learn much from what he *says* in his prophesying, and now in these chapters we are learning too from what he *says* in his praying. But here, as the sequence of confrontations – his protests and the Lord's responses – unfolds, we are to learn something very far-reaching also from what he *is*.

The first protest consists of three verses of appeal from Jeremiah (11:18-20) and three verses of answer from Yahweh (11:21-23). By the sixth protest, Jeremiah's appeals will have lengthened to twelve verses (20:7-18); already by the fourth, Yahweh will have stopped responding. But meanwhile He continues to give His servant a long series of messages to pass on to His people, which form the setting for the sequence of protests. The regular pattern seems to be that a passage of that sort of material sets the scene for the protest which then follows. If this is how we are intended to read them, there is

one exception, when the second protest (12:1-6) precedes the second scene-setting (which I take to be 12:7–13:27), instead of following it.

The setting of the first protest (11:1-17)

However convenient it may be to label these ten chapters the 'protest' section of the book, the protests themselves take up only one-fifth of the text, and we must not play down the importance of the rest. We should not embark on the first dialogue between Yahweh and His prophet till we have considered the prophecy of 11:1-17, which prepares the way for it.

This prophecy comes through Jeremiah, from Yahweh, to his people; that much may seem obvious.[4] But the placing of the 'from' phrases ('the word … from the LORD' and 'the LORD said') helps us to see the shape of the message, with three paragraphs beginning in turn at verses 1, 6, and 9. The 'to' phrases have Judah and Jerusalem, that is, the whole nation, in view; they appear at the same points, and also mark the end of the third paragraph at verses 12-13. A fourth paragraph then completes the prophecy.

Yahweh's theme is the covenant, and blow by blow He hammers it home, to the shocking climax that will provoke Jeremiah's first outburst of protest. The paragraph 11:1-5 states simple fact, to which all should assent. It is 'the words of this covenant', which one would think should be as familiar to his audience as the words of a national anthem (which in a way they are), that Jeremiah is here reiterating. At the centre of verses 3-5 Yahweh sums up the terms of the agreement, 'You obey me and I will bless you'. On either side of this statement He sums up the great rescue which is the core of the promised blessing, out of 'iron-furnace' land and into 'milk-and-honey' land, together with the words that had been commanded in Egypt and the oath that would be confirmed in Canaan. But the little chiasmus – out of, obey/bless, into – extends one step further in each direction; the pattern is not so much ABA as

---

4 Though who says what to whom in 11:2-3? As noted above (n. 2), these are 'problem' verses, because 'hear' is plural (so cannot be addressed just to Jeremiah), though 'speak' is singular. But with appropriate punctuation all is clear: Yahweh says to the prophet, '"Hear these words, you people" (this, Jeremiah, is what you are to speak to them).'

ABCBA, because to its end is added an unexpected 'Amen' from Jeremiah ('So be it, LORD'), balancing the ominous word 'Arar' ('cursed') that begins it: the people on whom Yahweh's eye is focused are the disobedient, who are under His curse, rather than the obedient, who may expect His blessing.

Allowing for that particular emphasis, the first paragraph of the chapter has put in a nutshell what God is saying to the people of Jeremiah's time, which is essentially just what He said to the people of Moses' time: 'Obey me … and I will be your God' (11:4 NIV). Now the second paragraph, 11:6-8, spells out how He is saying it. When the prophet reiterates to his contemporaries 'the words of this covenant', the exodus covenant, it is what Yahweh has been doing repeatedly for seven hundred years and more, from the day 'when I brought [your fathers] up out of the land of Egypt … even to this day.' He has sent them warnings, solemn and persistent. The word 'persistently' (frequent in these chapters) is literally 'rising early in the morning', as if, having sent His hearers off last night with His words ringing in their ears, He is on their doorstep first thing today to remind them yet again that action is required.

Yet in spite of all these exhortations they have repeatedly refused to keep their side of the agreement, even when He has 'brought upon them all the words of this covenant', meaning the punishments that He had assured them were bound to follow. Now for the third time in this chapter He speaks to Jeremiah about Judah and Jerusalem (11:9-13): yet again the accusation, 'they have turned back', and yet again the threat, 'I am bringing disaster'. Yet again, no doubt, they saw Jeremiah as a scaremonger, the boy who cried 'Wolf!' repeatedly and no wolf ever came. But there is something about this paragraph that should have given them pause. A conspiracy (11:9) has been found often enough in the story of the Israelite kingdoms, as various claimants to the throne have jockeyed for position, but there has not yet been one that has involved practically the whole populace; what Yahweh now sees pervading the nation is, as Mackay aptly puts it, not a secret plot but a 'consensus', a 'widespread meeting of minds'. It is hard to avoid a comparison with twenty-first-century Britain, and some other parts of the English-speaking

world, where there is just such a consensus, particularly in politics and the media, with the historic Christian faith which has shaped our culture now assumed to be the private interest of an irritating but negligible minority, over which the powers that be may ride roughshod with impunity.[5]

This was a new thing in Judah. The rejection of her traditional beliefs had never been so blatant or so widespread. It suggests strongly that chapter 11 does not belong to the reign of Josiah, when there was a top-down imposition of traditional standards, however much the people in general might resent it. Rather, Jehoiakim's is the reign in which the 'conspiracy' with which this paragraph begins comes into the open, to be fostered by those in power, resulting in the scene with which it ends – false gods worshipped in every town in Judah and their altars set up in every street in Jerusalem.[6]

Bracketed by the 'conspiracy' of 11:9 and the apostasy of 11:13, both of them near-universal, we have a cluster of further hints that in some sense or other 'the end is near'. The breaking of the covenant is 'bringing disaster … that they cannot escape'. Yahweh is about to close His ears to their prayers. The 'time of their trouble' is coming, and from it they will not be saved.

And thereupon we arrive at the fourth and last of these paragraphs, with a repetition of the doom-laden word spoken by Yahweh to His servant for the temple sermon that began the previous major division of the book, the 'Delusions' of chapters 7 to 10. As there, 'Do not pray for this people … for I will not hear you' (7:16), so here, 'Do not pray for this people … for I will not listen' (11:14). Instead of praying for them, says Yahweh, speak again to them, the message of 11:15-17. The rather difficult verse 15 seems to underline the warning that no amount of so-called 'worship' in the temple can compensate for His people's wickedness, and what should have been a beautiful and fruitful olive tree is destined to be destroyed.

---

5 In the immortal words of a turn-of-the-century political adviser (Alastair Campbell), 'We do not do God.'

6 In this interpretation the references to 'Judah and Jerusalem' have nothing to do with a supposed itinerant ministry of Jeremiah's in the time of Josiah, as suggested by some commentators.

The first protest: Jeremiah in the firing line (11:18-23)

So far, chapter 11 hangs together and has a clear structure. But what is the connection between this next paragraph, which in any case begins with a rather peculiar sentence ('Yahweh let me know, and I knew'), and what has gone before? At all events someone, at some stage, for some reason, caused 11:17 to be followed by 11:18, and there is no sound reason why it should not have been so dictated by Jeremiah and written down by Baruch. Here, I think, is an instance of the need for close attention to the text along with a disciplined imagining of the context – picturing, let us say, these two men now in exile in Egypt in the late 580s, working at a revision of the original scrolls that date from 604 (we shall learn of them in chapter 36).

'Jeremiah,' says Baruch diffidently, as he reaches the end of what we call verse 20, 'forgive my interrupting, but have I missed something? That first sentence at the beginning of this protest of yours, what does it mean: "Yahweh let me know and I knew"? And this "I" and "you" and "they" – who is who?'

'I'm not surprised that all this should seem rather incoherent,' responds Jeremiah. 'I too was completely thrown by it; it came as a huge shock. "They" were the people of Anathoth, my own friends and neighbours. I had an inkling that some plot was being hatched back at home while I was in Jerusalem, but I had no idea that I was myself its target, till Yahweh showed me. I had had His promise from the start, that I should be made a "fortified city" and an "iron pillar" (1:18), and the promise was put to the test, as you know, when Jehoiakim came to the throne. I had presumed that I was unassailable, for here I was, preaching with impunity under the nose of that wicked king, in the heart of his city. But my own kith and kin in my own village – a community of the priests of Yahweh! – were so incensed by what I suppose they took to be my blasphemies and my unpatriotic defeatism, that they were scheming to destroy me and silence the word of God. It would have been a sort of "honour killing", the execution of one who had brought shame on the family.'

'So what happened to them as a result?' asks Baruch, picking up his pen again.

'Few if any of them will have survived the war and the famine of these recent years. Any who have are now exiles in Babylon, and none will ever see Anathoth again.[7] But as you know, I do myself own some land there! People like you and me have "a future and a hope", such as will figure later on in our book.'[8]

The second protest: Jeremiah under a darkening sky (12:1-6)

In the first six verses of chapter 12 Jeremiah is obviously still protesting, and here as in the last six verses of chapter 11 he appeals to the righteous Judge, who tests the human heart, against the wicked men who surround him. If anything, these likenesses suggest two distinct protests based on the same kind of appeal rather than one longer, somewhat repetitious, protest that straddles the two chapters.

Up to the time when the plotting in Anathoth was exposed, he had been laying about him in fine style, castigating the nation at large for its manifold sins. Then in chapter 11 it was revealed to him that his own folks were tarred with the same brush, and that he personally stood in peril of his life because of it. Now he begins to see the pattern and connect the dots. He recognizes that the vicious antipathy felt by them towards him is the same as that which the nation at large feels towards Yahweh. This cannot be allowed to go on indefinitely. Hence the cry for 'vengeance' in the first protest (11:20) and for 'the day of slaughter' in this one (12:3).

This opens up for him the vexed age-old question of why the wicked prosper.[9] It is as if with the unexpected revelation of the plot against his life he suddenly sees the question whole. The personal hurt, 'How could they do this to me?', is only the most obvious part of it. Yahweh, who had planted the tree of Israel (11:16-17), had also planted these people, who then grew and produced fruit (12:2) – bad fruit! When and how had the horticultural experiment gone wrong? And with regard to literal 'growing things', the crops and creatures of the countryside (12:4), why was the blight of man's wickedness

7 Ezra 2:23 mentions the return of 128 men of Anathoth after the exile, seventy years later, so presumably of the next generation.

8 See Jeremiah 32; 29:11.

9 See Psalms 37 and 73; Habakkuk 1:12-13; Malachi 3:15.

allowed to spread and spoil his environment too? And since justice demands that somehow, somewhen, whoever bears the responsibility for all this evil must be held to account, then why, Lord, don't you get on and do it?

'Jeremiah,' responds Yahweh (12:5-6), 'you have certainly seen the magnitude of the problem. But you don't yet see its implications. Before I can give you answers, you need to experience for yourself what these people are capable of.' The double question of 12:5, though not without its difficulties, is a searching one. Whether verse 5a pictures a race between runners and horsemen (a slightly odd image) or a fight between infantry and cavalry, it warns Jeremiah that opponents will emerge far more powerful than his ill-disposed kith and kin in Anathoth. A translation that makes good sense of verse 5b is that of the NRSV: 'If in a safe land you fall down, how will you fare in the thickets of the Jordan?'[10] In other words, to quote G.K. Chesterton's famous lines,

'I tell you naught for your comfort,
    Yea, naught for your desire,
Save that the sky grows darker yet,
    And the sea rises higher.'[11]

For the present, however, it is enough for Jeremiah to learn the hard lesson of having to fear and distrust his own family.

The setting of the second protest (12:7–13:27)
At some point in the story, Jeremiah must have begun to suspect that there was more to his calling than simply standing firm through difficult days and proclaiming Yahweh's word faithfully, though you might have thought that that task alone would be as much as any man could reasonably be asked to cope with. This extra dimension to his ministry has begun to emerge in the second protest and Yahweh's response to it. The treachery that he sees thriving all around (12:1) has now come home to him; he himself has experienced it at the hands of his own kin (12:6).

---

10 The river valley, dangerous either because of overgrown jungle with its wild beasts (as here) or because of its periodic 'swelling' or 'flooding' (NKJV). 'Trusting' (ESV) is an alternative reading for 'falling' or 'stumbling'.

11 G.K. Chesterton, *The Ballad of the White Horse*.

What follows this conversation between Jeremiah and
Yahweh is another chapter and a half of prophecy, given
to Jeremiah for him to convey to the people. It seems, for
a reason that will become apparent, that these words belong
to a time some years later than that of the 'temple sermon'
in Jehoiakim's reign. From their beginning in 12:7 they are
directly related to what Yahweh has just said to Jeremiah
– 'Your brothers and *the house of your father* ... have dealt
treacherously with you' (12:6); and now through Jeremiah He
tells His people, 'I have forsaken *my house*'. The domestic rift
in Anathoth corresponds to a rift on the grand scale affecting
the whole nation. As Jeremiah has been rejected by his family,
so Yahweh has been rejected by His people. For it is, of course,
Israel whom He calls 'my house ... my heritage ... the beloved
of my soul', and with whom His relationship is now broken.

It may be Jeremiah's privilege to feel, in some small
measure, the pain of rejection by his own people that Yahweh
feels. But it is not for him to go the next step and react as
Yahweh reacts. For the whole of this prophecy, 12:7–13:27, is
about how Yahweh responds to His rejection by Israel; which
is, to put it plainly, that *He* rejects *her*.

'Righteous are you, O Lord' – so Jeremiah began his
second protest (12:1); and only the righteous Judge knows
how to apply the *lex talionis*, the tit-for-tat, eye-for-an-eye law
of retribution, righteously, and how to inflict punishment
justly. (He also knows how to temper it with mercy but, as
yet, in these chapters, we see no more than a glimpse of that.)
What we have here is a sequence of word-pictures like those
of chapter 2, not quite the dizzy kaleidoscope that we found
there, but still a series of memorable images.

The first, in 12:7-9, takes up Jeremiah's lament in 12:4, that
from a land so blighted by wickedness even the creatures of
field and farm have fled. Fled indeed, agrees Yahweh, to be
replaced by wildlife of a different sort: truly wild, a zoo of
predators – 'My own people have turned on me like a lion
from the scrub, roaring against me ... This land of mine [is]
a hyena's lair, with birds of prey hovering all around it.'[12]

---

12 Verses 8-9 NEB, agreeing with ESV (other translations follow slightly different
wording in the Hebrew).

The opening words of 12:10-13, 'many shepherds,' might suggest that Yahweh is next going to portray His people as sheep, as He frequently does in Scripture. In fact, the main picture here is not of a flock, but of a vineyard: 'shepherds' is simply a regular Old Testament term for rulers, and the 'enemies' of verse 7 are now seen to be kings, both foreign and home-grown, both before and during Jeremiah's time, trampling down what Yahweh calls 'my vineyard ... my portion ... my pleasant portion' (in parallel to the trio in verse 7, 'my house ... my heritage ... the beloved of my soul'). Yahweh's word through Jeremiah, however, makes it clear that when the policies of kings are allowed to hurt His people, this is 'the sword of the LORD' bringing punishment (12:12), and that the resulting hardship is their own fault (12:13).

Jeremiah should find that the 'worse-to-come' warning of 12:5, the threat of bigger challenges than he has till now anticipated, is offset by Yahweh's extraordinary statements in 12:14-17. He is taken back to the very beginning, when he was first commissioned, and 'set ... over nations and over kingdoms, to pluck up and to break down, to destroy and to overthrow, to build and to plant' (1:10). Before the two constructive commands, four that were destructive, and the first of these was 'to pluck up', to uproot. That has already been the fate of the northern kingdom, in 722; it will be the fate of the southern kingdom too, in 586. The uprooting of the nation, the destruction of the monarchy, are the climax towards which the whole book moves. And here indeed is Yahweh saying, 'I will pluck up the house of Judah'; but the context is astonishing, and points us back again to that original commissioning: 'I have set you this day *over nations and over kingdoms,* to pluck up ...'. He is giving Jeremiah what we might call a cosmonaut's view of the Bible lands, with a grid of political frontiers superimposed on it. He addresses Judah's 'evil neighbours', and looks ahead to a day when they in their turn will be uprooted, while a further uprooting of Judah 'from among them' will have brought her home again! Even beyond that, he looks into a remoter future, and glimpses a world in which every nation where the name of the living Lord is venerated will be back where it should be, among the people of God.

In 13:1-11 Jeremiah's experience of prophetic words from God is ratcheted up to a new level. From the outset it has been related to things he is shown, beginning with the almond branch and the boiling pot of 1:11-14. Now for the first time it involves not simply things he has to look at, but things he has to do. In this much-debated passage he is told to buy and wear an *'ezôr*, then to take it to *Perath* and bury it there, then later to retrieve it. But why? And what in any case is an *'ezôr*, and where is *Perath*?

The object in question is certainly an item of clothing; the translations vary. Moving outwards, as it were, from 'waistcloth' to 'belt' to 'sash', it might be something decorative, even showy, perhaps a visible mark of distinction. Moving inwards, it could equally mean a loincloth; few translators might venture to use the word 'underwear' in this connection, but the 'clinging' metaphor in 13:11 does suggest something next to the skin; so close, says Yahweh, is Israel to me.

Since the background to the whole book is the relation between Israel and the Mesopotamian superpowers, the place described here has regularly been assumed to be some point on the Euphrates, the great river on which Babylon stood. This raises the question of whether Jeremiah would really have undertaken a round trip of 500 miles, not once but twice, to set up a 'visual aid' whose intended audience would not be able to see it. Some suggest his achieving a similar effect by a piece of 'street theatre' in Jerusalem, telling his spectators that the wavy line he was drawing on the ground was the Euphrates, and so forth (though how about the burying of the loincloth, the interval, and the finding of it spoilt?). Much the most likely scenario is Jeremiah's assembling of his audience on two successive occasions, at a place by a stream not far from Anathoth, whose name was very like that of the great river,[13] so lending itself to his purpose.

At all events, the garment represents Israel/Judah, and it will somehow be rendered useless by its stay in 'Euphrates' country. Once we focus on this question – in what sense would

---

13 Whereas all but one of the fifteen Old Testament references outside this chapter are, explicitly or implicitly, to '*the river* Perath', and do refer to the Euphrates, all four references in it are simply to 'Perath'. The suggested site is Parah, with its spring ('Ain Fāra).

the nation actually 'perish' in the course of the Babylonian captivity? – several interpretations have to be ruled out.[14] The one that emerges, which we shall find reinforced as the story unfolds, is that what Babylon brought to an end was Israel's political structure as a kingdom.

Opinion is less divided over the conversation piece that follows, 13:12-14, but again we find that the meaning is not obvious, and that the tone is darker than in the two previous chapters. It may be that Jeremiah here broaches the subject of wine simply to engage the attention of his audience. 'Wine is for wineskins,' he announces: perhaps a common saying, not unlike 'horses for courses', to which his hearers respond 'Yes, we know, "wine is for wineskins"; so – ?' Whereupon what is a mere turn of phrase becomes an accusation: it is they who are full of wine. Too full; the whole of Israelite society, from the king downwards, seems to be pickled to the eyebrows in strong drink, to judge by its witless response to the current political situation. All are doomed to destruction, even 'the kings who sit on David's throne'. The promise of an everlasting Davidic kingdom is going to hold good, but not in the way they think. The sons of Josiah will find their version of it shunted into a dead end.

The two chapters that begin with Jeremiah's second protest are now completed by another passage in verse, 13:15-27. It is almost impressionistic, a patchwork of vivid word-pictures: deepening gloom, a flock taken away into exile and captivity, the 'foe from the north' reappearing, the inescapable pains of childbirth, an immoral woman exposed, wickedness as indelible as the colour of an African's skin or the spots of a leopard; chaff blown away by the desert wind; an inheritance (the 'lot' and 'portion' of verse 25) as unlike the 'land of milk and honey' as you could imagine.

It is to Jerusalem, which of course stands for 'the whole house of Israel and the whole house of Judah' (13:11), that this terrible message is addressed, by Yahweh, through Jeremiah, and we may note two outstanding features of it. One is general: the pervading sense of a judgment which is final,

---

14 The faith of Israel was contaminated first by Canaanite, later by Assyrian, religion; the Babylonian exile was in the event a purifying process rather than a damaging one.

inescapable, and imminent. The other is particular, the picture of 'the king and the queen mother' (13:18), and surely anchors these chapters to a year that we can date. The last such time-reference was the 'temple sermon' in chapter 7, which almost certainly belongs to the reign of Jehoiakim in the 600s. In 598 Jehoiakim died; his widow Nehushta took on the influential role of queen mother, and his son Jehoiachin became king. The Babylonians had already been interfering in Israelite politics, and within three months they had removed both mother and son. Hence this picture: both were dethroned, and he lost his crown.

If this is the background to chapters 12 and 13, it touches on one of the great questions which have exercised God's people repeatedly down the years, and Jeremiah among them. For to the prophet himself, and indeed to anyone who is trying to 'hear and give ear' (13:15) at this time, the disasters he threatens really do seem imminent. The darkness does deepen, enemies do approach from the north, some of us have already gone into exile, and now the final generation of David's descendants is on its way to Babylon. No doubt there are futurologists right here in Jerusalem who have calculated that the world is going to end in 598. What then are we to make of this Zedekiah, Josiah's last surviving son, placed on the throne of Judah by Nebuchadnezzar of Babylon? How can he be anything more than a regent – no, even less, a puppet – so long as his nephew still lives in exile? Does not this mean, in the prophet's striking phrase, that the 'beautiful crown has come down' (13:18)? Even so, clearly we are not yet actually at the end, life goes on, and in some sense or other the kingdom is still here; Jeremiah continues to prophesy, and the word of Yahweh continues to tantalize those who puzzle over the 'signs of the times'.

The setting of the third protest (14:1–15:9)

There will be a change in the tenor of Jeremiah's prophesying once the deportation of 597 has taken place and Zedekiah has been installed as king. For the present, it seems that Jeremiah and Baruch are still busy with the doom-laden prophecies of the Jehoiakim years; there have been many of these, despite the king's attempts to silence the prophet (of which we

shall read in chapter 36), and they have provoked a violent reaction, as the third protest is about to tell us. We are still in a time when Yahweh is saying, 'Do not pray for the welfare of this people, for I will not hear' (14:11, as in 7:16 and 11:14). This is the generation which is beyond reprieve, and is to be destroyed 'by the sword, by famine, and by pestilence' (14:12).

Drought, explicitly threatened long ago as a punishment for the breaking of Yahweh's law,[15] has clearly become a recurring problem in Jehoiakim's reign,[16] affecting every level of society,[17] as well as the creatures of the wild. Jeremiah sets this forth in 14:1-6 as a nationwide crisis – 'Judah mourns,' 'the cry of Jerusalem goes up' – and then finds himself uttering words which are perhaps as unexpected to him as they may be to us: the people's cry is not just a complaint about bad things happening *to* them, but a confession of sin, of bad things done *by* them. And a thoroughly heartfelt cry it would seem to be (14:7-9). It could be adopted (and would not need to be adapted!) by any gathering of the people of God, in any age and any place, as a penitential approach to prayer and worship. Confession tends to be soft-pedalled in modern liturgies, but these three verses are up there with the classic heart-searchings of the 1662 Prayer Book: 'We have erred and strayed from thy ways like lost sheep ... Have mercy upon us, miserable offenders.'

So much the more shocking, then, is Yahweh's reaction to this apparent penitence. 'Thus says the LORD concerning this people: "*They have loved* to wander thus; they have not restrained their feet; therefore the LORD does not accept them; now he will remember their iniquity and punish their sins ....* Though they fast I will not hear their cry."' As then, so now, a fitting form of words is immensely valuable, but only if there is a truly penitent heart. The finer the prayer, the greater the condemnation of those who say it without meaning it.

At the end of chapter 14, another confession on the part of the people is going to be followed by another rejection on the

---

15 Leviticus 26:18-20, Deuteronomy 11:13-17.

16 Touched on in 3:3 and 12:4, and the word here in 14:1 is plural ('droughts', as in NKJV).

17 'Farmers' (14:4) would be better translated 'farm labourers', a social contrast with 'nobles' in 14:3.

part of Yahweh. First, however, Jeremiah raises a real problem of his own. We think of him as 'Jeremiah *the prophet*', but he is only one among many prophets, and when he passes on Yahweh's threat of sword and famine, every other prophetic voice in the land is raised to contradict it. What should he do next? What can he say more? He might be excused for feeling in desperation that he is simply being outgunned by the enemy.

Step by step, therefore, Yahweh coaches him in the next stage of his thankless task. He can be sure that sword and famine are indeed on their way, and will devastate Judah, with first among their victims those who are betraying their calling as the mouthpieces of Yahweh: sword and famine they deny, so 'by sword and famine those prophets shall be consumed' (14:13-15). But he is not now to engage in a war of words, confronting and denouncing; instead he is to bypass the controversy and become himself the tragic figure who will picture for Judah the fate that awaits her. He is to go forth as the 'weeping prophet', representing her as grievously wounded, exposing her leaders as the charlatans they are, and exclaiming with horror at the scenes he can already see with the prophetic eye, of slaughter outside the city and of starvation within it (14:17-18).

Then he is given in 14:19-22 the text of the second confession of sin. It is again one such as she might use, even more heartfelt than the first one, grasping even more realistically the facts of the case, now that (in his vision) the day of wrath has arrived. The words put into her mouth could not be more abjectly penitent; and so, once again, all the more terrifying are the words that are put into his mouth, in 15:1-9. For it will be too late. The day of grace will be past, the door of opportunity will be shut. Yahweh would have her look beyond His servant Jeremiah to three other memorable figures in her history. The powerful prayers of Moses and Samuel (15:1) might plead for Israel to be pulled to safety, as had happened in the lifetime of each of those great prophets.[18] But the wickedness of King Manasseh[19] is pulling in the opposite direction, and whatever

---

18 Exodus 32:9-14; 1 Samuel 12:23.

19 2 Kings 21:10-15, 23:26-27.

eloquent words of confession she might babble under duress, that is where her unregenerate heart lies.

People who say that the God of the Old Testament is a bloodthirsty tyrant usually know very little of what the Bible actually says; show them Jeremiah 15:1-9, and they might have grounds for their accusation! But they would still need to grasp that this is the kind of punishment, described by the prophet as though it had already happened, which awaits those who *do not want* God's mercy.

The third protest: Jeremiah the object of calumny (15:10-21)
'The time is out of joint,' says Hamlet, in the reign of a Danish king almost as wicked as Jehoiakim of Judah; 'O cursèd spite, That ever I was born to set it right!' To such an extremity Jeremiah feels himself driven in this, the third of his protests, as he will also in the sixth and last of them ('Cursed be the day on which I was born,' 20:14). He is provoked to it because he is himself the object of cursing by others, 'a man of strife and contention to the whole land'. Does 15:10 indicate a trumped-up charge of some sort of financial double-dealing, such as regularly rouses the self-righteous anger of the general public? If so, he is not guilty. All he has done is to tell them the truth.

The wording of Yahweh's response in 15:11-12 is extraordinarily difficult to translate. The NIV makes perhaps the best sense of verse 11: 'The LORD said, "Surely I will deliver you for a good purpose; surely I will make your enemies plead with you in times of disaster and times of distress."' Jeremiah will indeed find himself, ten years down the line, still alive in the reign of a king who though unwilling to support him publicly will nonetheless be pleading for his advice.[20] And in the context, the iron and bronze of verse 12 must look back to the prophet's original calling, to be 'an iron pillar, and bronze walls'; his enemies 'shall not prevail' against him (1:18-19). Exactly so will Yahweh round off his second, longer response at the end of this present chapter (15:20).

As if to confirm to Jeremiah that he is in the right place, doing the right thing, and will continue to be a central figure in the divine plan, Yahweh gives him another message for Judah and Jerusalem. It seems to arise directly from the

---

20 Zedekiah, in chapters 21 and 37-38.

accusation that was apparently being levelled at him. What should concern them far more than the state of Jeremiah's finances is the prospect of the total loss of their own, together with the renewed threat of exile and slavery (15:13-14).

There is something worse than the sniping of ignorant people on that particular topic. The prophet shows in 15:15-18, the four-verse extension of his one-verse protest in 15:10, what is really hurting him. We remind ourselves that its setting is the scandal of false prophecy, which has been exposed in 14:13-16. For my part, Jeremiah tells Yahweh, 'your words became to me a joy and the delight of my heart'; but the prophets of untruth shut their ears to his preaching of those words. And as has happened repeatedly down the years, contradiction of the message is followed by persecution of the messenger. Is the true prophet's witness to have no effect? Is Yahweh, who called Himself 'the fountain of living waters' in 2:13, now going to be 'like waters that fail' (15:18)?

At his lowest point yet, Jeremiah is simply given in 15:19-21 a reiteration of the original call and promise. He is to keep his face turned towards Yahweh; if there is to be any turning round, it must not be on his part but on Judah's. Jeremiah is to proclaim Yahweh's truth; Yahweh will guarantee Jeremiah's safety. The people may accuse him of fraudulent dealing and their leaders may accuse him of false teaching, but he is in good company. As Luke tells us at either end of his two-volume New Testament history, the crucified and risen Christ is 'a sign which will be spoken against,' and His church likewise 'is spoken against everywhere.'[21]

---

21 Luke 2:34 and Acts 28:22 (NKJV). Luke uses the same word, *antilego*, in each place.

6

Protests: The Second Group
(Jeremiah 16–20)

'Emotion recollected in tranquillity'
'The word of the LORD came to me: "You shall not take a wife"'
(16:1-2). That statement begins to set the scene for Jeremiah's
fourth protest. But first we should notice something implied
in it which might easily be overlooked.

Many translations set out large parts of Jeremiah's book
in the form of poetry, and many commentators base theories
about its meaning and composition on the distinction between
prose and verse. But the whole book, prose and verse alike,
would be covered by the phrase which William Wordsworth
coined to define poetry, 'emotion recollected in tranquillity'.
We should once again imagine Jeremiah and Baruch in Egypt
in the late 580s, in the relative tranquillity of exile, putting
together what had been said and done by both the prophet
and his Lord, and by his people, and by his opponents,
everything that had been of significance in those tumultuous
sixty years – an emotional roller coaster if ever there was one.

Within this complex 'recollection in tranquillity' of all the
ups and downs of Jeremiah's life there are curious dislocations
of time, when the text seems to hop to and fro across the
reigns of the three kings, on to Jehoiakim, then back to Josiah,
then forward again to Zedekiah; grist to the mill of critics
who reckon there must have been editorial work, long after
the event, rearranging chapters for a variety of conflicting
reasons. The point at issue with this verse (16:2), Jeremiah's

being forbidden to marry, is that by the end of chapter 15 we thought we were also at the end of Jehoiakim's reign, by which time Jeremiah would have been in his late forties; so almost certainly (in the normal course of events) he would have married already, had not Yahweh forbidden it, presumably while he was still a teenager.[1] In other words, the prohibition of 16:2 must date from long before the other events of these chapters, and someone has been rearranging the text.

But there is no reason why Jeremiah should not himself have been that someone. It is entirely justifiable to picture him saying to Baruch, 'The word of the Lord came to me, *long before all this,* telling me that I was never to marry.' His remaining a bachelor, a real oddity in that society, would no doubt have caused comment locally as the years went by, a point in his disfavour which would prepare the way for the later unpopularity in Anathoth, which in its turn would eventually culminate in the attempt on his life. But now, as Baruch writes up these protests which date mostly from the turn of the century and the later part of Jehoiakim's reign, Jeremiah brings forward this earlier word from Yahweh, to take its appropriate place in the sequence.

For there is a sequence, a progression. The prophet has just pointed Baruch back to the time when Yahweh had said 'You shall not take a wife', but he is actually working his way forwards, through an increasingly dismaying series of experiences. Having preached freely at first, he has been shocked to find in Anathoth the butcher's knife being whetted for the pet lamb (Protest 1), then to hear the warning that there will be worse to come (Protest 2), then to be the object of slander from the general public and contradiction by the religious leadership (Protest 3). The sky grows darker yet, and the sea rises higher.

The setting of the fourth protest (16:1–17:13)

It has been apparent from the start of the ten 'protest' chapters that they are concerned not only with what Jeremiah says, but also with what he is. As now we come within sight of the

---

1 The suggestion by M.D. Goldman that Jeremiah already had a broken marriage behind him, and was being forbidden to remarry (Thompson, pp. 403f.), is something of a curiosity, and unnecessary if the above reconstruction is correct.

fourth protest, which awaits us in the latter part of chapter 17, we find ourselves confronted in a new way by what he *does*. We have, of course, already seen him in action, prophesying and preaching, and more recently burying and then unearthing the ever-memorable loincloth. But here in chapter 16 we find Yahweh instructing him to turn his whole lifestyle into an acted prophecy.

This time the setting is made explicit. For Jeremiah's next group of prophecies, and his protest at having to utter them, the scene is set 'in this place', 'in this land' (16:2-3), as distinct from the land to which so many of Jeremiah's hearers are soon to be exiled, other lands where they will in due course be scattered (16:15), and yet others further afield to which we shall find his words addressed before we are done (25:15 and chapters 46–51). At this point the land of Judah is both the setting and the subject of the prophecy he is about to proclaim; and to give his hearers a picture of what their future will be, he is presenting himself.

Over the years he has clearly become a well-known figure. What he has said in recent times, while Jehoiakim has been on the throne, has been sufficiently public to rouse the ire of the authorities. What he has done, for example the hiding and retrieving of the loincloth, has similarly had the desired publicity, and there will now be many more such deeds. At this point, however, we focus again on what he is, namely a man so eccentric as to be still unmarried when some of his contemporaries no doubt have grandchildren. This likewise is common knowledge, and it forms the starting point for his next acted parable, which is spelled out in 16:1-9.

Look at me, he says. I have no wife. Being a bachelor, I have no children either. You will notice furthermore that on Yahweh's instructions I never nowadays attend funerals or weddings, so I am cut off from sharing in the community's sorrows and joys. Look at me, because *I represent Judah*. This is what our nation is soon to become, with the whole fabric of its society, its web of relationships, torn apart.

Yahweh has warned him what the reaction to this will be. Some may be alert enough to see the writing on the wall, to take the prophet seriously, and to ask the big 'Why?' questions of 16:10 with real anxiety. These people regard

themselves as Yahweh's people; in our day they would be thought of as 'regular churchgoers'. Yet they simply cannot see the difference between their show of religion and a real relationship with the true God. Today such people would be outnumbered by others whose tone of voice as they ask these questions would convey not anxiety but disbelief, dissociating themselves from ranters like Jeremiah, speaking not of 'sin that we have committed against the LORD our God' but of 'sin that *you allege* we have committed against the LORD *your* God.' Either way, the prophecy will be fulfilled. Judgment in the sense of verdict has been reached; judgment in the sense of punishment will inevitably follow (16:10-13).

At first glance, what 'the LORD says' in the next two verses (16:14-15) is something so out of key that it stops us in our tracks. After the deepening darkness of the 'protest' chapters as a whole, and of the present chapter in particular, why this sudden light – 'I will bring them back to their own land'? It is naïve to imagine Yahweh checking Himself, wondering if He has perhaps been a bit too harsh, and slotting in a promise which says, 'Things won't be quite as awful, or as final, as I might have led you to imagine.' In any case, He reverts instantly in 16:16-18 to the black days that lie ahead, with a new image, that of fishermen and hunters, and His rebellious people being fished out, hunted out, from every hole and cranny where might try to hide; and they are to be repaid 'double' for their sins. The word ('twofold') can mean 'twice as much'; but the meaning 'doubled over' suggests one half of a folded paper reproducing what is written on the other half, and so in this case a punishment that exactly fits the crime, which is quite frightening enough. In the context, it seems that the emphasis of verses 14-15 may be on the dark rather than on the light; not so much a promise of deliverance as a warning that though there will be a second deliverance, it will be from a captivity even worse in some respects than the Egyptian one.

The prophet's eyes do all the same find far distances, in terms of both time and space, opening up before them, with a dazzling future hope. From his backward look to the exile in Egypt, he turns to look forward: he sees many remoter lands in which God's people will in due course find themselves

exiled, and a remoter day when 'nations ... from the ends of the earth' will acknowledge how great is Yahweh the God of Israel (16:19-21).

Since we can give to several of the people who were there at the time 'a local habitation and a name', whereas such later editors as some suppose to have reorganized Baruch's manuscripts are shadowy, anonymous figures (if indeed they exist at all), we are free to picture the two friends working at those earliest drafts of the book, and deciding, for example, that the passages we call 16:1-21 and 17:1-13 should be written down in that order. We accept that we may sometimes be at a loss to know why they would do this kind of thing; but in this case, at any rate, there are links that seem to connect chapter 17 with what has gone before.

Might we have here three paragraphs, of nearly equal length, designedly linked by the word 'heart' in the first verse of each (17:1, 5, 9)? And since they have been preceded by the account of a dramatic presentation in which Jeremiah had taken the role of Judah under judgment, might he have understood that drama to represent the outward appearance of the coming calamity, while these verses explain the inward cause of it?

The heart of the nation – that is, her mind and will – is first represented, in 17:1-4, as a stone tablet (like those on which the finger of God wrote the Ten Commandments), and Judah's sinful nature is there engraved, as unchangeable as God's righteous law. Whatever glimmer of future hope there may have been in 16:14-15, there is none here; only God's anger, 'a fire ... that shall burn for ever'. Their religion, their family life, their land, all have 'sin' written indelibly across them.

Then comes one of the most memorable passages in the whole book (17:5-8), where Judah's heart is represented as turning away from the Lord. The wilful, unbelieving nation, determined to make its own way in life and trust in its own abilities, is like a shrub barely surviving in waterless soil. There follows immediately, in what is surely meant as a reference to Psalm 1, the beautiful picture of the believer as a tree planted by a river, its leaves 'green ... in the year of drought', to point up by contrast the folly of those who go the way Judah has chosen, and the disappointment that awaits them.

Finally, in 17:9-13, we stand back to look not just at the heart of Judah but at the heart of Everyman, as seen by the eye of Yahweh, which (in a figure we remember from the 'judgment' chapters) tests it as an assayer tests metals. What does He see here? The universal urge to amass one's own resources and not to be beholden to divine grace. But still, as always, Yahweh presides from His throne over the whole of His creation, and still there is a true Israel: all who pin their hopes on Him alone, and in yet another familiar metaphor find in Him the 'fountain of living water'.

The fourth protest: Jeremiah facing both ways (17:14-18)

After quite a complex setting of the scene comes the briefest of Jeremiah's 'confessions'. We notice that for the first time Yahweh is not going to speak in response to what Jeremiah is about to say; but then He is not being asked for a response. It is as if the prophet is putting together a series of statements and requests, to all of which the Lord need only nod His agreement.

Like much of the book of Lamentations, these five verses have the ABA pattern of a palindrome, expressing deep feeling within what might seem an artificial form. They are a prayer, and in the first of them the Yahweh to whom they are addressed is the one who heals (and Jeremiah will be healed!) and the one who saves (and Jeremiah will be saved!). Then when we set verse 14 alongside verse 18a, we notice both a likeness and a difference; for in the latter, Yahweh is the one who shames (and it is now not Jeremiah but his opponents who will be shamed), and the one who dismays (and it is not Jeremiah but his opponents who will be dismayed). With the Lord's powers and the prophet's needs in such accord, 'protest' may not after all be such an appropriate term for this section; I for one find in it a much more positive frame of mind than some commentators will allow.

We notice too the striking titles given to Yahweh. After the opening statement, Jeremiah calls him 'my Praise'; before the closing statement, though he is 'my Refuge' His enemies will find Him to be their Terror. Yahweh-my-Praise is scoffed at by the prophet's hearers, who see no sign of His threats coming true. But Yahweh-their-Terror is about to 'bring upon them

neither Yahweh nor his prophet is saying anything worth
hearing, and that the firm can carry on business as usual –
the law, the counsel, the word – without all this interference
from head office. No doubt it can, in a way; you do sometimes
wonder how long all the apparatus of the modern church
might, through sheer inertia, keep trundling on, if one day
(*per impossibile*) the Holy Spirit were to abandon it.

The fifth protest: Jeremiah at the end of his tether (18:19-23)
Israel's rejection of Yahweh as evidenced by her Sabbath-
breaking is followed by His rejection of her as a potter's vessel
spoiled, and then both attitudes are confirmed, in 18:12 ('we
will follow our own plans') and 18:17 ('I will scatter them').
These verses now lead into another protest which like the
fourth one will receive no immediate response. It is a cry
of real distress and anger from Jeremiah, in the face of his
nation's final decision to turn her back on Yahweh and His
prophet. That is the real point at issue, and explains his
extreme language about his enemies.

Even in the midst of such emotional turmoil, he falls
naturally into expressing himself in the forms of Hebrew
poetry. What he says reads like an ABA chiasmus, not indeed
in its detail but in its broad outline:

> LORD, listen to their plotting,
> > when I have spoken up for their welfare!
> > > Let them suffer the consequences of their malice;
> > for they have plotted my death.
> LORD, deal with them in your anger.

He has long been standing where Yahweh stands, representing
Yahweh to Israel. Now when he turns round, as it were, to
represent Israel to Yahweh, he must feel himself torn in
two. He himself is Israel as Israel ought to be, in touch and
in tune with her Maker and Redeemer, while the Israel that
he represents is in fact hell-bent on going her own way.
He is filled simultaneously with anger at her flouting of
the 'steadfast love' of her Lord, an anger which is entirely
justified, and with agony at the judgment soon to fall on her.
He sees a correspondence between what he is going through
now at her hands, and what she will soon have to go through

at Yahweh's hands. We might ask who would ever want to be in his position, but we know it has in some measure been the experience of many devoted servants of the Lord.

The setting of the sixth protest (19:1–20:6)

Another visit to the potter's workshop will prepare the way for the sixth and last of Jeremiah's protests. This time he goes, at Yahweh's behest, not to watch the process but to buy the product; and we are going to find the clay of Israel hardened, the opposition of her leaders sharpened, and the despondency of the prophet deepened.

We are well aware (and both the following facts are to be noted) that wet clay is malleable and dry clay is not. Already, in 18:3-4, Jeremiah has seen the potter with a pot in the making decide that it is not as he wants it, and set about remaking it. Even so had he and Josiah, nearly thirty years earlier, set about the renewal of Judah, the prophet by his preaching and the king by his reforms. With Josiah's death in 609, it had soon become apparent that there was little or no change in the hearts of the people, certainly nothing like the remaking of a nation. The clay began to harden, and Jeremiah's prophecies of warning began to sound increasingly like prophecies of doom. So now, perhaps halfway through Jehoiakim's eleven-year reign, Jeremiah buys an earthenware jar, the clay not only dried but fired, finished, and hard. There will be no remoulding of *this* item if it proves unsatisfactory.

He makes his way out to the valley that lies below the southern walls of Jerusalem, having got sundry prominent citizens to accompany him. By the Potsherd Gate,[6] at that part of the city's rubbish dump where is heaped whatever cannot be destroyed by the fires of Hinnom further along, he smashes the jar, and the fragments are scattered among a million others. 'Thus says the LORD of hosts: So will I break this people and this city … so that it can never be mended' (19:11); so speaks the prophet, with much more in similar vein.

Then he turns, goes back into the city and through the streets to the temple, and there in the great court speaks to the

---

6 When as a child I first met this word, I assumed on the analogy of 'shepherd' and 'goatherd' that it meant a person who looked after a herd of pots. Alas, no. Potsherd, not pots-herd; a shard of broken earthenware.

same effect 'to all the people' (19:14), presumably repeating the same blistering words, a dozen verses of them, and even that, perhaps, only a summary of something much longer. Were we called to speak these words, we might read them aloud from the printed page, or possibly recite them from memory. But it is not difficult to understand how Yahweh could speak this entire chapter, and more, into Jeremiah's mind, so that the ear-tingling divine judgment would burst forth spontaneously, incisively, to the ears of the prophet's wincing audience, and still be there word for word when in due course Baruch would be writing it down for him.

The natural understanding of the two 'potter' incidents is that just as one follows the other, both in our Bibles and in Jeremiah's experience, so the clay is at one stage workable and at a later stage unworkable. At first there is hope for Judah, but then the chance has passed and hope is gone. And that is true to the facts; it is what actually happened. We might even suppose that both incidents involve the same pot, and the same potter at two successive stages of his work, first making and then selling. But there is another connection between them, one which is even more significant. It is brought into focus by the incident which follows immediately, the sharpening of the opposition to Jeremiah described in 20:1-6.

Here for the first time we find him physically assaulted: arrested, beaten, and imprisoned, even if only briefly. It was Pashhur, the 'chief officer in the house of the LORD', who had thus set about silencing him. When he was released the following morning, Pashhur found him no whit abashed, but with denunciations fiercer than ever, sparked off by his night in the cells.[7] Pashhur might have been appointed over the affairs of the temple, but he, Jeremiah, had been appointed 'over nations and over kingdoms'![8] Pashhur might at present be in control of all that went on around him in God's house,[9] but before long it would be terror that he would see all

---

7 The object of the punishment described as 'stocks' could have been uncomfortable, even painful, confinement, rather than public humiliation. On the other hand, the word might mean a pillory; a prisoner with arms outspread and held for hours by the wrists in acute discomfort, while crowds ridiculed him, would have an extraordinary aptness in view of the obvious New Testament parallel.

8 'Officer' (20:1) and 'set ... over' (1:10) are the same word, *paqad*.

9 The name Pashhur may reflect this: see Thompson, p. 455n.

around![10] Pashhur had 'prophesied falsely' (20:6), whereas to Jeremiah Yahweh had said 'I have put my words in your mouth' (1:9)! But however freely the prophet may express himself, the fact remains that opposition has now become persecution, and that, shocking to relate, at the hands of the religious establishment.

It has been suggested that this was a major turning point in Jeremiah's ministry, the point at which the burden of his prophesying was no longer warning but doom. Up to this time, there had been the possibility of repentance, but now, the day of grace had passed, and there would be no turning back. Up to now he had had freedom to preach and friends to support him, but henceforward all that would change. In terms of the potter and his pot, the time when the clay was still malleable had come to an end, and the pot had hardened into a shape which the potter could not approve and would destroy.

In one respect all this is true. Judah/Jerusalem is indeed to be smashed 'so that it can never be mended'. The day will come, only twenty years or so from the date of these events, when Jeremiah's generation will see the city sacked and the surrounding country laid waste, with vast numbers of its people killed or deported. But this is not perhaps a critical point of the kind that some suggest. There have actually been bitter opposition and premonitions of doom from the start, and there will, in fact, continue to be gleams of hope and friends at court right to the end. For every Pashhur, intent on silencing Jeremiah, there will also be people of repute like those of 19:1, willing to go along with him and take note of what he says and does. Even when in due course the king himself publicly rejects the words of Yahweh and burns Jeremiah's scroll, in chapter 36, there will be men in high places ready to defend and protect God's man.

However, there is something deeper than all this that God's people have to learn from the two 'potter' incidents. The pot does indeed represent Israel, and from one point of view it is first made and then unmade. But it represents Israel in two different senses, and the making of the one Israel and the unmaking of the other are going on simultaneously. An ancient

---

10 'Magor-Missabib,' 20:3 (NIV), meaning 'Terror on every side', as at 6:25.

Israelite liturgy began with the words 'A wandering Aramean was my father' (Deut. 26:5), and traced the story of the family of Abraham till it became a nation brought out of Egypt by Moses and led into Canaan by Joshua. After that, God 'gave them judges' (so Paul recounts the story in Acts 13:16ff.); 'then they asked for a king'; and the kingdom too, as a political structure, would have a limited life, which was due to end – when? The answer, says Jeremiah as he dashes the pot into fragments, is: *'Any time now.'*

Whereupon we turn back from chapter 19 to chapter 18, where the clay is still wet, and the potter is still at work. The pot takes shape, but the potter has a better shape in mind for the finished article, and we watch it being 'reworked … into another vessel' (18:4). It is not the clay, but only the vessel, which has been spoiled. The political kingdom has become the vessel of chapter 19, which under the disastrous rule of the sons of Josiah has hardened beyond the possibility of reworking and is due to be thrown away. The true Israel is the clay of chapter 18, which is about to be reshaped as the Potter wishes. She has been an oriental monarchy for the past 450 years, having previously been something rather different, and is about to be turned into something different again. But from now on she will know how to think of her God in terms of royalty, faintly foreshadowed in the best of that line of monarchs who have reigned in Jerusalem, and she will hope that perhaps one day He might give her in some unimaginable way another sight, a clearer view, of His kingly majesty. The hope will become reality, in a measure, when 600 years later crowds will acclaim One riding a donkey's colt into that very city – 'Blessed is the coming kingdom of our father David!' – and in its fullness on another day yet to be revealed, 'when the Son of Man comes in his glory, [to] sit on his glorious throne.'[11]

The sixth protest: Jeremiah in agony (20:7-18)
The last chapter and a half have brought into focus the move away from a message of warning (the clay that could be recycled, 18:4) to a message of doom (the pot that would be broken, 19:11). Arising directly from this, the prophet's final protest is a remarkable passage, in some ways the central

---

11 Mark 11:10; Matthew 25:31.

point of the entire book. It falls readily into three sections, and
for the first of them the word 'derision' in 20:8 might provide
an obvious heading: 20:7-10, 'The prophet derided'.

These verses unfold like a scene in an opera, let us say
one of Wagner's monumental music dramas, with larger-
than-life characters, a stirring score, memorable scenery, and
a world-embracing plot. At this point in the drama we see
Jeremiah centre stage. Behind and above him sits the King,
who imagines himself (quite wrongly) to be presiding over
these events. The Lord stands, of course, at the right hand of
the Prophet,[12] who addresses Him accusingly, indicating the
chorus – the People – ranged to his left: '*You* have deceived me;
they all mock me' (20:7). That is what we see. What we hear, in
20:10, is a Wagnerian *leitmotiv*, a 'leading theme', a significant
phrase which runs like a tie rod through the opera: *magor
missabib*, 'terror on every side'. We have heard it elsewhere,[13]
and shall hear it again.[14]

The King takes no part in the proceedings, though we
need to be aware that he is there. He is not named, or even
mentioned, but he must be Jehoiakim. He was put on the
throne of Judah by the Egyptians when they removed his
brother Jehoahaz in 609, and has since changed sides as the
balance of power has shifted so that Babylon is now in the
ascendant. He has regularly 'gone with the wind', whichever
way it blows.[15] For him, the words 'terror on every side' are
mere words, a slogan that he can ignore, unless it can be spun
to his own advantage.

The People have heard Jeremiah harping on *magor missabib*
so long, to no apparent effect, that the 'terror' has become
an empty threat and he has become a nuisance (20:7b-8, 10).
He is like a disreputable eccentric parading a placard which
bears some such legend as Flee from the Wrath to Come, or
The End of the World is Nigh, or Prepare to Meet thy Doom,

---

12 Psalms 16:8, 109:31. Psalm 110:5 is, I believe, saying something rather
different: see my *The Message of Psalms 73–150* (Nottingham: IVP 2001), p.166,
n.413.

13 Psalm 31:13, Lamentations 2:22, Jeremiah 6:25, 20:3.

14 Jeremiah 46:5, 49:29.

15 The novel and the film borrowed their title from Ernest Dowson's poem *Non
sum qualis eram*, where it meant not 'blown away by the wind' but 'veering as the
wind veers'.

and 'Magor Missabib' is what they call him behind his back. It is all so unseemly. Thanks on the one hand to Jehoiakim's political balancing act, and on the other to their formal nod to Yahweh's religious requirements, they are sitting pretty. They can do without this unpatriotic preacher of doom, and would be glad to be rid of him. He still has his friends and supporters, but they are few and far between.

The Prophet is deeply distressed. To himself he seems to be the only person in any way perturbed by the 'terror', though he knows in his bones (20:9) that it is on its way. He is even more distressed by the gap that seems to have opened between him and his Lord. He is indeed 'the prophet derided' by Judah, but a better summary of this section might be 'the prophet deceived' by Yahweh (20:7a). Does a link between Old Testament and New come to our mind, the quoting of the first verse of Psalm 22 ('My God, why have you forsaken me?') at the climax of the gospel story?[16] The climax of Jeremiah's story is certainly near.

The Lord, of course, knows the story from beginning to end. His 'word', which so far as Jeremiah is concerned has become, for the moment, 'a reproach and derision all day long' (20:8), takes all these factors into account, past, present, and future. As the fire of verse 9 burns both in Jeremiah's heart and at the heart of the four 'terror' verses 7–10, so the 'terror' itself and even more importantly Jeremiah's suffering because of it, lie at the heart of this tremendous book. So far from being out of step with his Lord's will, he is right at the centre of it.

He needs to be reassured of this, because (as we are about to find) 'the sky grows darker yet, And the sea rises higher.' So first a shaft of light shines briefly into the gloom, like the angel coming to strengthen Jesus in Gethsemane.[17] Just so is it for Jeremiah: 'The LORD is with me as a dread warrior.' He has felt himself to be 'the prophet deceived', but here he is 'the prophet defended'. In this middle section, he is able to see first what is in store, indeed what is already in process, for his persecutors, on their way to failure and shame and 'eternal dishonour' (20:11). Then from what will be happening to them he turns to what in his own case has already happened. He

16 Matthew 27:46, Mark 15:34.
17 Luke 22:43.

for his part has committed his cause to Yahweh, and will see
a just outcome from these troubles both for them and for him
(20:12); and Yahweh for His part has set up what the grammar
books call a 'future perfect', meaning that as one day we look
back from the end of time we shall see that the deliverance of
God's people, which by then 'will have been' completed, was
as good as done already in our own time (20:13).

Traumatic events must take place before that 'future perfect'
is achieved. We plunge now into the nightmare of 20:14-18,
'The prophet distraught'. Is there anything quite like this,
anywhere else in Scripture, on the lips of a devout servant of
God? A curse on the day of his birth, and then another on the
person who brought the news of it, for failing to kill the child
(and inevitably its mother too) before it was born! And what
has given rise to this outburst? Simply, it seems, an increasing
unpopularity, which has escalated from indifference to dislike
to plotting, and finally to assault and arrest and a night in jail.
Is that it? Is that all? The apostle Paul lists a score of hardships
that he has had to endure, far worse than this, and reckons
that they are simply par for the course (2 Cor. 11:20-29). What
is extreme about Jeremiah's suffering, for goodness' sake?
Why is he so distraught?

He knows, of course, and Yahweh knows even better, that
Judah is terminally sick; a 'failed state', we might say today.
Could David have looked four centuries into the future and
seen what his God-centred kingdom was going to become, he
would have been horrified. Her historic threefold leadership,
by prophet, priest, and king, is still in place, but it is an
empty shell; her last four kings will go down in history as
utter failures, her last high priests as total nonentities, and
practically all the prophets of these days as traitors to their
high calling, with this one glorious exception. Judah may be
blind, but she is not yet deaf; she has all but lost sight of her
God, yet she cannot help but hear Him when Jeremiah speaks.
What was foretold at the beginning of his book has come
true: 'The Lord said to me, … "To all to whom I send you,
you shall go, and whatever I command you, you shall speak.
Do not be afraid of them, for I am with you to deliver you,
declares the Lord"' (1:7-8). But though Jeremiah has given
himself heart and soul to bringing these truths home to the

rebellious nation, none of his warnings registers, *because none of his threats has come true*. Hence his emotional crisis. Yahweh has deceived him and Judah derides him.

The mention of David's name may remind us that others besides Jeremiah figure in the Bible story as men appointed to 'face both ways', the pattern we found in 17:14-18. David himself was one such, and he too was an unlikely choice. The youngest of a big family, and overlooked as the runt of the litter (1 Sam. 16:11), he surprised everyone when he burst on the scene as the slayer of Goliath. But he became one of the great go-betweens. I have written elsewhere of his 'remarkable dual role', as it emerges in so many of the Psalms. 'As God looks at him, he is one with his people (and with the rest of us) in his frail and fallible humanity. But as Israel (and we) look at him, he stands alongside God in his delegated majesty as the Lord's anointed.'[18] He represents Israel to Yahweh, and he represents Yahweh to Israel.

We find the same pattern in Samson. 'That archetypal buffoon … who could never resist either a joke or a girl,'[19] he too represented Israel. His faults were those of his people writ large, in taking worthless things seriously and treating serious matters as trivialities. In Milton's poem *Samson Agonistes*, his fellow-Israelites call him the 'mirror of our fickle state'. Yet when he turns round, as it were, and represents Yahweh to them, they see him at the last delivering the nation by his superhuman strength. At the climax of their enemies' triumph, 'Samson grasped the two middle pillars on which the house rested, and … bowed with all his strength, and the house fell upon the lords and upon all the people who were in it. So the dead whom he killed at his death were more than those whom he had killed during his life' (Judg. 16:29-30).

We must note that it was *in his death* that Samson demonstrated the power of God to save His people, because that brings us back to our present passage. In Jeremiah, Yahweh again takes hold of unlikely material – this time a diffident, retiring youngster – and makes of it something tough and immovable, 'an iron pillar, and bronze walls' (1:18).

18 *The Message of Psalms 1–72* (Nottingham: IVP, 2001), p.25.

19 J.A. Motyer (2006), *Discovering the Old Testament* (Nottingham: IVP/Crossway), p. 91.

Even so, what this man represents to Yahweh is an Israel full of questioning and doubt, throwing uncertainties and challenges at her inscrutable God. When, however, we look at the other face of Jeremiah, when he turns round to represent Yahweh to Israel, what do we see? What is the counterpart here of David's showing us something of God's glory and majesty, and of Samson's showing us something of God's power and strength? It is a picture far different from those. Here in contrast to the majestic king and the mighty judge is one 'despised and rejected' by his own people, 'a man of sorrows, one acquainted with grief,'[20] all of whose ministry seems to come to nothing. If this is what Israel's God is like, then (from what people see of Him in Jeremiah) His well-intentioned efforts must be under some sort of curse, and He is a helpless, suffering God, to all appearances a failure. To think that an outcome as wretched as this should be the end result of so many years of obedient, persevering ministry!

But the apparent failure is not, in fact, the end, and it should not in any case seem strange to the people of God. Isaiah 53 has set forth the classic portrait of the suffering servant; Jeremiah here embodies it, and Israel herself is soon to tread the same *Via Dolorosa*. All these foreshadow the sufferings of *the* Servant, whose death is the central, and literally the crucial, point of the whole biblical revelation. In the words of John Bowring's hymn,

> In the cross of Christ I glory,
>> Towering o'er the wrecks of time;
> All the light of sacred story
>> Gathers round its head sublime.

The pattern is equally observable in our own half of history. Today the persecution of the servants of Christ is more widespread than it has ever been. We do well to protest at such suffering and try to put a stop to it, but there is no denying that now as always 'the blood of the martyrs is the seed of the church,' as Tertullian put it in the early days of the Christian era, and these lesser crosses have an extraordinary power to draw sinners to repentance and faith.

---

20 Isaiah 53:3.

7

Betrayals

(Jeremiah 21–23)

Time: several years later. Scene: the same but different
'That nightmare was my lowest point,' says Jeremiah, 'but in
the mercy of God I did wake up. Or, rather, in the *plan* of God.
He had intended the nightmare as well as the awakening; he
wanted me to put my protests into words.'

'What you awoke to was hardly less unpleasant,' objects
Baruch. 'When Jehoiakim died we were certainly glad to be
rid of him, but young Jehoiachin was scarcely installed as his
successor when Nebuchadnezzar's army was back here, the
boy was taken off to Babylon, and we found the kingdom
being run by Uncle Zedekiah. Some improvement! You know
very well you're suffering more in his time than you ever did
in his brother's.'

'True enough. But I see the plan unfolding, and I begin to
grasp how the kingdom has to die in order to be reborn. The
pot smashed, yet the clay reshaped – there's an intriguing
picture!'

'It's one I find hard to grasp. Especially the smashing of the
pot. What will have been destroyed? And what will be left?
For generations past our nation has been like – oh, forget the
clay pot for a moment, think instead of a three-legged stool:
prophet, priest and king, all three necessary if it's to stand.
You, we know, had promises from God at the very beginning
that will certainly hold good, so Israel will still have a prophet.
But you seem to be foreseeing the end of Jerusalem, which

must mean the end of the temple and the throne. No more priests? No more kings?'

'If temple worship does come to an end, Yahweh will see to it that true believers still have access to Him somehow, wherever they may be,' says Jeremiah. 'I'm more concerned about the ending of the line of kings. And, for that matter, about whether the line of prophets will continue; because although Jerusalem seems to be awash with people claiming to speak for Yahweh, there are precious few who have actually met Him as I have… If you're ready for some more dictation, Baruch, we ought to get down in writing the most recent word that Yahweh gave me for Zedekiah. I have no great hopes of him, but at least he's looking for advice in the right quarter.'

As this imagined conversation indicates, times have changed. In the latter part of Jehoiakim's reign, towards the turn of the century, Jeremiah was protesting that no one, least of all the king, believed his prophecies of doom. Now, in (let us say) 588, it is Zedekiah's reign that is drawing to a close, and the truth of the prophet's earlier warnings is all too obvious; the enemy is at the gates. Baruch is right; paradoxically, for reasons that will become clear later in the book, Jeremiah suffers more in the reign of Zedekiah, who has considerable regard for him, than he did in that of Jehoiakim, who despised him. But now he is back on an even keel, confident, sure of his Lord, his protests laid to rest, imprisoned though he may be amid more tangible horrors than the nightmare of chapter 20. And he has a message from Yahweh for this last king of Judah (21:1–22:9), then a message about each of his four predecessors (22:10–23:8), and after that a message about the prophets whose calling it is to guide them and their nation (23:9-40).

Speaking prophet; listening king? (21:1–22:9)

What a surprise as the spotlight turns to Zedekiah – a son of Josiah who actually *wants* to 'enquire of the Lord'! And equally surprising is the response of Jeremiah, who at the end of chapter 20 (a dozen years earlier in real time, but only a moment ago as we read the book) was choked with his own despair and the prospect of his nation's doom; whereas now he is composed, his response is measured, and as city and

nation are facing their final agony he even offers a gleam of hope.

Not for Zedekiah, though, as we are about to see. In the early stages of what is going to be a prolonged siege, the Chaldeans (a term Jeremiah uses regularly for Nebuchadnezzar and his Babylonian armies) have a blockade in place around Jerusalem, but are still being engaged from time to time by Israelite sorties from the city. The days of that kind of fighting 'outside the walls' are numbered, says Yahweh (21:4). He foresees soldiers and weapons back inside the fortifications, shut up in the city along with disease and famine. The miseries of such a siege are the burden of Yahweh's first word to the king's representatives (21:4-6). It will end, says his second word (21:7), with the sacking of the city and the pitiless slaughter of those who have survived the siege. A third word (21:8-10) is then directed not to Zedekiah but to the people at large: anyone 'who goes out' while the opportunity is still there 'and surrenders to the Chaldeans … shall live'. Yahweh is just and merciful; no one need perish in the coming catastrophe.

But there is no denying that many will, and that leads on to three further words from Yahweh. Unlike the first three, each of these in turn is addressed to '*the house* of the king of Judah'. They give a range of meanings to that phrase. In 21:11-14, the 'house' means the dynasty, the 'house of David', charged from generation to generation with the just government of God's people. In 22:1-5, it is defined as a 'place', a building, namely the palace, with its gates and its throne-room. At the same time it is also the court that is based there, the royal household, 'kings … and their servants and their people.' And in 22:6-9, the 'house' appears to be the city, Jerusalem, which Yahweh threatens with devastation. In fact in every sense of the phrase, the house of the king of Judah is doomed.

Though later chapters will give us a more detailed picture of Zedekiah, we can see already that he has a respect for Jeremiah, a belief (of sorts) in Yahweh, a fear of Babylon and an inability to cope with advisers more strong-minded than he is. But merely to be sorry for him, and to hope that we might do better in similar circumstances, is to miss the point of these verses. He is more than an individual; he is, for better or worse, the king, and 'the house of the king of Judah' is his

responsibility. He may recoil from a task for which he feels inadequate. But if he does, he is in exactly the same position as Jeremiah was when he was called to be a prophet; and Jeremiah, having proved the power of Yahweh for himself, is on hand to offer the same resource to Zedekiah.

No excuses, then. But in the event Zedekiah would fail, and the kingdom would fail with him. His hope had been that Yahweh would do one of 'his wonderful deeds' (21:2) to save the situation, and he presumed it would be not just the kind of miracle recorded in the ancient scriptures, like the deliverance from Egypt in the days of Moses, but a repeat of the actual deliverance of his own city Jerusalem, only a century earlier, from the Assyrians, in the days of Hezekiah. That however was not going to happen. In the plan of God, the only way forward was to leave the beleaguered city and to surrender to the Babylonians. To his consternation Zedekiah had the divine intervention, God's 'wonderful deed', spelt out for him as the very opposite of what he hoped for – 'I myself will fight *against* you,' said Yahweh through His prophet (21:5). And he would discover in due course that the 'surrender' of 21:9 would betoken a much more far-reaching thing, namely the surrender of Israel's sovereignty, with her status as a political kingdom revoked for all time. When a year or two later Jerusalem was 'given into the hand of the king of Babylon', who would 'burn it with fire' (21:10), it was not just a conglomeration of buildings but a 450-year-old institution that was being consigned to the flames.

These were events not only foreseen but also intended by God; but that does not exonerate Zedekiah. Though as an individual he may cut a pathetic figure in the pages of Scripture, we have to remember that he also had public responsibilities; in fact they are the reason for his being there at all. The care of God's kingdom had been placed in his hands for the final eleven years of its history, and he knew both how to 'enquire of the LORD', and who would give him God's answers. If he had put himself wholeheartedly into Jeremiah's hands, he could have coped. But he didn't. For himself, he has to be reckoned a failure, and his sad end (of which we shall learn more later) was his own fault. More serious was the fact that the fate of many others was linked to his. He had been

entrusted with the kingship, and his epitaph has to be that of one who betrayed his trust.

In that he was not alone. Jeremiah now calls in review the whole line of Josiah's family, and his relationship to it, through four reigns and twenty-three years between the accession of Jehoahaz in 609 and the removal of Zedekiah in 586.

Kings who betray their trust (22:10–23:8)

Jeremiah does not draw attention to the following facts, but the histories record as part of the kingdom's timeline that Jehoahaz reigned for three months, Jehoiakim for eleven years, Jehoiachin for three months, and Zedekiah for eleven years. This might seem too neat to be true, but detailed research leaves us with little doubt about the dates.[1] We also know that when Nebuchadnezzar came to power in Babylon, his campaigns in what he called 'Hatti-land' (meaning the territories of Judah and her neighbours) resulted in three major deportations of local kings and leading citizens. The first, in 605, included Daniel and his friends.[2] The second, in 597, took Jehoiachin into captivity; and the third followed the sack of Jerusalem in 586, and removed Zedekiah.

There is an analogy between what we found in Lamentations, where fervent emotion is channelled, not choked, by strict poetic forms, and what we find here, where real history, normally so untidy, may nevertheless be shaped in memorable patterns. So Jeremiah can dictate his prophecies about the sons of Josiah and the last days of Judah in a remarkably symmetrical way. Here is a first draft:

Shallum/Jehoahaz, 3 months (22:10-12)
Eliakim/Jehoiakim, 11 years (22:13-19)
    Judah and her allies (22:20-23)
[Je]coniah/Jehoiachin, 3 months (22:24-30)
Mattaniah/Zedekiah, 11 years (23:1-8)

But is that the right label for 23:1-8? Surely Zedekiah, in whose time this whole section of the book was put together, has been dealt with already, with a chapter and a half (21:1–22:9) in which

---

1 2 Kings 23:31, 36; 24:8, 18. See Mackay, vol. i, pp. 35-51, and vol. ii, pp. 603-616; McFall, 'Sixty-Nine Weeks', pp. 712-13.

2 Daniel 1:1-7.

he, like his predecessors, stands condemned. So who is it that follows Jehoiachin in chapter 23? Let us move chronologically along the portrait gallery and find out.

We are told elsewhere that 'all Judah and Jerusalem mourned for Josiah' when he was killed in battle in 609, and he is remembered 'in their laments to this day.'[3] But as the New Testament says of David, 'he had served the purpose of God in his own generation,'[4] and with those laments was mingled a deep appreciation of what Yahweh had done for His people through one of the greatest of their kings. With Josiah's passing, however, we arrive (says Jeremiah) at a stage in the history of Israel which really is lamentable. As Shakespeare puts it when another great ruler dies, if you have tears, prepare to shed them now.[5]

For a mistake was made which could have cost the nation dear. The officers of state, who presumably had Josiah's confidence, believed his youngest son Shallum (22:10-12) to be the right man to carry on his father's good work. They anointed him king, with the throne-name of Jehoahaz, and almost at once everything went wrong. 'He did what was evil in the sight of the Lord,' in the tradition of the worst of his ancestors,[6] and perhaps it was fortunate that his reign came to an end as soon as it did. As we know, it was in trying unsuccessfully to stop an Egyptian army on its way to a war zone in the north that Josiah had perished, and the pharaoh, leading his troops home three months later, decided that Jehoahaz was likely to be equally anti-Egyptian. Being in his own eyes overlord of these smaller states, he took it on himself to replace the young king by his older brother Eliakim, and took him off into exile. Had Judah been rescued from a bad king, or deprived of one who might have reformed? Either way, he was a lost soul and a cause of bitter grief. What Yahweh says about the journey of Shallum/Jehoahaz into Egypt should have been a stark warning to those who in chapters 42 and 43, twenty-odd years later, were going to suppose that that might be a place where Judah's remnant might survive, and

3 2 Chronicles 35:24f.
4 Acts 13:36.
5 *Julius Caesar*, III ii.
6 2 Kings 23:32.

even perhaps revive: 'There shall he die, and he shall never see this land again' (22:12). Egypt is a place where hopes drain away into the sand. Josiah's youngest son had not had long to show whether he would measure up to the responsibilities of kingship but in the short time that he did have, it became clear that the answer was no.

We are not told immediately whose portrait it is that hangs second in the gallery (22:13-19). But need we ask? So much that we have seen up to now of Jeremiah's ministry, and certainly the ten chapters that cover his protests, has been set against the background of a reign which is at odds with everything he stands for. The spoiled loincloth, the unsatisfactory clay jar, and the prophet's own wretchedness, represent the real state of the nation, while Judah shows herself more and more plainly to be in denial, repudiating his allegations. And the king who is presiding over this fool's paradise is Eliakim, better known to us by his throne-name Jehoiakim. The damning evidence would be obvious to any fair-minded jury: to say nothing of 'dishonest gain ... shedding innocent blood ... oppression and violence' (22:17), there in the background to the portrait is a palace, brand new and quite unnecessary, being built a few miles from Jerusalem, by forced and unpaid labour, with ridiculous extravagance ('more and more cedar', 22:15 NIV). It was perfectly possible, as Josiah had shown, to live in regal style without descending to this sort of showy nonsense. As in the parable of the man who built himself bigger barns, God would shortly be saying to Jehoiakim, 'Fool! This night your soul is required of you.'[7] When that night came, there would be no classy royal funeral, with its formal cries of 'woe, woe', says 22:18; Yahweh had already condemned the unlamented monarch with the 'woe' of 22:13,[8] and 'with the burial of a donkey' he would be buried, 'dragged and dumped beyond the gates of Jerusalem' (22:19).

Halfway along the row of portraits is something different: a landscape, a depiction of the country of Judah, with her neighbours in the surrounding highlands – Lebanon to the north, Bashan to the north-east, and Abarim to the south-east

7 Luke 12:20.

8 It is the same word (hôy) which ESV translates as 'Woe' in the one verse and as 'Ah!' in the other.

(22:20-23). Five different images combine in these four verses. We may take 'lovers' to mean pagan allies, and 'youth' to mean earlier periods of Israelite history. The 'wind' is Babylonian aggression; the 'shepherds' are kings; and the 'pangs' of birth represent (for the moment, at any rate) unavoidable suffering. There, then, at the centre of the complex little picture, are the kings who betray their trust, the main concern of this section of the prophecy: shepherds who have failed to shepherd their flocks, and so will themselves be herded off 'into captivity'.

Next in line, in 22:24-30, is Jeconiah (Coniah is an abbreviation, and he is more often called by his throne-name Jehoiachin). A carbon copy of Jehoahaz, each of them exiled after a three-month reign? Not really; though to save ourselves from wasting misplaced sympathy on either of them, we should note something else they had in common: each made the most of his brief reign to do 'what was evil in the sight of the Lord.'[9] The most obvious difference between them had to do with the dramatic shift in the balance of power in the Middle East during the last decade of the seventh century B.C. Within five years of the Egyptian interference which deprived Jehoahaz of the throne of Judah and gave it to Jehoiakim, Nebuchadnezzar had come to power in Babylon and was himself interfering right, left, and centre in the politics of the surrounding countries. He actually captured Jerusalem in 597, when the middle one of the three deportations took place and Jehoiachin (with the queen mother Nehushta, noted already in 13:18 as well as here in 22:26)[10] was exiled to Babylon. Like Jehoahaz in Egypt, they would die in exile, and never see their native land again.

But there is something curiously ambivalent about the Coniah/Jehoiachin passage. Noticing its length, twice as long as the Shallum one, we notice also the queries, explicit and implicit, that it contains. *Is* Coniah a broken pot (22:28)? Does the question expect the answer 'yes' or the answer 'no'? And he may be a broken pot, but were we not shown alongside the broken pot of chapter 19 the refashioned clay of chapter 18? And he may have been childless as far as the 'throne of David', the royal succession, was concerned (22:30), but he

9 2 Kings 23:32, 24:9.
10 See also 2 Kings 24:8-17.

did have children in exile, did he not? Was the the breaking of the pot perhaps the termination of the reigning royal line, and the continuance of the actual bloodline the remaking of it in a different shape? And did not that line survive the exile and re-emerge at the restoration, with Zerubbabel, and even extend into New Testament times, with Jesus Himself?[11] Jehoahaz may have been doomed to extinction in Egypt, and Jehoiakim to a donkey's grave outside Jerusalem, but there seem to be gleams of hope in this third portrait.

We might expect that the fourth would depict Zedekiah, as in the symmetrical outline suggested above. But there is no mention of his name (though Yahweh's name figures nine times in eight verses!). Instead, the first paragraph concerning this final portrait (23:1-4) is about the shepherds, that is, the kings, in general – what they have not done, namely attend to the flock, and what they have done, namely destroy and scatter the sheep. So Yahweh will duly 'attend to' the wicked shepherds with an attention they will not enjoy, and will Himself take over the care of the flock, and restore it.

He will do this, says the second paragraph (23:5-6), through another king. Two dazzling verses picture this kingdom that is yet to come with a cluster of new images to add to the profusion that already adorns these chapters. This will be *David's* kingdom, going back to the prototype and starting afresh with everything as it was originally meant to be. It will be ruled by *the Branch*, one of a group of words most familiar perhaps from Isaiah 11:1 ('a shoot from the stump of Jesse, and a branch from his roots'), and here used as a royal title.[12] And we are told His name: 'The Lord is our righteousness', 'the Lord' being *Yah*, and 'righteousness' being *zedek*; so the last portrait is that of Zedekiah after all, but *zedek* and *Yah* taken up and turned round and made into something new and very special.

We know, of course, that the new Zedekiah will never betray His trust, being none other than 'Christ Jesus, whom

---

11 1 Chronicles 3:17, 19; Ezra 2:2, 3:2; Matthew 1:12-16.

12 See also Isaiah 4:2 and Zechariah 3:8, 6:12. The English word 'branch' is slightly unfortunate if it suggests an off-centre side shoot, less important than the main trunk.

God made ... our righteousness.'[13] As the third and last of these
paragraphs (23:7-8) puts it, when the Lord Himself brings
all His people out of captivity and into the Promised Land,
that will be the fulfilment of a pattern that goes back beyond
Jeremiah, even beyond David, to the original redemption of
Israel in the days of Moses.

So, perhaps surprisingly, where Jeremiah was given
prophecies of warning in the days of Josiah and prophecies
of doom through three of the reigns that followed, we see
a change in his ministry, even as 'the sky grows darker yet'
and the Babylonian menace grows greater. He himself has
torments yet to endure at the hands of ill-wishers whom
Zedekiah has not the courage to restrain, worse than anything
he suffered at the hands of Jehoiakim. But he finds a renewed
confidence, and stands steadfast as 'a fortified city, an iron
pillar'; and against the background of a parade of kings
who one and all betray their trust, prophecies of hope begin
to shine. 'How you will be pitied', he said to Judah and her
allies, 'when pangs come upon you, pain as of a woman in
labour' (22:23); but as Jesus Himself would point out, that
kind of anguish is regularly followed by the joy of a new birth
(John 16:21). We can therefore revise the chiastic pattern of
Jeremiah's words to the sons of Josiah in this way:

Jehoahaz (22:10-12): doom in exile
Jehoiakim (22:13-19): doom at home
        Judah and her allies (22:20-23): a place of doom and hope
Jehoiachin (22:24-30): hope in exile
'Zedekiah' (23:1-8): hope at home

Prophets who betray their trust (23:9-40)

As the kings were entrusted with the governing of the people,
so the prophets were entrusted with the guiding of the kings.
To judge from Jeremiah's book thus far, that might seem to
mean in his time three kings in particular, with one prophet
(himself) appointed as guide to each of the three in turn. But
a very cursory reading of the story shows that things were
not as simple as that. Jeremiah was by no means the only
prophet of his day. Contemporary with him were others who

13 1 Corinthians 1:30.

have left us books of their own (Habakkuk and Zephaniah in Judah, Daniel and Ezekiel in Babylon), and others again whose calling was simply to speak God's word (Huldah, Uriah),[14] to say nothing of men like Hananiah, whom we shall meet shortly, preaching poisonous untruths in the name of Yahweh. To judge by chapter 23, there was plenty of this last kind of prophesying.

Prophecy generally, whether true or false, was addressed to the public at large as well as to the reigning king; and everyone was well aware that prophets might sometimes contradict one another. When that happened, what were people to think? How was anyone, king or commoner, to tell which of the conflicting messages did indeed come from Yahweh?

We have just seen Josiah's sons deservedly pilloried for betraying their trust as kings, but they were aided and abetted in doing so by such people as Hananiah, when he betrayed his trust as a prophet. To Jeremiah, as a genuine prophet of Yahweh, fell the double task of exposing such falsehood and proclaiming the truth that it denied.

So he speaks 'concerning the prophets'. First, Hananiah and his kind are strangers to the law of Yahweh; they do not themselves live according to it (23:9-17). Because the 'heart' in Scripture represents the mind and will rather than the emotions, the broken heart in 23:9 means not that Jeremiah is grief-stricken (though he probably is), but that he is nonplussed, simply staggered by the way 'the LORD and ... his holy words' are treated by the false prophets. Surely it is obvious, he would say, that the word of prophecy and the word of law belong together? How can these people claim to be servants of the first while their whole lifestyle ignores the second? 'For the land is full of adulterers ... their course is evil ... From the prophets of Jerusalem ungodliness has gone out into all the land' (23:10, 15). The northern kingdom's prophets 'prophesied by Baal and led my people Israel astray', which was perhaps only to be expected up there in Samaria. But the southern kingdom's are no better; down here in Jerusalem 'they commit adultery and walk in lies' (23:13-14). According to Deuteronomy, a false prophet may be identified in two ways: either his predictions do not come true (Deut. 18:21-22),

---

14 2 Kings 22:14; Jeremiah 26:20-21.

or they do come true, but he himself practises and preaches an ungodly way of life (Deut. 13:1-3). He predicts a rosy future for people whose sins are actually dragging them down to ruin. As Jeremiah puts it succinctly here in verse 17, such prophets 'say continually to those who despise the word of the Lord, "It shall be well with you"; and to everyone who stubbornly follows his own heart, they say, "No disaster shall come upon you."'

He moves on to speak of them as being strangers also to the council of Yahweh (23:18-32). Summing up the previous paragraph, about high-sounding optimistic prophecy that takes no account of people's sins, he has already indicated where the false teachings of these prophets come from: 'They speak visions of their own minds, not from the mouth of the Lord' (23:16). 'Who among them', he now asks, 'has stood in the council of the Lord to see and hear *his* word?' The picture of 23:18, Yahweh sitting in council like a king discussing policy with his ministers of state, is one familiar to the Bible writers,[15] but nothing like it has been the experience of Jeremiah's opponents. He, by contrast, *has* experienced it. His claim to have seen and heard Yahweh's word is validated by the fact that even now that word is being fulfilled: 'Behold, the storm of the Lord! Wrath has gone forth' (23:19). That is the true word, and 'if they had stood in my council,' says Yahweh (23:22), that is what they would now be proclaiming, and they would be urging their hearers to turn from the sins that have provoked it. But they have not had that experience, they have not heard Me or seen Me as I truly am. Of Me, He says, they see only what they want to see. But I see them, and everything about them (23:24).

What is more (Yahweh continues), I hear them; 'I have heard what the prophets have said,' and it is all mere dreams (23:25). He is not here speaking of the kind of dream which demonstrably, both in Bible times and since, brings a message from God that ties in with everything else He is doing and saying. That is precisely what the false prophets do not bring. Yahweh is distinguishing between two utterly different messages. We might paraphrase verse 28, and the passage in which it is set, something like this: 'Know that what Jeremiah has is My word, and he speaks it faithfully; and know that

15 Cf. 1 Kings 22:19-23; Job 15:8; Psalms 82:1; 89:7.

when these people tell a dream, a dream is all it is. *He* relays a word from Me that has power to nourish the soul like wheat, to burn the conscience like fire, to break hard hearts as the hammer breaks the rocks. *They* find some agreeable thought emerging from their subconscious, or they consciously invent one, or they simply repeat what the next man has said. These dreams are lies' (the word is 'delusion', as repeatedly in chapters 7-10), 'and their effect is to lead My people astray.'

As they reject Yahweh's law, and have no experience of Yahweh's council, so the false prophets are strangers also to Yahweh's burden (23:33-40). That term may itself seem strange to modern readers, especially when they find that some English versions render it as 'oracle', the voice of a god. But our word 'burden', like the Hebrew word *massa'* which it translates, lends itself to a grim pun that may be the point of this sentence. The root meaning of 'burden' is something you 'bear', or lift up; as here in 23:33, for example, where the messenger comes 'bearing' a message from Yahweh, and His people are asking what it is. But a delivery man might come to your front door 'bearing' a weighty and cumbersome package that he will be only too glad to be rid of. Hence the brusque exchange in some of the versions: 'What is Yahweh's burden?' 'You are! And I am about to rid myself of it.'[16] For Yahweh has heard more than enough of people who claim to know how things are, and how they are going to develop – as such 'prophets' might pompously put it, what is the true analysis of the present situation and what the outcome is undoubtedly going to be. How dare they call such opinions the 'burden' of Yahweh? That sort of message is merely 'every man's own word,' he tells them, 'and you pervert the words of the living God' (23:36).

A rueful look around the English-speaking world of today, with its institutions and its culture shaped by centuries of Christian tradition, will show us something very similar. In what the media say and what the government does, they take on the roles of prophets and kings, paying lip service to truth and justice and compassion, but all too often adapting these values to the supposed requirements of the modern age. Nowadays (we are told) principles that were central in

---

16 This translation follows the Greek Old Testament, the Septuagint (RSV, NRSV, ESV); others translate as 'What burden?', following the Hebrew text (KJV, RV, NASB, NIV).

the thinking of the men of the Reformation and the Puritan divines and the leaders of the Evangelical Revival and the philanthropists and missionaries of Victorian times are of historical interest only.[17] The nations of the West appreciate the grandiose building they have inherited, but not the old-fashioned foundations on which it was built. All honour to those who hear and obey the call to be God's Jeremiahs in this secular twenty-first century version of Zedekiah's Judah!

Even so, it is today's church rather than today's world that is expected to learn from Jeremiah's account of trusts betrayed. It was God's people who at the turn of the sixth century B.C. were let down by kings to whom they looked for leadership and prophets to whom they looked for guidance. Every so often in their history a chapter closes, humanly speaking because of some flaw or failure, but from God's point of view as the necessary way forward to a new development; and this was one such ending. For us today, the New Testament makes it clear that we are living in the final chapter, awaiting the close of the whole story and then 'the renewal of all things'.[18] Jeremiah's messages of warning, doom, and hope are as necessary now as they were in Bible times for all who foresee the death of our world and look forward to a rebirth beyond it. Here in this sinful world they are called to be salt to prevent decay and light to banish darkness;[19] but it is not so much to the world around them, as to them themselves, that these words from the final years of the kingdom of Judah are really directed. The kings and the prophets, the governments and the media, have their equivalents among the people of God today. We are being shown the need for a church leadership shaped and directed in all things by the Scriptures—living according to the law of Yahweh, listening to what is said in the council of Yahweh, proclaiming the 'burden' of Yahweh. This is one of the darkest passages in the long tale of the Hebrew monarchies from Saul to Zedekiah, but it has a great lesson to teach us.

---

17 For example, at the time of writing 'equality' is far more important than religious conviction. But in the nature of things, that statement could be out of fashion by the time you read this, and the day may come when people are flabbergasted that any generation could have been taken in by such nonsense.

18 Matthew 19:28 (NIV).

19 Matthew 5:13-16.

8

The View from Jerusalem
(Jeremiah 24–25)

The call

At the beginning came the call: 'Before I formed you in the womb I knew you, and before you were born I consecrated you; I appointed you a prophet to *the nations*' (1:5). At the end we shall find the 'word ... concerning *the nations*' that Yahweh had called Jeremiah to proclaim (46:1) expanded to no fewer than six chapters. And here too, at the book's midpoint (a hinge like those on which most of the poems in Lamentations pivot), we find the same calling noted, indeed intensified: 'all the words ... which Jeremiah prophesied against *all the nations*' (25:13).

Up to now, though, his book has been concerned almost exclusively with his own nation. And you can see why. He will be keenly aware of an earlier call, namely Israel's calling to be a channel of blessing to the rest of the world; like the prophet, the nation also was consecrated to a God-given vocation before it was born, with the promise first made to Abraham,[1] then repeated to his descendants,[2] and now renewed through Jeremiah. But Jeremiah has had to qualify his message with a big 'If', for Israel is in no fit state to be the bearer of these glad tidings. '*If* you return, O Israel' (that is, repent), '*if* you remove your detestable things from my presence, ... *if* you swear "As the LORD lives" in truth, in justice, and in righteousness, *then*

---

1 Genesis 12:3; 18:18; 22:18.
2 Genesis 26:4, 28:14.

nations shall bless themselves in him' (4:1-2). As things are, the holy nation has a lot that needs to be put right before it can be a blessing to anybody else; there has to be plucking up and breaking down before there can be building and planting (1:10).

Then there is a third call, besides Jeremiah's and Israel's. Josiah has done all that a king can do to reform his kingdom's structures; Jeremiah has done, and is still doing, what a prophet must do to touch its heart. But the kingdom is not listening, and now, therefore, it has to be taught a sharp lesson – the sharpest imaginable. It is to that task, the disciplining of a wilful, incorrigible Israel, that the other nations are called. Their arrogance and greed and cruelty are to be given free rein to bring it to its knees, and eventually to its senses. They cannot destroy it as a nation, but they will destroy it as a kingdom. And then, having accepted that call – freely, and with disgusting, lip-smacking relish – they in their turn will be judged by the God of all nations. As these central chapters say, this is His word not only *to* them but also *against* them. Great is the mystery of freely chosen wickedness and of the way God uses it for His own good purposes.

The place

The place is of course Jerusalem. Here Jeremiah is based for almost the whole of his ministry, certainly for the four decades between his call in 627 and the calamity of 586. It was different for others of the great prophets. The last forty years of Moses' life were one long journey, a succession of significant places, because he had been called to lead his people on their great migration. Samuel 'went on a circuit year by year' round the towns of Israel,[3] because by the time he was called to be its judge the nation was settled in its new land. Now we find Jeremiah staying put in the capital; a different calling, but on the same principle. This is the place where God wants him. No doubt many in Judah are assuming that if the worst comes to the worst, Jerusalem at any rate will be indestructible (don't the Scriptures say 'God is in the midst of her, she shall not be moved'?).[4] Jeremiah knows better. This place will be no safer

3 1 Samuel 7:15-17.
4 Psalm 46:5.

than any other on the day of judgment. But Jerusalem is, and will be to the end, the kingdom's capital. Here the last five kings of the House of David are to preside over its decline and fall. Here, then, Jeremiah must remain, with his repeated prophecies of warning and doom for them. But it is also from here that he will be sending forth prophecies of challenge to the nations beyond their frontiers, and even, remarkably, prophecies of hope to the remnant that will survive the death of the city.

The time

Whatever shape a commentator may claim to find in this complex book, it will not be that of a straightforward narrative. We may notice this in many of its chapters, but it is particularly obvious as we read these two. Chapter 24 is set in the 590s, the first decade of the new century, according to our modern reckoning of the years. The young king Jehoiachin has been deported to Babylon, and Zedekiah is now on the throne (24:1, 8). Chapter 25, however, is set in the 600s, the last decade of the old century, several years earlier, and Jehoiachin's father Jehoiakim is still on the throne (25:1). Would it not be more helpful to have events narrated in the order they happen?

Yes, for certain purposes, no doubt: for example, so that modern readers would find it easier to get a clear outline in their minds of what happened when. The account of the seven kings through whose reigns Jeremiah lived, on pages 34-35 of this book, is an attempt to provide something of the sort.[5] Much more wide-ranging have been the various modern accounts of the whole life and ministry of the prophet, with the Bible text abridged and rearranged imaginatively so as to tell a coherent story. The results can be illuminating; such are the twentieth-century studies of Jeremiah by George Adam Smith, Alexander Stewart, J.O. Hannay, and David Day.[6]

But Bible history is written with other aims than the construction of a chronological grid for people who find that

---

5 My *In the Days of the Kings* (Tain: Christian Focus, 2010) aims to offer the same kind of background narrative to the overall story of the Hebrew kingdoms.

6 George Adam Smith (1923), *Jeremiah* (London: Hodder & Stoughton); Alexander Stewart (1936), *Jeremiah* (Edinburgh: Knox); J.O. Hannay, writing under the pen-name George A. Birmingham (1956), *God's Iron* (London: Geoffrey Bles); David Day (1987), *Jeremiah* (Leicester: InterVarsity Press).

sort of thing helpful, or even the narration of a stirring true story. What might be the purpose in the mind of God when He causes this book first to be put together, and then to be preserved down the ages, in the shape in which it now comes to us?

A sneak preview of chapter 36 will show us Jeremiah recalling and dictating the substance of more than twenty years of prophesying, and his friend Baruch writing it all down, some as the prophet speaks it ('Then I said …'), some as Baruch reports it ('Then Jeremiah said …'). Nothing is more likely than that the collaboration should have continued after the dreadful days of 586, when the two of them, having survived the sack of Jerusalem, had been taken to live in exile in Egypt. We may picture Jeremiah finding that he could remember more and more of the tremendous words that Yahweh had given him, especially if he had kept notes at the time, and Baruch acting as prompter and secretary and editor. It would have quickly become apparent that along with the content of these prophecies Jeremiah was aware of theological patterns underlying them. The book that was taking shape would be something more than, indeed quite other than, just a glorified diary. Mere chronology was taking second place to some more significant scheme for the organizing of the mass of material.

'It was the message about the figs that you wrote down yesterday, wasn't it, Baruch?'

'Yes, the one you delivered to King Zedekiah after the second deportation – the big deportation, that took so many of our leading lights away into exile, and left him on the throne in place of his nephew. You'll have plenty more for me to record from the rest of his reign, I'm sure.'

'I shall indeed… But today there comes back to me the word I was given a few years before that, about how the fate of the nations would be tied up with the fate of Israel.'

'I remember that well. Go ahead. Once I have it copied down, I presume you'll want me to slot it in where it belongs chronologically, back before the "figs" vision.'

'No; I think not. We need to make it clear that there were two stories, with an overlap between them. What you have just written takes the first story to its end in 597, with Zedekiah

and the "figs" prophecy; this is the point at which we should begin the second story, even though it means going back seven years, to the "nations" prophecy of 604 while Jehoiakim was still king.' (Not of course that this imagined conversation would have used our BC dates!)

The end of the line

'The end of the line' – for what? For whom? We are only at chapter 24, and nowhere near the end of the book. True, the renegade northern kingdom had come to an end more than a century earlier, in 722, when the Assyrian empire overran most of the smaller states of the region. Here in the south, the three decades of Josiah's reign and the three months of that of his son Jehoahaz were each in turn brought to an end in 609 by the armies of Egypt, and in 598/7 the reigns of Jehoiakim and his son Jehoiachin were likewise terminated in quick succession as Babylon came to dominate the Middle East. Many endings! But the vision described in chapter 24 carries a powerful double message, and the first part of it is that the imminent doom of Jerusalem does not in fact spell the end for Israel.

For the basket of good figs represents those whom Yahweh intends to preserve through the coming catastrophe. They are 'regarded as good' not because of any good *in* them, but because of their willingness to accept the good that He plans *for* them. This basket, like the other, is set down 'before the Temple of the Lord,' that is, the place where Yahweh pledges to meet with His people, because in 'the land of the Chaldeans' just as much as in 'this place' (24:5) Israel will find herself in His presence. And to those already in exile in Babylonia He makes extraordinary promises (24:6-7) to which we shall return in a moment.

But the second part of this chapter's message does signal an end, in fact several ends. 'The bad figs that are so bad they cannot be eaten' (24:8) are, as Jesus said in a similar connection, of no use even 'for the soil or for the manure pile', but are fit only to be 'thrown away'.[7] This is the end of the line for Zedekiah, of whose final days we shall read in chapter 39. It will be the end of the line for the royal family, such as is left

---

7 Luke 14:35.

of it in Israel; for even if he still had a crown, he would have no one to bequeath it to – after his capture he will see his sons 'slaughtered … before his eyes' (39:6). Furthermore, it is the end of a dynasty, a continuous line of kings that stretches back four centuries: Zedekiah does not know it, but he will be the last descendant of David ever to rule as king in Jerusalem. And (what is in some ways even more important than any of these considerations, and will turn out to be at the heart of Jeremiah's ministry) it is the end of something that goes back even further, in fact nearly nine centuries, to the days of the exodus. For there is a sense in which as Zedekiah's reign and David's dynasty come to an end, so too does Moses' covenant.

The story of that covenant begins with the arrival of Israel, led out of captivity by Moses, at Mount Sinai. In fact, it is summed up in a mere eight verses at the beginning of Exodus 19: Yahweh speaks to the people through Moses, '"If you will indeed obey my voice and keep my covenant, you shall be my treasured possession among all peoples…" All the people answered together and said, "All that the LORD has spoken we will do"' (vv. 5, 8). They didn't, of course. 'For about forty years he put up with them in the wilderness,'[8] then they tried His patience with their disobedience for another 400-plus years in the time of the judges, and for a similar period under the rule of the kings. Zedekiah's reign marks the end of the line for the kind of agreement which one of the parties won't, or can't, keep. Israel has 'exhibited,' says Gordon McConville, 'apparently definitively, her incapacity to be faithful to the covenant.'[9]

All change

When I, being a railway enthusiast, hear the words 'the end of the line', what is likely to come first to my mind is something rather more mundane than a historical succession of kings. One night the last train leaving London Victoria for the south coast, the 1 a.m. to Brighton, stopped halfway, at a deserted, dimly lit station. (I know, I was on it.) 'Three Bridges,' said a voice, 'this train terminates here.' It doesn't, it can't do, I'm booked through to Brighton, this is not the end of the line! For

8 Acts 13:18.
9 McConville, p. 174.

that train, however, it was. 'All change, please,' said the voice. 'Buses are waiting in the station forecourt to take Brighton passengers forward.' A slower, bumpier, colder ride, but we got there in the end.

All change, therefore, for Israel as a political kingdom. That train is going no further.[10] All change for the attitude that takes for granted the inheritance of the land of Israel, the guidance of the law of Moses, the rule of the Davidic kings, and the security of the city of Jerusalem, without any heartfelt commitment to any of them, or to the God who has set them in place. All change for the notion that Yahweh is here among us, and not out there among the heathen; those who cling superstitiously to this place will find He has deserted them, those who accept exile in Babylon will find that He is there. All change, similarly, for the assumption that His prophets must always say soothing, comforting things, and for the deaf ear turned to Jeremiah's message of plucking up and breaking down, destroying and overthrowing, as well as of building and planting (1:10).

And the biggest change of all will be the setting up of a new covenant between Yahweh and His people. The terms will not have changed, and the response Yahweh expects will be the same; it is not in that sense that this covenant will be new. The difference will be that it will address the fundamental problem that has bedevilled the relationship ever since it was set up at Sinai: the sinful hearts of God's people. Throughout the days of the exodus, and the days of the judges, and the days of the kingdoms, Israel demonstrated repeatedly that she neither could nor would keep her side of the contract. When even under the rule of Josiah, that godliest of kings, when even under the preaching of Jeremiah, that most persistent of prophets, the nation still refused to mend its ways, God acted: first, the captives of the 597 deportation were 'sent out of this place for their own good, into the land of the Chaldeans' (24:5, NKJV), then in 586 the 'bad figs', not accepting the discipline of that earlier exile, would be driven out anyway, delivered 'to trouble into all the kingdoms of the earth, for their harm' (24:8-9, NKJV). And out of the turmoil, in the first group would eventually emerge the new covenant: Yahweh says, 'I will

---

10 See *In the Days of the Kings*, pp. 166f.

give them a heart to know that I am the LORD, and they shall
be my people and I will be their God;' they will both return
to this land, and 'return to me with their whole heart' (24:7).
More of that anon.

The view from Jerusalem
Having seen the first story end where so much else ended,
with Zedekiah in chapter 24, we now backtrack several years
to where the second story begins, with Jehoiakim in chapter 25.

It would have been in Jeremiah's home village of Anathoth
that the teenage boy one day found his attention riveted by
an almond branch and a cooking pot, and on learning what
they meant, heard himself being called to be a prophet to
the nations. The city visible from the high ground above the
village drew him, and for the next forty-one years he would
be based in Jerusalem. From there he would first look out over
the kingdom whose capital it was. What he saw was Yahweh's
people caring little for the God to whom they belonged, but
being made to fall into line, at least outwardly, by a young king,
Josiah, who cared very much for that God. Then he looked
further out, to the lands beyond. More powerful nations began
to make their presence felt, as had not happened for some time,
and it was thanks to an Egyptian pharaoh that Josiah died in
battle and that Jehoahaz, the son who briefly succeeded him,
was replaced by another son, the Jehoiakim of this chapter.
Now, four years into this man's reign, it is a Babylonian king
who arrives in Jerusalem, and Jeremiah sees a number of its
leading citizens taken to Babylon as hostages. The year is 605.

What will he see next? A Jehoiakim who, having had to
accept Nebuchadnezzar as overlord, foolishly rebels, and
finds Babylon-sponsored hostilities breaking out all round
him (2 Kings 24:1-2); then the return of a vengeful Babylonian
army to capture Jerusalem and dethrone Jehoiakim's son and
successor Jehoiachin, and another deportation, the 'good
figs' of 597; then leading up to 586, Judah's final bid for
independence under Zedekiah, followed by the final assault
on Jerusalem and the doom of 'the bad figs ... the king of
Judah, his officials, the remnant of Jerusalem who remain in
this land, and those who dwell in the land of Egypt ... They
shall be utterly destroyed' (24:8-10).

In spite of all this finality, however, story no. 2 has begun and is going on. The notorious 'seventy years' of 25:11-12 have caused much debate,[11] but we should notice that here this period has to do not so much with Israel's exile as with Babylon's dominance. In fact, the description of what Jeremiah now sees from Jerusalem concerns not only the people of Yahweh but 'all the nations' (v. 13). His vision has become worldwide – not indeed in our terms, but certainly in terms of what his world knew about itself. So after Judah it ranges over lands, peoples and rulers to her south (Egypt), west (Philistia), east (Edom, Moab, Ammon), and north (Tyre and Sidon), and then over the rest of the Babylonian empire; verses 15-29 show that Yahweh has purposes for all of them, though none of them recognizes the fact, and that Babylon herself (here called Sheshach)[12] will then pay the price for her power-hungry arrogance, and be brought down in her turn. All of this is going to be opened up at length in the six chapters of 'oracles to the nations' (46-51) which will bring us almost to the end of Jeremiah's book.

This God is a God like no other. Verses 30-38 set forth His power by a battery of metaphors: the roar of a lion, the thunder of a storm, the trampling of a winepress, the approach of a hurricane. The downfall of political leaders ('shepherds') is His doing. The remarkable thing – and it should be hugely encouraging – is that the view from Jerusalem shows every event, every development, in every nation, being overseen by the God of Israel. We cannot miss the insistence in chapter 25 on the word 'all'. All, great and small, in Israel or in Babylon or at the ends of the earth, in our times as in biblical times, – all, whether they revere Him or hate Him or simply ignore Him, whether or not they are aware of the hurricane, and (if they are) whether or not they recognize that it is His work, are ultimately in His hands, for good or ill.

11 Of the period which in my view best fits this description, and does so exactly, the first year is 605 (the year of 2 Kings 24:1a, Jeremiah 25:1, Daniel 1, and the first deportation), and the seventieth year is 536 (the year of 2 Chronicles 36:22f., Ezra 1:1-4, Jeremiah 29:10, and the first repatriation). See Leslie McFall, 'Do the sixty-nine weeks of Daniel date the Messianic mission of Nehemiah or Jesus?', *JETS* 52/4 (December 2009), pp. 688-93.

12 This 'athbash', a kind of code (SSK = BBL, the first letter of the Hebrew alphabet being replaced by the last, the second by the next to last, etc.), is obviously related to the palindromes that are such a feature of Lamentations. See p. 17.

9

Intentions
(Jeremiah 26–29)

'These things shall be'

We have been at a pivotal point in the structure of the book.

Chapter 24 took us on into the sixth century B.C., and the end of the story of Israel as a political kingdom. The first verse of that chapter refers to the year 597, when 'Nebuchadnezzar king of Babylon had taken into exile' Jehoiachin king of Judah, with the cream of Judah's leadership, and we were then pointed forward to 586, when that young man's replacement Zedekiah would also bite the dust, and 'the remnant of Jerusalem' would be 'utterly destroyed' (24:8-10).

But then chapter 25 took us back into the seventh century B.C., and the start of a new story, already begun before the other one ended. The first verse of *that* chapter told us that the new beginning was in 605, 'the first year of Nebuchadnezzar king of Babylon'. He instantly took centre stage on the international scene, with what the New Testament writers would almost certainly have called his 'parousia', the word they use for the appearing of Christ at the end of time. A startling image – the iron rule of the great conqueror, whose advent spreads terror across the world![1] But this pagan tyrant was being made to serve the purposes of God constructively as well as destructively. For with three great deportations which took thousands of God's people into exile, while back home the political kingdom writhed in its death agony, there

---

1 Matthew 24:27-30; 2 Thessalonians 2:8; Revelation 19:11-16.

in Nebuchadnezzar's Babylon an Israel of a new kind was coming to birth.

Yahweh, of course, was overseeing both processes. Doom was shortly to fall on those 'who remain in this land', the 'bad figs' of 24:8-10: 'they shall be utterly destroyed'. Hope was promised to those 'whom I have sent away … to the land of the Chaldeans,' the 'good figs' of 24:5-7: 'I will bring them back … build them … plant them.' All was under His eye and included in His plan.

Under His direction Jeremiah now sets about telling the second story. He introduces it by going back even before Nebuchadnezzar's arrival on the scene in 605, back to the 'temple sermon' which we remember from chapter 7, and which the first verse of chapter 26 dates 'in the beginning of the reign of Jehoiakim'.[2]

Set the two accounts of the temple sermon side by side, and notice the difference. The chapters that began at 7:1 consisted almost entirely of spoken words, those of Yahweh mingled with those of Jeremiah, the latter often protesting and expostulating. Here were storm and stress, and the awareness of approaching doom. All that was what we are labelling the first story. In contrast, the parallel section that begins now with chapter 26 is full of incident and the interplay of different characters, including several prophets besides Jeremiah: action as well as words. When the words are Jeremiah's they are without question Yahweh's also, positive statements about what He intends to do, and how He deals with those who contradict Him. This is the second story. In a nutshell, it sets forth God's long-term intentions. 'These things shall be!'

A memory from my early schooldays is of morning assembly with a hymn sung from a blue book, a junior version of the once-fashionable *Songs of Praise*. One in particular sticks in my mind. Young though I was, I did not feel quite at ease

2 This can be a technical term for a king's 'accession year', meaning the months between his accession and the start of the next calendar year, when (according to that method of reckoning) his official 'Year 1' would begin. It can also have a more general sense (i.e. the earlier part of the reign), as in 28:1, where 'beginning' = the 'fourth year' of Zedekiah's eleven. If 26:1 does refer to Jehoiakim's accession year, it shows how quickly the nation had abandoned Josiah's high standards once he was no longer there to enforce them.

with John Addington Symonds's lines, set to an ominously minor-key tune:

> These things shall be! A loftier race
> Than e'er the world hath known, shall rise
> With flame of freedom in their souls
> And light of knowledge in their eyes.

How soon might we expect a takeover by these supermen, this master race? With what sinister kind of freedom? With what depraved sort of science? As a child of the 1930s, I thought the prospect rather creepy. I couldn't then have put it into words, but the fact was that Mr Symonds sounded rather too much like Mr Hitler. Give me Jeremiah any day. His prophecies face the worst and offer a way through. 'These', fortunately, are the things that really 'shall be'.

Jeremiah and Uriah (26:1-24)
As we have just noted, the 'temple sermon' took place 'in the beginning of the reign of Jehoiakim' (26:1). This phrase links it with the prophecy of the next chapter, given 'in the beginning of the reign of Zedekiah' (27:1), and with the letter reproduced in chapter 29, sent to the people exiled to Babylonia with Jehoiachin.[3] Three kings, therefore, and three prophetic messages from Jeremiah; each message is followed by the mention of another prophet or prophets, and these chapters as a whole open up for the reader what Yahweh's intentions are as one story ends and the other begins.

In the early part of Jehoiakim's reign, the shadow of the great Delusion described at length in 7:1–8:3 was already darkening the minds of the people of Judah, in spite of the thoroughgoing reforms his father had carried through. The combined efforts of Josiah and Jeremiah, in the years leading up to 609, had been meant to warn their people not to 'sin away the day of grace', and here in the early years of the new reign comes one final word of warning: 'It may be they will listen, and every one turn from his evil way,' says Yahweh (26:3). However, when Jeremiah threatens the destruction of Jerusalem ('If you will not listen … I will make this city

---

3 Here called Jeconiah (and elsewhere Coniah); but Jehoiachin is the name by which he is most commonly called, and so is the least confusing.

a curse,' 26:4-6), there is such a strong reaction on the part of the religious establishment, with Jeremiah in his turn threatened with death for saying such terrible things (26:8), that it simply confirms his condemnation of his nation's leaders. What was a message of warning is now a message of doom.

But Yahweh does not intend His servant's ministry to be cut short at this point, or ever. Hearing the uproar in the temple courts, the lords of Judah[4] arrive and intervene, and the fracas becomes an official inquiry, eerily reminiscent (or prescient) of the trial of Jesus before Pilate, with the nation's religious leaders claiming, 'This man deserves the sentence of death' (26:11; cf. John 19:7). We are relieved to find that although the times may be changing there are still people of integrity and influence who are prepared to stand up for one who speaks 'in the name of the LORD our God'. In support of Jeremiah's words, they quote those of Micah a hundred years earlier, a prophecy with similar import and undiminished force.[5]

Between them, the lords (26:16) and Ahikam ben-Shaphan (26:24), of that noble family that so often stands by the prophet in time of need, rescue Jeremiah from his enemies. We are meant to see that he has been in mortal danger; it is from death that these God-fearing allies have rescued him, for what the priests and the prophets wanted was the silencing of this mouthpiece of the word of God. But before the chapter ends with Jeremiah set free, we need to be told that it is not always so. Here in 26:20-23 is the only mention of the prophet Uriah, and he is introduced only to remind us that many of Yahweh's servants have died, and do die, 'for the sake of the Name'. His words were 'like those of Jeremiah', and in his case it was not just the priests and the prophets but the full powers of the state that were mobilized to put him out of action. He was not even safe beyond Judah's frontiers, for in those early years of Jehoiakim's reign there were still treaty obligations between Judah and Egypt, and having sought refuge in the pharaoh's

---

4 *Sarim* is a difficult word to translate. 'Princes' in the older versions sounds like members of the royal family, 'officials' sounds like bureaucrats; both are misleading. The basic idea is 'people of high rank'; hence the suggestion 'lords' (as in Lord Mayor or Lord Chancellor).

5 26:18 = Micah 3:12.

dominions, Uriah was duly extradited and brought home to a shameful death.

His story may look like a tragedy, but we know only its outline, and can be sure that no detail of it was outside the plan of God. 'Precious in the sight of the LORD is the death of his saints.'[6] We may not have our curiosity satisfied, but on the one hand we know that the Lord is no man's debtor, and on the other we see that when He buries His workmen His work goes on regardless. Jehoiakim, for his part, stands condemned both for his vendetta against the man and more importantly for his rejection of the message. But not even his best efforts (of which another prime example awaits us several chapters ahead) can silence the word of God.

Jeremiah and Hananiah (27:1–28:17)

With chapter 27 we move on from the early part of Jehoiakim's reign to the early part of Zedekiah's. As Jehoiakim had been given one last chance to hear the message of warning proclaimed in his father's time, although because he refused to listen it became for him a message of doom, so those doom-laden threats are still real to Zedekiah, but now with a surprising message of hope shining through them.

Will it be recognized, though?

'You know, Baruch, I preached that word not once but three times over. The envoys from Edom and Moab and the rest heard it, so did Zedekiah in a private audience, and so did the priests and a gathering of all the people. I think we'll record all three. There will be repetitions, but that will underline how important those occasions were... It was in Zedekiah's fourth year, when the news from Babylon was of trouble elsewhere in the empire, and some people at our end wondered whether Nebuchadnezzar's grip on power was quite as strong as it had been. Zedekiah, you remember, hosted a conference for representatives of half a dozen of us western nations to debate whether this might be the chance for us to reassert our independence. Whether or not they seriously believed that Nebuchadnezzar would not hear about it, or that if he did he would sit back and let it happen, Yahweh had something to say on the matter. The king of Babylon *would* hear, he *would*

---

6 Psalm 116:15.

deal with those other problems and then turn his attention back to us here in the west, and what was far more important, Yahweh Himself had intended that this should happen. As the God who "made the earth", he had "given all these lands into the hand of Nebuchadnezzar." Babylon would rule the Middle East for a certain period, after which Nebuchadnezzar's dynasty would be conquered by other great powers that were yet to arise.'

'And all this was illustrated by the sign of the yoke,' observes Baruch.

'Exactly. A wooden frame designed to fit the shoulders of the oxen that pull the plough, and a metaphor for enslavement. I made one for myself, and marched into the conference wearing it.'

'And they took you seriously, and got the message.'

'I made it clear to them: Fight the Babylonians and you will be destroyed; accept the Babylonian yoke and you will survive. It seemed defeatist and unpatriotic, but it was actually a message of hope.'

'The envoys from Tyre and Sidon must have been shaken to hear the God of Israel taking the trouble to warn them, as well as His own people, about what lay ahead.'

'Yes; they too had their false prophets, telling them that they would not have to "serve the king of Babylon", and for them too that was all part of the Lie, the great Delusion. You could say that that original calling of mine to be a prophet to the nations was beginning to be fulfilled.'

'I remember you said as much to King Zedekiah in your audience with him afterwards. It was all "as the Lord has spoken concerning *any* nation that will not serve the king of Babylon." But, of course, it was the effect the Lie was having on our own nation that he should have been dealing with.'

'He was not good at that. When I was sent to speak to the priests and the people generally, it was I who had to spell out the implications for them. Misguidedly, they were most concerned about the temple furnishings that Nebuchadnezzar had taken away from Jerusalem four years earlier (as if there were not far greater issues at stake!), but they hoped that since the prophets were now promising rescue from Nebuchadnezzar, all those things might soon come back.

On the contrary, I had to say, everything else will be going to Babylon too, and staying there until Yahweh completes his plans for these present times.'

****

Obviously this kind of reconstructed dialogue does not square with the common view that the book as we have it dates from long after Jeremiah's own time. But if he and Baruch were themselves its architect and its builder, so to speak, we ought to be able to make sense of its structure, and to find reasons why even at the time it might have seemed right to them to order their material in the way they did.

Which is something to bear in mind as we reach chapter 28. The question they would have asked themselves repeatedly – 'How does such-and-such an incident fit into the overall plan of our book?' – is the kind of question Jeremiah had already had to ask himself in respect of the prophecy of Hananiah. The prophets of Judah were numerous, and almost all of them prophesied lies (the great Delusion); yet Hananiah is not here labelled a false prophet. On the contrary, as in this chapter his opponent is repeatedly styled 'Jeremiah the prophet', so he himself is equally often styled 'Hananiah the prophet', and his way of introducing his prophecy corresponds exactly to Jeremiah's: 'Thus says the LORD of hosts, the God of Israel' (28:2 = 27:21). He even uses the very artefact which Jeremiah has used as a visual aid, the wooden yoke; that prophet makes it, this one takes it and breaks it.

What is more, Hananiah has gone so far as to specify dates and times: 'Within two years I will bring back' both the goods and the people taken to Babylon by Nebuchadnezzar, says Yahweh (28:3-4). Jeremiah knows that all this is false, but how is he to counter it? The test of true prophecy in Deuteronomy 18 is that its predictions come true, a test which in this case is of no immediate use. And to that aspect of Hananiah's prophecy Jeremiah responds, with a grace which his rival does not deserve, 'Amen' – yes, it would indeed be gratifying if things were to happen that way; though he knows they won't.

The test of prophecy set forth in Deuteronomy 13, however, is another matter. Alongside the forward look we need the backward look. Are the prophet's words in line with what

Yahweh has said and done in the past? Jeremiah's life and ministry have certainly been under the authority of the divine *law* given through Moses, which enables him to see clearly why Israelite religion in his day needs root-and-branch overhaul. But he has also been given an overview of the divine *plan* working out through the Davidic monarchy, and indeed through the whole Bible world of the first millennium before Christ. As he tells Hananiah, he sees his own ministry to be at one with that of 'the prophets who preceded you and me from ancient times', and who 'prophesied war, famine, and pestilence against many countries and great kingdoms' (28:8). In contrast, Hananiah's prophecy is merely a piece of wishful thinking which takes no account either of Israel's wholesale breaking of the law or of her total ignorance of the plan. He is one of those who 'speak visions of their own minds, not from the mouth of the LORD'; he has not 'stood in the council of the LORD to see and to hear his word' (23:16-18). Yahweh's snapshot in 23:28 captures the two men precisely, and the fundamental difference between them: 'the prophet who has a dream', and the one 'who has my word'. The dreaming man has no awareness of the waking world; the waking man, aware of both worlds, knows what dreams are, and keeps them in their place.

To this particular dreaming man, who has wilfully shut his eyes to the truth of Yahweh's word, and has uttered a grandiose prediction which will not come true, is given a personal prediction which will. He who foretold deliverance within two years is told that he himself is doomed, and within two months he is dead.

Jeremiah and three prophets in Babylon (29:1-32)
The word sent from Yahweh in 'the reign of Jehoiakim' (26:1) and that sent in 'the reign of Zedekiah' (27:1) are followed by one sent to the exiles who are in Babylon with 'King Jeconiah', that is, Jehoiachin (29:2, 4). Three kings, as we noted earlier, but not a straightforward sequence. In 598 Jehoiakim was succeeded by his son Jehoiachin; but, as we know, the Babylonians removed that young man only three months later, and put his uncle Zedekiah on the throne in his place; so for the next eleven years there were simultaneously a king

in exile in Babylon and a king reigning in Jerusalem. Which was the true king of Judah? For most people, a real quandary, something like that faced by England in the 1700s, with Protestant monarchs on the throne and Catholic 'pretenders' in exile; except that in the case of Judah this unhappy dilemma had been forced on the nation by a feared and hated enemy.

To Jeremiah it was no problem. Each of these two men, uncle and nephew, would be the last of the line, but in two different senses. Zedekiah would be the last king to reign in Jerusalem and would perish with the demise of the political kingdom. To underline the finality of what would be happening in 586, his sons would perish too; their execution, the extinction of his line, would be the last thing he would see before his captors put his eyes out. Jehoiachin, on the other hand, would be the last of the line to be called a king, but we have already been given Yahweh's word concerning him in 22:30: a 'childless' man, in the sense that 'none of his offspring shall succeed in sitting on the throne of David', but children he would have, through whom in the fullness of time a new kind of kingdom would come into being.

So it is no wonder that in those dark days when Zedekiah presided over the collapse of the monarchy, and Jeremiah was repeatedly harassed and threatened by enemies whom the ineffectual monarch could not control, the prophet was nevertheless given an extraordinarily upbeat message to pass on, a message which after all the words of earlier days, words first of warning and then of doom, was now a message of hope. This chapter contains one of the most memorable passages in the entire book: 'I know the plans I have for you, declares the LORD, plans for wholeness and not for evil, to give you a future and a hope' (29:11). And with his plan comes his promise: 'You will seek me and find me. When you seek me with all your heart, I will be found by you, declares the LORD' (29:13-14).

The practical import of these promises is that the exiles should accept their present situation and make the best of it, while Nebuchadnezzar, 'and his son, and his grandson,' rule the world of their day, 'until the time of his own land comes' (ominous phrase) when 'many nations and great kings shall make him their slave' (27:7). Meanwhile this word from

Yahweh comes to His exiled people in a letter from Jeremiah –
accorded the dignity of being sent in the diplomatic bag carried
by official emissaries from King Zedekiah to his overlord in
Babylon! In this heathen land, we remind ourselves, Ezekiel's
prophetic ministry flourishes, and Daniel even rises to high
governmental office under these pagan kings.[7] In all sorts of
ways this is a far cry from that other captivity, centuries earlier
in Egypt; and the difference is evident also from the surprising
contents of Jeremiah's message. What Yahweh wants the exiles
to expect, and to make use of, is (of all things) *normality*. They
have been deported, but certainly not enslaved. Whether or
not they have been fearing something like those dreadful
years of misery in the Egyptian brickfields, here in Babylonia
they are to 'build houses and live in them', to 'plant gardens
and eat their produce', to prosper and increase, and even to
'seek the welfare' of Babylon (29:5-7).

Oddly enough, this does not please them. It seems natural
to them to hate Babylon and to believe in the false prophesying
of Hananiah, back in Jerusalem: that is, his assurance that the
Babylonian yoke will be broken and the exiles repatriated
within a couple of years (28:2-4). Such things are being heard
in Babylonia too. It is all dreams and lies, of course, another
aspect of the grand Delusion (29:8-9). We need not doubt
that at the root of all this is the hankering for the old formal
religion of those last days of the monarchy, where you could
be sure that as long as so-called worship went on in the temple
in Jerusalem all would be well and you could live as you
pleased. The exiles have to be disabused of this, the lie which
is bringing the old order of things to the brink of destruction.

For Jeremiah personally life back in Judah is becoming
ever more stressful. But he is the man chosen by Yahweh
to say, from a distance, what the exiles in Babylon need to
hear, and he is prompted to say it by the news that there too,
among them, false prophets have appeared. Two of these are
introduced in 29:21. Dismiss the thoughts that might instantly
spring to mind concerning these men – that is, their initials
A and Z (no, it doesn't work in Hebrew!) and the familiarity
of the names (no, this is not *the* Ahab and not *the* Zedekiah).
In respect of these pseudo-prophets, Jeremiah has two things

---

7 Ezekiel 1:1-3; Daniel *passim*.

that have to be said. The first is that they also, like the false prophets in Jerusalem, are telling lies, presumably saying that the future will be as Hananiah has been predicting, namely a resurrected kingdom back there in Judah in two years' time. Such teaching is pernicious nonsense, because that Judah, the one ruled since 609 by the sons of Josiah, is cursed – its people are the 'bad figs' of chapter 24 (29:17-19 with 24:8-10). The political kingdom is doomed. The second thing Jeremiah has to say about Messrs A and Z is that their pretentious words are belied by their immoral lives; once again Deuteronomy 13 comes into play as a key test of a true prophet. Whatever prompted the extreme judgment of 29:22, that these two be 'roasted in the fire', it is ironic that a Babylonian court should be used to bring home Yahweh's justice to two of Yahweh's unfaithful servants.

The last part of chapter 29 is a little complicated. The order of events seems to be that Shemaiah, the third of the false prophets to appear in this chapter, learns the content of Jeremiah's letter, as it tells the exiles to prepare for a long stay in Babylon. He has the temerity to cast himself in the role of Jeremiah-in-reverse: he not only sees himself as Yahweh's true voice to the exiles (29:31), but also reckons that he can write to Jerusalem denouncing Jeremiah's pretensions, just as Jeremiah is writing to Babylon to denounce his. So he sends a complaint to Zephaniah, the priest who has just succeeded Jehoiada as overseer of the temple (29:26), both about Jeremiah's prophesying and about his (Zephaniah's) failure to do his job properly by disciplining this 'madman'.[8] 'Zephaniah … read this letter in the hearing of Jeremiah', whereupon an answering letter went back to 'all the exiles' prophesying Shemaiah's doom. The final verse of chapter 29 promises once again 'the good that I will do to my people, declares the LORD', but Shemaiah and all who think as he does are not going to see it.

We have to take note of one particular intention in the mind of Yahweh which to many of the deportees must have seemed

---

8 It seems 'Zephaniah had only recently succeeded to that post, and on that basis Shemaiah makes so bold as to instruct him in the duties of his office' (Mackay, vol. 2, p.175). How to win friends and influence people! On the popular view, among unsympathetic people, of prophets as 'madmen', cf. 2 Kings 9:11; Hosea 9:7.

the most bizarre of all. They had, of course, to accept the fact of the exile. Furthermore, if they were sensible they believed Jeremiah when he said it would last a great deal longer than the false prophets made out. They schooled themselves to accept all this, and to adjust their lifestyle and expectations accordingly. But however humanely they were treated in that foreign land, there was no denying the terrible things that the Babylonians had done, and would yet do, to Judah and Jerusalem. 'By the waters of Babylon, there we sat down and wept, when we remembered Zion' (Ps. 137:1).

Such things were hard to forgive. But to be told then that they were expected not simply to forgive, but actually to 'seek the welfare of the city where I have sent you' (29:7), that surely was beyond reason! This however was Yahweh's intention. The community of faith lives in two worlds simultaneously, being both God's holy nation, distinct from all others, yet also a people immersed in the affairs of this godless world and concerned for its true welfare. In the sixth century BC this principle took the shape of a great company of deportees, expected to 'sing the LORD's song in a foreign land' (Ps. 137:4), who might, and probably did, say frequently to God in words like those of the old hymn 'Thine exiles long for home',[9] but who nevertheless learned to pray for the peace not only of Jerusalem (Ps. 122:6) but also of Babylon.

Jeremiah 29:11 ('the plans I have for you ... a future and a hope') provides a massive underpinning for any believer's faith, but Jeremiah 29:7 is hugely important in a different way. I owe a great personal debt to lifelong contact with the work of the London City Mission, in whose ranks my father served as an evangelist for many years; and this is a text to which the L.C.M. has returned repeatedly in its long history: 'Seek the welfare of the city where I have sent you.' In an increasingly urbanized world these words challenge an increasing number of God's people. But actually Babylon is all around us, not just among the ancient ziggurats or even just among the modern skyscrapers. Every aspect of society needs our prayers and our witness. What is more, we notice that the responsibility was being placed not so much on Jeremiah, the 'holy man', the specialist, as on 'all the exiles' (29:4). But if the prospect seems

9 Henry Alford, 'Ten thousand times ten thousand.'

daunting, we remember that behind the whole enterprise stands our great God, with His 'plans for wholeness and not for evil', plans which it is His sovereign intention to carry through. These things shall be.

10

Promises

(Jeremiah 30–33)

The heart of Jeremiah's message

We may regard chapters 24 and 25 as the hinge of Jeremiah's book, corresponding to the midpoint of the palindromes of Lamentations; but the heart of it is to be found in these four chapters, 30 to 33.

Not many can now remember, but all of us can imagine, the bombing raids of World War II, with defence systems that aimed to catch enemy aircraft in the converging beams of searchlights. The prophecies Jeremiah is given here are illuminated in a similar way from several different directions. For a start, the section we have just been reading points towards what now follows as being something further of the same kind, but made sharper and brighter in a particular way: those chapters stated Yahweh's intentions, these proclaim His promises. The intentions become personalized. 'What God intends to do' is remarkable enough; 'What God intends to do *for you*' is even more special.

Then again, we may be aware that chapters 30–33 are known 'in the trade', so to speak, as the Book of Consolation. The more one reads them in that light, however, the more they seem to demand a different label. Rather as the *mot juste* for chapters 11–20 is surely something sturdier than 'confessions', and hence my preference for 'protests', so the *mot juste* for chapters 30–33 is surely something altogether tougher and more bracing than 'consolation'. Are they really

no more than a soothing mantra to go with a sympathetic hug – 'There, there, you'll get over it'? Should not a grasp of their message produce a frisson of excitement, a new spring in the step, a new light in the eye, a confident, even buoyant, spirit? So 'promises' is a very apt description of them.

'One *reads* them' – a telltale phrase in that last paragraph. All Israel's prophets were gifted with the spoken word, and some of the greatest of them were gifted with the written word as well. A few, Jeremiah being one, were explicitly told to turn their preaching into writing. Now why, we might ask ourselves? Since Jeremiah's story is very much that of a *preaching* ministry, forty years of it, in a very specific place and time, geared to very particular events, why would Yahweh say to him, '*Write in a book* all the words that I have spoken to you' (30:2)? The answer is that though his prophecies were of course intended in the first instance for his immediate hearers, they were intended also for people in another place (Babylonia) and another time (the coming seventy years of exile); in fact, as it would turn out, for people everywhere and in every coming age.

Chapters 32 and 33 are both dated in the tenth year of Zedekiah, when he and his kingdom were only months away from destruction, and when Jeremiah was 'shut up in the court of the guard … in the palace of the king' (32:2). Chapters 30 and 31 no doubt belong to the same period, but even if they were given to Jeremiah earlier, the final editing of the book – by the prophet himself, in my view – seems to treat the four chapters as a unit. Now no one is going to hear these prophecies except Jeremiah's jailers and visitors passing through the court of the guard (though his enemies, as we know from 38:1, reckon that that is quite public enough!); therefore they are written down, like Paul's 'prison epistles' in New Testament times, so that what may be heard in Jerusalem may be read in Babylon. And in view of their long-term significance, as they look ahead to Babylon's 'seventy years' (25:11ff.) and beyond, and of their wide-ranging vision, encompassing many other nations besides Israel and Babylon, it seems clear that from the outset Yahweh has intended a book, and not just a voice, to take Jeremiah's message out to the ends of the earth and on through all the ages.

Something that will come into focus in these four chapters is the indication of certain 'days' relating to the promises. Chapter 30 speaks of a day of distress (v. 7a) and a day of deliverance (v. 8), but the real point of the chapter emerges in its last line: 'In the latter days you will *understand* this' (v. 24). The brightest and best of the promises in the glorious chapter 31 is about 'the days [that] are coming … when I will make a new *covenant* with the house of Israel and the house of Judah' (v. 31). Chapter 32, a word given when 'the king of Babylon was besieging Jerusalem' for the last time (v. 2), promises the destruction of the city that had aroused Yahweh's *wrath* 'from the day it was built to this day' (v. 31). But hard on its heels comes His final word, with chapter 33: 'the days are coming … when I will *fulfil* the promise' (v. 14). If all of these prophetic promises are being given in the tenth year of Zedekiah, the next twelve months are going to bring the sack of Jerusalem, the end of the monarchy, and the death of the dream that that might have been the permanent final form of the Davidic kingdom. As he foresees the shattering of that dream, Jeremiah now sets before us the days of understanding, the days of covenant, the days of wrath, and the days of fulfilment: four aspects of the waking reality.

The days of understanding (30:1-24)
Zedekiah's reign is the overlap of the two epochs, with the Israelite monarchy at its last gasp in Judah and the seeds of its successor already germinating in Babylon. It is time for Jeremiah to clarify what Yahweh is saying to His people at this juncture, and so long as we are aware that not all the English versions are equally helpful in the way they divide a chapter like this into sections, we should find it sufficiently clear.

'In the latter days you will understand this' (30:24). There is a faint air of mystery about the words 'latter days', scarcely a phrase the man in the street is likely to use, but one felt to have special significance by some students of biblical prophecy. In fact, there is no real reason for it to mean anything more obscure than 'in due course', or 'in days to come' (NIV). Chapter 30 is a God's-eye view of the exile and its sequel, and in due course, as the sixth century progresses, the events it predicts will begin to happen. It is to be written down so

that both this generation and those that follow will be able to benefit from the very words of Yahweh through His prophet.

Make no mistake: the overall promise is a thoroughly positive one – the return of the nation to its God-given land (30:3). But notice how this promise is unpacked. First must come the day of distress (30:4-7a). Yahweh here uses 'Israel' in its narrower sense to mean the northern kingdom, which by Jeremiah's time is long since defunct; so the panic and terror, with 'every face turned pale', sum up the disasters that are about to destroy Zedekiah's little domain as they have already destroyed its sister kingdom. Hence 'Israel and Judah'. As the political monarchy now comes to an end in the south as well as in the north, we find the term 'Jacob' used to denote the twelve-tribe nation as a whole. The striking picture of a man having to cope with the (to him) unimaginable pains of childbirth sums up this dreadful day.

Jacob 'shall be saved out of it', Yahweh continues (30:7b-10). Without missing a beat, He next tells us what will happen 'in *that* day' – in the 'deliverance' day of verse 8, as distinct from the 'distress' day of verse 7a. Out of those pains of childbirth something new is to be born. A new life will begin. It will still be a life of service, for no one can help but serve some overlord or other; but instead of serving 'foreigners', under their yoke and bound in their bonds, Jacob will be brought out of 'captivity' and brought home from 'far away', to serve Yahweh, and to do so in 'quiet and ease.'

At the centre of the chapter Yahweh has His people stand back to see His plan for them set side by side with His plan for their enemies (30:11). His object is to deal with evil wherever He finds it. Of the nations who have attacked His people He 'will make a full end', for even though He Himself sponsored the attacks ('I scattered you', He says), those nations were more than willing to be the aggressors. But of His own people He 'will not make a full end', richly though they deserve it. An end there will be, an end of many things that they have, quite wrongly, come to regard as indispensable, and they 'will suffer loss,' as Paul puts it in 1 Corinthians 3:15; however they themselves 'will be saved, but only as through fire.'

The full end of the nations and the partial end of Israel are then opened up, with a paragraph for each, but in the reverse

order. On the one hand, Israel: the 'punishment' dealt out by a 'merciless foe' is actually Yahweh dealing His own people 'the blow of an enemy' (30:12-15). On the other hand, the nations: while Yahweh 'will restore health' to Jacob (30:16-17), those who have caused Jacob such suffering will themselves be plundered and devoured, made captive and a prey.

The chapter is completed by an extended vision, in the most positive and lyrical terms, of Jacob's future glory and greatness (30:18-22), while just two verses at the end of it are enough to set forth Yahweh's fierce and final punishment of the wicked (30:23-24).

As time goes by, those who have paid attention to all these words will see them coming true. The chapter ends with as plain a promise as one could wish for: Watch how Yahweh works, and it really does begin to make sense.

In the light of this, we can see something of the shape of what Yahweh is doing. Two further sources of illumination are less obvious, but they make the promise of this chapter stand out almost three-dimensionally. The first has to do with a link word in verse 7 and another in verse 16. We would expect in each of these places what is called an 'adversative conjunction', meaning (in plain English) a word like 'but': 'Bad things have been happening, *but* I am going to put a stop to them.' In fact, as McConville points out, Yahweh is not saying that. In neither place do we find a 'but'. Verse 7 should read, 'It is a time of distress for Jacob, *and* he shall be saved'; verses 14-16 read, even more surprisingly, 'I have dealt you the blow of an enemy, *therefore* all your foes shall go into captivity.' In each case we are tempted to object: That doesn't follow, it's a *non sequitur*; 'the thought-flow is illogical;'[1] it should be *but*, not *and*; it should be *but*, not *therefore*. Surely (we think) these are two of those grand Scriptures that enable us to face the fact of evil, and to counter it with the words 'But God'. Many an encouraging sermon has been preached on such texts.[2] The point of Jeremiah 30, however, is not that the power of evil is more than matched by the power of God, though that, of course, is true. It is the even grander fact that the power of evil

---

1 McConville, p. 95.

2 For a well-known example, see the words of Joseph to his brothers in Genesis 50:20: 'You meant evil against me, *but God* meant it for good.'

is actually incorporated into the plan of God, and is thereby defeated, a truth that we see in all its completeness at the cross of Calvary. Christ has died, *but in spite of that* there will be new life? Oh, no. Christ has died, *and because of that* there will be new life. It is Yahweh who through the Babylonians is destroying Zedekiah's kingdom, and He is doing so *in order that* the true kingdom may arise from its ashes. Everything, bad as well as good, will in the end be seen to have served the inexorable purposes of Yahweh. Now there you have a cordial to cheer the most despondent heart.

The second of these extra searchlight beams is the fact that the final verses of this chapter, 30:23-24, are repeated from 23:19-20. Such repetitions are not infrequent in Jeremiah; an obvious one is the temple sermon in chapters 7 and 26. Why might Yahweh want the prophet to reiterate now what he said on that previous occasion?

In the earlier chapter, Jeremiah was in conflict with the false prophets, who had not stood in Yahweh's council (23:18-22), and did not understand His purpose. To them this true prophet had spoken of 'the storm of the LORD' which would 'burst upon the head of the wicked'. But (in McConville's words) their activity 'served only to draw a veil over that purpose and hasten the punishment.' Now, however, with the final catastrophe only months away, they are silenced, and the purpose is being made plain. 'It is the renewed promise, coming to its climax in the theology of new covenant, and written in a book by the prophet who *did* know the mind of YHWH (30:1), that constitutes the plans of his mind.'[3] That covenant is the theme of the next of these four great chapters.

The days of covenant (31:1-40)

The 'latter days' when an understanding of Yahweh's plans is promised to His people (30:24) are also the setting for His promised new covenant: 'At that time ... I will be the God of all the clans of Israel, and they shall be my people' (31:1). These words, standing at the head of this chapter and reiterating what He has just said in the previous one (30:22), are the basic definition of the covenant between God and His people all the way from Exodus 6:7 to Revelation 21:3. Here, He is

---

3 McConville, p. 93.

going to head three paragraphs with the words 'See, the days are coming when … ' (31:27, 31, 38 JB). But before He arrives at these promises He gives us another series of vivid word-pictures like the ones we have seen (as a portrait gallery, or as a kaleidoscope) in earlier chapters where all was warning and doom. Here, in contrast, we are shown scenes of hope. There are five of them, marked out by the statement 'Thus says the LORD' or its equivalent, and in each a memorable phrase catches our attention.

First, 31:2-6. 'An everlasting love', says Yahweh in 31:3, is one that spans the centuries. He seems to be looking back from some future standpoint and linking those who will have 'survived the sword' of the Babylonian wars with those who 'found grace in the wilderness' in escaping from Egypt nearly a thousand years before. His love for His people assures them, with a threefold 'again', of the end of present misery: once more there will be building, and merrymaking, and fruit-gathering, and festivals that will reunite Ephraim and Zion, north and south, in the worship of Yahweh.

Secondly, 31:7-9. 'A great company', says Yahweh in 31:8, will be brought back from exile. How varied it is, and how needy; what cause it has for both 'gladness' and 'weeping'; how gently and surely its heavenly Father leads it home! And it includes those we might have reckoned to be lost beyond recall, for again Ephraim is specially noted, resurrected from the death of the northern kingdom back in 722.

Thirdly, 31:10-14. 'A watered garden' is what Yahweh in 31:12 says His ransomed people will look like to their neighbours. This beautiful simile takes over from the classic image of a shepherd and his flock, which is how Israel's testimony will come across to the wider world (31:10); but the extended picture here, for those who gather 'on the height of Zion', is that of rejoicing in harvest, with feasting and gladness, abundance and satisfaction.

Fourthly, 31:15-20. '[A family] restored', 'children … come back', is what Ephraim longs for (31:17-18). Again the greater miracle is in view, a twelve-tribe nation reconstituted. Jeremiah's immediate audience is the still identifiable population of the southern kingdom, only recently deported to Babylon – that community might envisage itself being

brought back home more or less intact. But how on earth could the lost tribes of the north, long since scattered far and wide across another empire, the Assyrian, which has itself now disintegrated, ever be brought together again? 'They are no more,' laments Rachel, the best-beloved wife of Jacob/ Israel and the mother of the tribes that formed the core of the northern kingdom.[4] Not so; 'keep your voice from weeping,' says Yahweh; 'there is hope for your future,' they 'shall come back to their own country'.

Fifthly, 31:21-25. 'A new thing' is what Jeremiah foresees in 31:22. There is agreement among translators that the new thing is 'a woman' who 'encircles a man' (ESV), or words to that effect; there is no agreement among commentators as to what that means. For one ancient view that is worth looking at afresh, we might begin by highlighting the names Ephraim and Israel. Each of these can be a label for the northern kingdom, and in the first four paragraphs of this chapter there are four mentions of the name Ephraim where it does indeed mean that. But it is also the name given to God's people when they are viewed as Yahweh's firstborn (31:9) and His dear son (31:20), while Israel is the name given to them when they are viewed as Yahweh's virgin daughter (31:4, 21, 22a) – and therefore, perhaps, identical with the woman who figures in the mysterious saying of 31:22c.

It is in this context, this picture-language of Yahweh's people being not only His 'son' but also His 'daughter', that we are told of the creating of the 'new thing' (31:22b). This must be a major event, an act of supreme importance, on a par with what God did when He made the worlds, what He will do when he remakes them at the end of time, and what He does when an unbeliever is born again ('if anyone is in Christ, he is a new creation').[5] And as chapter 31 proceeds it tells us of one outstanding event which fits this description like a glove: 'the days are coming … when *I will make a new covenant*' (31:31). With New Testament hindsight, we know that that promise is to take shape in the person of Jesus; and once we have the incarnation of the Son of God in mind, we may well

---

4 Rachel's two sons were Joseph and Benjamin. The tribes in question sprang from Joseph's sons Ephraim and Manasseh.

5 Genesis 1:1; Revelation 21:5; 2 Corinthians 5:17.

conclude that perhaps Jerome's comment on verse 22, back in the fourth century, was not so far from the truth. He believed the phrase in question to be about the birth of Christ, as when John Donne's Christmas poem speaks to the Virgin Mary about 'Immensity cloistered in thy dear womb'. An even truer picture is of the Christ being born not to that particular individual, but to 'Virgin Israel', Yahweh's chosen people, as when an earlier John was given, in the book of Revelation, a vision of a woman who 'gave birth to a male child … who is to rule all the nations'.[6]

For the moment, the promised Messiah is still in the womb of His mother-to-be. 'A woman encircles a man.' But now that lengthy introduction is to be followed by three tremendous promises, the central one being the promise of the new covenant.[7]

The two that flank it are brief but far-reaching statements about Yahweh's people (31:27-30) and Yahweh's city (31:38-40). Since the chapter immediately following this one belongs to 'the tenth year of Zedekiah' (32:1), we may picture Jeremiah as being near the end of his ministry; and 31:28 transports him back across the entire forty years of it (and us back across thirty chapters) to that dismaying moment when as a boy in Anathoth he first heard the voice of the Lord. '*What do you see, Jeremiah?*' '*I see the branch of an almond, a wake-tree.*' '*And I also see; I am awake, overseeing the destinies of my people, to pluck up and to break down, to destroy and to overthrow.*' This is it, Jeremiah. You are seeing it happen. But you remember that Yahweh also said '*to build and to plant*'. And that precious promise is for a nation which will find itself once again made whole, Israel and Judah together (31:27), and at last prepared to accept responsibility, to confess its sin and not blame someone else for its troubles (31:29-30).

To this promised replanting corresponds the promised rebuilding in 31:38-40. It does not matter that we may not today be able to identify all the locations and features of Jerusalem

---

6 Revelation 12:5.

7 The unusual note at 31:26, that the visions of the previous 25 verses had apparently come to Jeremiah in dreams (God-given dreams, not those of 23:23-32), sets what they have shown him of the joyful future over against what his waking eye sees of the gloomy present. 'The contrast', says Kidner (p.108), is 'poignant', but 'enhances the delights he has glimpsed in vision'.

that are mentioned there; the point is that 'the city shall be rebuilt for the LORD.' Nor are we expected to find dates for the fulfilment of these two prophecies somewhere along the biblical and post-biblical timeline. Each promise – restored people, restored city – was later fulfilled partially, beginning with Zerubbabel's return in the later sixth century and Nehemiah's in the fifth, but neither will be fulfilled completely until this world ends and we see 'the new Jerusalem, coming down out of heaven from God', and the whole 'Israel of God' drawn 'from every nation ... standing before the throne'.[8]

The Lord, Yahweh, whose declarations these are, sees to it that the very structure of the chapter is designed (as we found with Lamentations at the beginning of our study) to make a point. The two flanking promises, like heraldic supporters on either side of a coat-of-arms, focus our attention on the central one, the extended promise of 31:31-37. The covenant between Yahweh and His people is what it always has been, and 31:33b states it in its simplest form: 'I will be their God, and they shall be my people'. But in this setting there is something different about it. Yahweh Himself underlines this: it is 'not like the covenant that I made' in the days of the exodus (verse 32). His people repeatedly broke their side of that agreement for the simple reason that they had not the power to keep it. All that will change, though for the time being they can know the change only in prospect, not in actuality. But the day is coming when Yahweh will reveal Himself in His trinitarian New Testament fullness as it is set out here (in Old Testament terms, of course, for Jeremiah's generation) in verses 33-34: God the Father made known by the indwelling work of God the Spirit to all whose sins have been dealt with by the redeeming death and glorious resurrection of God the Son.

Not surprisingly, those who know this God see aspects of His character reflected in the world He has created. What He Himself points out in connection with the covenant He has made with His people is the 'fixed order' of creation (vv. 35-36) and its size and complexity (v. 37). The breaking of His covenant with His people is as inconceivable as the collapse of the one, or man's discovery of every last detail of the other.

8 Revelation 21:2; Galatians 6:16; Revelation 7:4-9.

The days of wrath (32:1-44)

We notice a slight difference between the two halves of the 'Book of Promises', in that chapters 30 and 31 are almost entirely the words of Yahweh, and are undated, while chapters 32 and 33 are set in the last year of Zedekiah's reign and include some of his words and some of Jeremiah's besides those of Yahweh. But all four do belong together, even if the 'days' motif comes through slightly differently in chapter 32. Elsewhere, the significant phrase is 'See, the days are coming when…' Here, however, the word 'day' figures twice in one verse when Jeremiah is speaking to Yahweh, and twice in one verse when Yahweh is speaking to Jeremiah. The prophet reminds Yahweh of the wonders He has done from the time of the Egyptian captivity 'to this day', and of the name He has made for himself 'at this day' (32:20). Yahweh, in His response, says that Jerusalem has angered Him 'from the day it was built to this day' (32:31).[9]

A bird's-eye view of chapter 32 shows first King Zedekiah talking to Jeremiah, whom he has had 'shut up in the court of the guard' (a paragraph of five verses), and then Jeremiah, in a curiously oblique response, negotiating from his prison the purchase of a field in his home village of Anathoth (ten verses). The pattern is then repeated on a larger scale: now it is Jeremiah who begins, with an address to Yahweh (ten verses), which is followed by a response from Yahweh (nineteen verses). In each half the response is the weightier part.

When we consider each of these paragraphs in the light of the others, the connections and the flow of events begin to emerge. The protracted siege of Jerusalem is in progress. As Jeremiah has been shut up in the court of the guard by Zedekiah, so Zedekiah is himself shut up in the city by the armies of Babylon. He hopes Egyptian forces may be coming to his rescue, and to his mind Jeremiah's prophesying that this won't happen is bound to spread alarm and despondency. Hence his indignant, accusing, question 'Why?' in 32:3. Why does the prophet talk like this? Does he really have to go on

---

9 The NIV translators disapprove of repetition (which for the Bible writers was intentional and important). Here they remove one of the four 'days' ('from the day it was built until now'), so that we miss the link between Jeremiah's two (32:20) and Yahweh's two (32:31). This is characteristic of the NIV. *Caveat emptor.*

so about *Dies irae, dies illa* – 'that day of wrath, that dreadful day' – being only just around the corner?

It may have been a temporary relaxing of the siege because of the rumour of Egyptian intervention that enabled Jeremiah's cousin to get into Jerusalem to visit the prisoner. To cheer him up? Oh, no. Hanamel only came because he wanted to dispose of a field in Anathoth, no doubt with a view to moving right away from the war zone, with some cash in his pocket, while he could. Jeremiah was his next of kin, so would Jeremiah please, according to ancient custom, buy it from him?[10]

This 'untimely proposition', as Derek Kidner calls it[11] – 'was there ever a more insensitive prison visitor?' – was Jeremiah's God-given opportunity (32:8) to show everyone in the palace that though the city and the kingdom as they knew them were doomed, there was still a future for Israel. Let them see him pay, in cash, in public, in the presence of many witnesses, with the deeds signed and lodged in a sealed container by the faithful Baruch (who though we have heard about him already is here named in the book for the first time), for a piece of real-estate, *ownership of which is meaningless unless it will one day be possible to enjoy it*. It is a fact that the wrath of God will fall upon the kingdom of Zedekiah, and that that dream will die. It is a greater fact that a later generation will awake to the next stage of Israel's development: equally real and solid, with 'houses and fields and vineyards … again … bought in this land', but a step nearer to the ultimate reality. The threat of the day of wrath is actually a promise of hope.[12]

Jeremiah knew that 'the word of the Lord' was behind Hanamel's visit and the proposal that he should buy Hanamel's field (32:8). But we may wonder how far he was able to conceive the transaction to be something actual rather than merely theoretical. From what he now says to Yahweh in his prayer of 32:16-25, he seems to be doubting whether Israel the land, with Israel the nation owning properties in

---

10 Leviticus 25:25-31; Ruth 3:12, 4:1ff.

11 Kidner, p. 112.

12 And, we may note in passing, a sign that we shall one day find life beyond death to be itself not less, but more, real and solid than this present world.

it (as he himself is now technically a landowner),[13] has any realistic future. He cannot see how the threat of destruction relates to the promise of restoration. He is trying to grasp the overall pattern of God's work in history, specifically what was happening when Hanamel turned up at the guardroom not to bring sympathy and family news but to beg a thoroughly selfish favour. What made Jeremiah agree to the deal, and why did he find himself saying that Israel's property market would eventually pick up again?

Sensibly, wisely, like the experienced believer that he is, as he comes to God in prayer he first marshals the facts. What he sees in the wonders of creation tells him that 'nothing is too hard' for Yahweh (32:17). Furthermore, this is the God of love and justice, 'great in counsel and mighty in deed' (32:18-19). He has been demonstrating His power throughout all nations (32:20) from the time of the exodus 'to this day', so that His name is known 'at this day' as – well, as what? As a God who, having richly blessed His people, has found them impossibly ungrateful and disobedient, and who now, therefore, is bringing upon them the consequences of their sin and the punishment they so richly deserve: the city, the land, the nation destroyed. Which is what you said would happen, Lord, and now 'behold, you see it' (32:24). And I see it too, says Jeremiah. What I do not see is how a prosperous future for Israel – houses and vineyards and fields, one of them now belonging to me – fits into this (32:25).

If you are an honest seeker after truth, you will regularly find that God takes facts you have become aware of but do not understand, and shapes them into a pattern which suddenly makes sense. So here in 32:27 Yahweh begins where Jeremiah began in 32:17, saying in effect, 'Yes, you are right, nothing is too hard for me. And yes, you are right, I am giving Jerusalem over to Nebuchadnezzar and his armies. And as you say (32:23), this disaster is a punishment, because My people have never obeyed My voice or walked in My law.' We have noticed how in verse 31 (ᴇꜱᴠ) Yahweh even takes up the repeated 'day' from verse 20. It is here that He makes explicit what kind

---

13 This is how the man in the street would describe the situation (an *ad hominem* argument). Biblically, the land is Yahweh's and the people are His tenants (Lev. 25:23).

of 'days' these are. He speaks of those who 'provoke me to anger', who 'have done nothing but provoke me to anger', who have 'aroused my anger and wrath' from the day the city was built to this present day, and of 'all the evil ... that they did to provoke me to anger' (32:29-32). These truly are the days of wrath.

'Now,' continues Yahweh as the paragraph 32:36-41 begins, 'concerning this city you say – you, Jeremiah, and the few people who love truth as you do[14] – that it is doomed to destruction. And you are right. It will burn, and its people will be taken into exile. *Therefore* I will bring them back...'

'*Therefore*'? How can it be '*therefore*'? Surely He must mean that they are going into exile, *but* He will bring them back?

We have been here before, when we were puzzling over 30:16; and this time the force of that unexpected word is spelt out even more clearly. It is not a case of people being free to do bad things while Yahweh is preoccupied somewhere else, *but* then He comes back and puts matters right. It is a case of a colossal drama that He Himself is producing, overseeing its every detail, and one act of the drama will be completed by the Babylonian exile; *therefore* the stage will then be set for the next act.

As we see the storm clouds gathering over Judah in those closing scenes of the 'kingdom' act, our minds may go centuries ahead to one of the memorable hymns of William Cowper, a timorous believer who knew nevertheless how to put his fears to rest:

> Ye fearful saints, fresh courage take;
> The clouds ye so much dread
> Are big with mercy, and shall break
> In blessings on your head.[15]

The promise of 31:31-34 was that 'after those days', when the wrath was over and done, the era of the new covenant would begin. Here in 32:36-41 we find that it is not only new, but also 'everlasting', and here its glories are greatly developed. It would be many a year yet before the dawn of the Christian era and the coming of the Spirit would make the promise of a changed heart a reality, but as a foretaste of promises yet

---

14 The 'you' in 32:36 is plural.
15 William Cowper, 'God moves in a mysterious way'.

to be fulfilled it would not be quite so long before Jeremiah's acquisition of his field at Anathoth would be followed by a faith-affirming upsurge in the property market all over the reoccupied land.

Two great facts for faith emerge from Yahweh's response to Jeremiah. 'Thus says the LORD: Just as I have brought all this great disaster upon this people, so I will bring upon them all the good that I promise them' (32:42). He is in control of everything that happens. Isaiah presents the same fact against an even broader backdrop: 'I form light and create darkness, I make well-being and create calamity, I am the LORD who does all these things' (45:7). But over and above that is the connection that McConville points out: Jeremiah is prophesying the imminent doom of the city and the nation and the dynasty precisely *'in order that* they might ultimately be saved!'[16] It is necessary for Israel that she should move on both from a kingdom and from a covenant neither of which could ever in that Old Testament form measure up to their ideals. They were the chrysalis. She is destined to be the butterfly that is to emerge from it.

The days of fulfilment (33:1-26)
At the centre of chapter 33, the motto of this section of the book is stated one more time – 'See, the days are coming, declares the LORD' – and now he is speaking of the days 'when I will *fulfil* the promise I made' (verse 14).

This then is the climax of the Book of Promises. Here, as in 32:17, and before that in 31:31-37, Yahweh speaks as the Creator (33:2, 20-21, 25-26). Once again the complexity, the order and the reliability of His creation serve to assure His people that His plans as their Redeemer are no less complex, yet no less ordered, and no less reliable. Now they are to hear 'great and hidden things' about those plans that go beyond anything they have heard so far. This revelation of the future will of course be couched in terms of their sixth-century world; if it were not, they would find it simply incomprehensible. But for readers further down the timeline, such as ourselves, Jeremiah's prophecies will be sufficiently 'elastic' to carry ever bigger meanings as the plan unfolds.

---

16 McConville, p. 101 (my italics).

The details of 33:4-5 are unclear, but these verses are the final reference to Yahweh's anger and wrath, and from here on everything is about restoration and rebuilding (33:6-7). One after another, the promises of the last three chapters are recalled. First comes the new covenant's basis in the forgiveness of sin (31:34); be sure of it, says Yahweh now – you are guilty, sinful, and rebellious, but I will cleanse you and forgive you (33:8). Then 30:10 promised 'quiet and ease'; a 'watered garden', said 31:12; 'safety' and 'good', said 32:37 and 41; and all these promises come together in glad thanksgiving as Judah sees Yahweh 'restore the fortunes of the land' (33:10-11). Where the closing verses of chapter 32 saw property being regained in every direction, the same six place-names have by now developed into prosperous sheep country (33:12-13).

Here too, from an earlier chapter, is 'the Branch' of 23:5, the promised royal scion of the House of David under whose reign all will be put to rights (33:14-17). Then the promises for the future begin to reach further into the past, to the priesthood that was central to the life of Israel before kings were even thought of (33:17-22). Back and back ranges Yahweh's overview, highlighting one after another of the great names that have defined His people down the centuries, beyond the kingdom of David to the priesthood instituted by Moses, to the nation born to Jacob in Egypt, to the family of Abraham in Canaan. As the Babylonians' grip tightened on the beleaguered city and the remnant of Israel penned up in it, it must have seemed that the promise Abraham was given in Genesis 22:17, of a family as numerous 'as the stars of heaven and as the sand that is on the seashore', was about to be extinguished. Yet to Yahweh's people, seemingly in the process of being destroyed, is given the promise of this extraordinary future.

The contents of these chapters, first put into Jeremiah's heart and mind by Yahweh 'in the tenth year of Zedekiah', presumably reached the ears of others almost at once, for Zedekiah himself had actually been talking with him about these things. Once spoken, they could have been committed to writing (as the prophet had been directed, 30:2) there and then. It was some time since the faithful Baruch had begun

to do this for Jeremiah, producing first the scrolls that King Jehoiakim would destroy, as we shall learn in chapter 36, and then their enlarged second edition. There is no reason why he should not have been on hand now, seventeen years later, in the besieged city, able to visit the imprisoned prophet and record these latest messages. How would they have been understood at the time? What, in the year 587, did the future hold for God's people – the kingdom, the priesthood, the nation, the family?

Top of the list is the kingdom. Here is King Zedekiah in person, in conversation with Jeremiah. It is all very well for the prophet to tell him that 'David shall never lack a man to sit on the throne of the house of Israel' (33:17); how is that to be squared with the statement that no descendant of his nephew Jehoiachin would 'succeed in sitting on the throne of David' (22:30), and the fact that his own sons are to be 'slaughtered … before his eyes' after the sack of Jerusalem (52:10)? For us, this whole question has already been thrashed out in the hinge chapters 24 and 25. The kingdom in its political form is doomed. The idea that it might be resurrected in that form is a mere dream. Kingdom, priesthood, nation, family: the kingdom is the most recent of the various shapes that Israel has taken, and the shortest-lived of those shapes – there have been only 450 years between David's reign and Zedekiah's; last in, first out. Israel will continue to be a 'kingdom', but henceforth in some transcendent, spiritual sense, with Yahweh as its king.

Similarly, what are we to make of 33:18: 'the Levitical priests shall never lack a man in my presence … to make sacrifices for ever'? After the exile the priesthood would be reinstated, in a rebuilt temple; it began earlier than the kingdom and would last longer. But for seventy years the continuing Israel in exile would have had to survive, spiritually, somehow, without it; no temple, no sacrifices for sin, no priesthood in the form that Moses had set up nine centuries before. As Yahweh is saying, 'A kingdom, yes, but not in that form,' so He is saying, 'A priesthood, yes, but not in that form.' And the day will come when that revived post-exilic temple, too, with its priests and its sacrifices, will prove to be a dream from which God's people will awaken, to discover the reality behind the Levitical priesthood as well as that behind the Davidic kingdom.

In fact, the whole Israelite nation is eventually to undergo the same chrysalis/butterfly transformation. In the final verse of the Book of Promises, Yahweh speaks of 'the offspring of Jacob', the original Israel, the father of the twelve tribes. Every Israelite bringing his offerings to the annual Festival of Firstfruits would recite the liturgical statement about how his great ancestor 'went down into Egypt and sojourned there, few in number, and there he became a nation, great, mighty, and populous.'[17] The nation was to last even longer than the kingdom or the priesthood. In one sense, it has lasted to this present day, and many would see worldwide Jewry, or the modern state of Israel, as its present shape. But Jeremiah would have seen even the nation as a dream from which there would one day be an awakening. His prophesying to the nations, to all the nations, was not a call summoning them to admire blessings that Yahweh intended for Israel but would not be offering to anyone else. It was the offering of the same blessings to all from every nation who would turn to Yahweh in repentance and faith. And for us in New Testament times it should be blindingly obvious that the 'holy nation'[18] has become an international community, the church of Jesus Christ; not, heaven forbid, that Old Testament Israel has been 'replaced' by the Christian church, as some misread the evidence, but that the true Israel of those times has *become* the true Israel of these times.

So we wake up to the fact that the kingdom of David, the priesthood instituted by Moses, the nation sprung from Jacob, are all pictures of the reality, which is Christ. We look back even to Abraham, the father of the original family (33:26), and find in him the prototype of saving faith: 'In Christ Jesus the blessing of Abraham [comes] to the Gentiles ... through faith.'[19] One thing remains that still today is something we see only in dreams, and that is the New Jerusalem, where His glory will one day appear. But on the analogy of the rest, Christ's people look forward with total confidence to the last great awakening.

---

17 Deuteronomy 26:5.

18 1 Peter 2:9.

19 Galatians 3:14; and see Galatians 3:7-9, Romans 4.

11

Failures
(Jeremiah 34–36)

The view from Nebo and the view from Sinai
Three places on the map are linked with the three places in
his book where Jeremiah is called a 'prophet to the nations'.
Through his eyes we have seen in his youth the view from
Anathoth (1:1-6), and in his prime the view from Jerusalem
(25:1-14). We shall see in his later years the view from
Tahpanhes in Egypt (43:8 and onwards). It would not be
surprising if he thought of these present chapters, the Book of
Promises (30–33) and those we may call the Book of Failures
(34–36), in terms of two other viewpoints, well remembered
from the story of his famous predecessor Moses. At the end
of Israel's forty-year pilgrimage through the wilderness that
other great prophet had looked out from Mount Nebo at the
panorama of the wonderful country Yahweh had prepared
for His people; while forty years earlier he had looked down
from Mount Sinai on a rebellious nation that did not deserve
such a destiny.[11]

As chapter 34 opens, it is of course only in his imagination
(and ours!) that Jeremiah may be seeing any such scene. But
he too is being given a similar privilege. He has set before
his readers in the last four chapters a view of an even more
wonderful land of promise than the one Moses saw from Nebo,
and in the next three he will be setting before them a view of

---

1 Deuteronomy 34:1-4; Exodus 32:7-20.

a nation that has failed to deserve it even more inexcusably than the faithless rabble Moses saw from Sinai.

So he is brought down from the climactic point of his prophetic inspiration, with its vision of a glorious future for God's people under the terms of a new covenant, to expose Israel's abject failure to grasp what He offers them. Retracing Judah's recent history backwards from his imprisonment in the very last days of the siege, he now recounts three events of which we have not yet read.

A goal not achieved (34:1-22)

From the last days of the siege of Jerusalem, when in the summer of 586 Nebuchadnezzar's forces will finally break into the city (incidentally releasing Jeremiah from prison), the prophet takes his readers back to an earlier stage of the war, when other cities besides Jerusalem are still holding out against the invader (34:1, 7).

We notice that the first of the three chapters of the Book of Failures, with its account of the first of these significant events, is itself composed of a threefold word that 'came to Jeremiah from the LORD' (34:1, 8, 12). In Word One (vv. 1-7), Yahweh tells Zedekiah that Jerusalem will be captured and destroyed, and that he himself will be sent into exile in Babylon (34:2-3). It is a curious prophecy, so selective that one might consider it downright misleading, in view of what chapter 39 will reveal of what was actually going to happen to Zedekiah, in all its horrible detail.

The shadow of Josiah, Zedekiah's father, the last godly king ever to reign in Jerusalem, lurks in the background of each of these three chapters,[2] as if to show that with his death in 609 the good ship Judah finally slipped her moorings and began to drift irretrievably to disaster. For though he is not named here, Yahweh's word that Zedekiah would 'die in peace' (34:5) is a clear echo of the ambivalent word that had come through the prophetess Huldah concerning Josiah, that he likewise would die in peace (2 Kings 22:20), when, in fact, he was going to be killed in battle. In each case, the message was one of those Delphic utterances that could come true in more ways than one. Josiah's kingdom was indeed at peace with

---

2 See also 35:1, 36:1.

the world when he decided to intervene in someone else's war and perished in the process; he was 'gathered to [his] grave in peace' in the sense that he did not live to see his country invaded by Nebuchadnezzar's war machine. In the same sort of way, Zedekiah too was going to die 'in peace' – in exile, in obscurity, bereaved and blinded, in the Babylonian 'peace' that would follow the obliteration of his kingdom. Neither man need have died in the way he did.

Zedekiah will have well remembered how 'all Judah and Jerusalem mourned for Josiah,' and how 'Jeremiah also uttered a lament for Josiah, and all the singing men and singing women have spoken of Josiah in their laments to this day' (2 Chron. 35:24-25). If he had ever reflected on his father's needless death, he might have grasped that the prophecy now being conveyed to him about his own future was similarly ambiguous. There were more ways than one of 'dying in peace'. Yahweh could have frightened him into repenting by spelling out in advance the gory and tragic details of what would happen if he didn't. But that would have confused the issue. The crucial demand was that here and now, regardless of consequences, he should finally make up his mind to trust and obey the word that came from Yahweh through his servant Jeremiah. That would be the proof of a true heart-repentance.

And that surely is the point of Word Two, in verses 8-11. It relates to a project that Zedekiah undertook in the course of the prolonged siege of the city, a 'proclamation of liberty'. For most modern readers, 34:8-9 is likely to be a minefield of misunderstanding and wrong assumptions. The words 'Hebrew' and 'Jew' and especially 'slave' are all misleading. We can sidestep some of the complications by using the word 'Israel' to cover 'all the people in Jerusalem', and by recognizing that none of them was a slave in the modern sense of the word. To put the matter in a nutshell, Yahweh's original intention had been that Israel should 'live off' the land He had given her, 'every man under his vine and under his fig tree'.[3] But in Israel in these later times there were many who for various reasons did not own land which they could farm, and who instead 'sold themselves and their services as

---

3 1 Kings 4:25.

a way of life because they were landless'.[4] This was, in fact, a way of life not unlike 'many kinds of paid employment in a cash economy' in the world of today.[5] In any case, all such so-called 'slaves' had to be released from their obligations after six years of service.[6]

Apparently for a number of such employees and employers the seventh year had arrived and passed, and amid the stresses of wartime and invasion the release that was due had been shelved. Since employers had considerable responsibilities to their bondservants, some might have been glad of the opportunity to cut down on expenses by 'letting them go', as we might put it today. But either way, Yahweh's law required the release, and He approved of its having been implemented, however belatedly: 'You … repented and did what was right in my eyes by proclaiming liberty' (34:15). Here was Zedekiah finding one command at any rate that he might obey in order to show loyalty to Yahweh, and he obeyed it. Perhaps to his own surprise, everybody fell into line (34:10).

Not, however, for long. Jeremiah's object in recounting these events is to draw attention not to the workings of this miscalled 'slave labour' system, but to the perversity of the people in first agreeing to implement the law of release and then going back on the undertaking, and to the weakness of the king in not enforcing his wishes. This is the gist of Word Three (vv. 12-22). Of the people, it has to be said that their change of mind may have been influenced by changes in the political situation (was the siege getting worse as the Babylonians tightened their grip, or easing off as rumours of an Egyptian army coming to Judah's help diverted Nebuchadnezzar's attention?). But what Yahweh is chiefly concerned with is the people's attitude to Himself, as indicated by the word 'turn' that figures repeatedly in Jeremiah's book. In this chapter we find that in respect of the proclamation of liberty, first 'they obeyed … But afterwards they *turned round* and took back the … slaves they had set free' (34:10-11). And again, 'you

---

4 Christopher J.H. Wright (1996), *Deuteronomy* (Peabody, MA: Hendrickson), p.197 (on Deuteronomy 15:12).

5 Wright (1983), *Living as the People of God* (Nottingham: IVP), p. 179. The whole section referred to in each of Wright's books will repay study

6 Deuteronomy 15:12-18.

recently *repented* [= *turned*] and did what was right ... But then you *turned round* and ... took back [your] slaves' (34:15-16). There is no point in simply turning for its own sake, turning and turning, as in the old Shaker song, until at some point you hope you may 'come 'round right'. The challenge was, and is, to make a practice of just one kind of turning, *from* sin and *to* God. You never know what may be your last, irrevocable, opportunity to do so.

Since the people have adapted the meaning of the word 'turning' to suit themselves, Yahweh too plays with words, adapting the meaning of the word 'liberty' to His own purposes (34:17). He sets them free from being His bondservants, free from the protection they enjoy when He is their master, free to make what they can of a godless world in which 'sword, pestilence, and famine' will now confront them at every turn. Since they do not want Him, they shall not have Him (which, when you come to think of it, is the biblical doctrine of hell summed up in eleven monosyllables). Then in 34:18-22 He takes up the word 'covenant', so central to Jeremiah's whole book, and unpacks the covenant-making procedure. A calf was slaughtered, and its parts were laid out in two rows, between which the parties to the agreement would then walk, saying, in effect, 'May I suffer a similar fate if I break this agreement.' You have, says Yahweh; and you will.

Word Three is addressed primarily to the people of Judah and Jerusalem, but the king, reappearing in verse 21, is equally at fault. The incident of the proclamation of liberty for bondservants might have been tailor-made to expose his personal failure. He had had the right idea, and set the liberation process in motion. He had had the strength of will to carry it through, so that everyone obeyed (34:10). He had had the backing of the law (in Deuteronomy 15) and of the prophets (in the person of Jeremiah). He had even been given a brief respite from hostilities while the Babylonians were preoccupied with the threat from Egypt (as appears from 34:21-22). So the only question was, would he have the resolve to carry it through? When the citizenry began to change its mind and go back on its undertakings, would he stick to his guns and show that he truly did mean to rule Yahweh's people in Yahweh's way?

No. The goal was not achieved, and the whole incident exposed Zedekiah for the failure that he was. The prayer attributed to the Elizabethan adventurer Sir Francis Drake is precisely to the point: that those who 'endeavour a great matter' should 'know that it is not the beginning, but the continuing of the same until it be thoroughly finished, which yieldeth the true glory.' For once in his life, Zedekiah had taken a godly initiative, but had not the spiritual stamina to see it completed. Had he already, perhaps years earlier, passed the point of no return? Was he already a lost cause? There are some signs that that may have been so. But this incident from the final months of the siege offers us just a glimpse of what might have been, and warns Jeremiah's readers not to hark back to a form of Yahweh's kingdom that had demonstrated, right to the end, that it simply could not deliver.

A lifestyle not understood (35:1-19)

Jeremiah had presented the 'liberation of bondservants' issue as a final test, in those last months before the city's fall, of whether Zedekiah and his people were able and willing to carry through a decision of straightforward obedience to a plain command from Yahweh.

They were not; and the prophet now sets alongside that narrative an earlier one, from the previous reign, to expose an underlying cause for their failure. It concerns a group of people mentioned nowhere else in the Bible story, and, as with the events just described in chapter 34, it may arrest our attention precisely by its uniqueness.

It was 200 years earlier that Jonadab ben-Rechab had founded the religious sect that bore his name, back in the days of the reforming king Jehu of Israel, who had recognized him as a kindred spirit (2 Kings 10:15-27). Like some modern Christian communities – the Amish of Pennsylvania spring at once to mind – it aimed to foster its inherited faith by preserving the culture of a bygone age. In the case of the Rechabites, this meant living as if they were still nomads newly arrived in the Promised Land; in tents instead of houses, and with no tilling of the ground (and therefore no vineyards and no wine). With the Babylonian threat all too real in the latter part of Jehoiakim's reign, they had abandoned their rural settlements

in order to move, no doubt very unwillingly, into Jerusalem for safety.

Yahweh had a message for 'the people of Judah and the inhabitants of Jerusalem' on this particular occasion (35:12-13), which was framed between two messages for the Rechabites. The first of these was simply that Jeremiah should visit their community, presumably encamped in some open space within the city walls, and invite them to a meeting in the temple precincts. There, it seems, they found members of the temple staff gathered, and tables set with jugs of wine and cups. They must have thought the whole situation surprising and peculiar, but there will have been no surprise about their reaction when Jeremiah invited them to drink. Certainly not, they must have said; you know very well that our community is a wine-free zone. 'We have obeyed the voice of Jonadab the son of Rechab, our father, in all that he commanded us,' they stated (35:8), and proceeded in the following verses to rehearse the rule of the community.

We can almost hear Jeremiah responding, as he shows them courteously to the door, 'Thank you, that is exactly what I knew you would say, and it gives me the springboard for my next word from Yahweh, which I now have to preach to the city at large.'

In fact, the public statement of faith that he has been able to draw from the leaders of the Rechabite community is not just a springboard, but the actual theme of his own next public prophecy, the second 'word from the Lord' in this chapter. They are only one clan among the tribes of Israel, and their community is relatively small, relatively new (though determinedly old-fashioned), and relatively insignificant, and does not find it easy to keep up its traditions in the modern world of 600 BC. The task may not be easy; but it is possible, proclaims Jeremiah. Here among you the Rechabites stand as a living witness to that fact. How much more should you, 'the people of Judah and the inhabitants of Jerusalem', value the far broader-based, far longer-established, far more directly God-inspired traditions that have shaped your nation as a whole!

That was the immediate message that Jeremiah drew from the incident at the time. Now that he is placing his account of it here in the Book of Failures, as a lesson for exilic and post-exilic

times, it acquires a further resonance. In Jehoiakim's Judah, with perhaps fifteen years yet to go before the kingdom's demise, the prophet was contrasting two kinds of religion – of the Israelite religion, that is; two ways of worshipping Yahweh. The Rechabite minority, though limited in its outlook, placed a premium on obedience, and lived faithfully according to the rule of its founder Jonadab. But the nation as a whole sat loose to the rule of its Founder and Redeemer Yahweh, and the prophet had repeatedly to charge it with disobedience.

With the lapse of years, the death of the kingdom, and the advantage of hindsight, we can see that Jeremiah's book at this point is actually setting forth not two but three kinds of religion, each regarding itself as the true faith of Yahweh. Back in the days of Jehoiakim the religious establishment was still powerful, with priests to staff the temple and prophets to give (supposedly) divine guidance to government and people. It is not hard to imagine how the Rechabites would have been regarded in those circles – negligible eccentrics with irrelevant ideas, not unlike that other maverick, Jeremiah; they, nonentities out on the conservative far right; he, a persistent nuisance on the radical left.

This would have been the view of Jehoiakim himself. We know he regarded Jeremiah with loathing, and may well have been heard to mutter (as Henry II would one day say, reportedly, about Thomas à Becket) 'Who will rid me of this turbulent priest?'[7] And we can be pretty sure that if he ever gave the Rechabites a thought, he would have regarded them as little more than a bunch of weirdos. But the fact of the matter was that that alignment of three parties – with establishment religion central and an eccentric fringe on either side – was a total misunderstanding of the situation. At the centre, in court and in temple, in politics and in religion, was a spiritual vacuum. What the prophet had tried to put across at the time, what now (after the fall of the city) he was reiterating in the writings he was putting together for the people of the exile, and what he would bequeath to later generations of Israel, was the crucial point about the Rechabites' lifestyle. They knew, and never forgot, that Yahweh had acted in redeeming His people from Egypt. They knew, and never forgot, that He had

---

7 Not too irrelevant to our prophet – see 1:1.

spoken in guiding them through into a new life. True, they had not grasped that He expected them to settle in the land of promise, to build houses and to plant vines.[8] But Jehoiakim and his ilk should have looked beyond their eccentricities to see at the heart of their community the reality of a living, acting, speaking God, such as Jeremiah himself, from his side, was constantly proclaiming. None of that registered with the powers-that-were in the Judah of the 600s.

The third of this chapter's three messages from Yahweh, like the first, is addressed to the Rechabites (35:18-19). Jeremiah understood what lay at the heart of their lifestyle, for all its inadequacies, and will have been glad to convey this very special promise, the reward of obedience: 'Jonadab the son of Rechab shall never lack a man to stand before me.' It echoes the promise concerning Judah's royal family, in 33:17: 'David shall never lack a man to sit on the throne of the house of Israel' – one of those promises that seem periodically to disappear underground, while first Jehoiakim and then Zedekiah lose the throne, and Jehoiakim's son survives but never regains it,[9] and his grandson returns from exile but with no royal rank,[10] and so on down the centuries until the coming of 'great David's greater Son', to claim the crown in a sense beyond the imagining of any of these Old Testament believers.[11]

A word not accepted (36:1-32)

In chapter 34, Jeremiah has set before his readers a classic example from the kingdom's last days of its failure to carry through Yahweh's will. In chapter 35, he then highlights from an earlier time an example of what lay behind that, its failure to understand Yahweh's ways. Now in chapter 36, he pinpoints an outstanding example of the attitude that lay behind both: the deliberate rejection of Yahweh's word.

---

8 Houses and vineyards were from the outset features of the land promised in Deuteronomy 6:10-11, and building and planting is a recurrent theme in Jeremiah's ministry, from 1:10 onwards. Of the Promised Land of the future, Ezekiel would write specifically, 'They shall dwell securely in it, and they shall build houses and plant vineyards' (28:26).

9 Jeremiah 22:28-30.

10 1 Chronicles 3:17-19; Ezra 2:2, 3:8

11 James Montgomery, 'Hail to the Lord's anointed'.

For the third time, we are reminded that the reign of good king Josiah is over and done (36:1). Instead of the prophecies of warning that were the norm in his days, his son Jehoiakim is to hear prophecies of doom. The times are changing, though Yahweh, of course, is calmly pursuing His own plans, making them known to His servant Jeremiah, and now having His words written down by Jeremiah's friend Baruch (36:4). In the year after this written record begins to be compiled, that is, in the winter of 604, Baruch is also commissioned to give it its first public reading.

We find ourselves suddenly in a scene of high drama, which more than any chapter we have read so far is crowded with characters and incidents. Jeremiah himself, whose imprisonments lie some years in the future, is at present a free man, though in sufficiently bad odour to have been 'banned from going to the house of the LORD' (36:5). In fact, he scarcely figures here at all. But he has friends at court, and negotiates access for Baruch to a vantage point in the temple complex in Jerusalem, presumably a window or balcony in the house of Gemariah ben-Shaphan which overlooks one of the main temple courts, at a time when a fast has been proclaimed, and a great crowd has gathered. From there Jeremiah's scroll can be read aloud 'in the hearing of all the people' (36:10). It is in a sense material that is already in the public domain – 'all the words', says Yahweh, 'that I have spoken to you … from the days of Josiah until today'; not exhaustive, as we know from the chapter's closing sentence, but comprehensive. And it is by way of being one final warning, so that even now the nation might hear, turn and be forgiven (36:2-3).

Gemariah's house provides Baruch with a pulpit, and Gemariah's son Micaiah, as he listens to the reading of the scroll, grasps the gravity of the occasion. He goes hotfoot to the palace to interrupt a meeting of the cabinet, of which his father is a member. This group at once abandons its agenda, to summon Baruch and hear the prophecies for itself. The picture comes across clearly in 36:11-20: at the highest level of government, there are still reverence for the words of Yahweh, respect, indeed concern, for the prophet and his spokesman, and a sense of responsibility for the welfare of the kingdom: on the one hand, as they all agree, the king must hear these

words, but on the other hand Jeremiah and Baruch must go into hiding.

In the next hour, their hopes for a sensible response to Yahweh's word are going to be blown away like chaff before the wind. The scroll is brought to Jehoiakim, sitting by the fire in the winter house, and as Jehudi ben-Nethaniah reads the words of Yahweh column by column, we see the king 'cut them off with a knife and throw them into the fire ... until the entire scroll [is] consumed' (36:23). Seven times its contents have been spoken,[12] and at the seventh, the word of the God of David is finally and totally rejected by this latest king of the line of David. At that point the die is cast, the cause is lost, the hopes of the faithful remnant – believing men of God in the highest echelons of government – are dashed, and the fate of the kingdom is sealed, even though it will take another eighteen years to die and Jeremiah will to the end be preaching the offer of repentance.[13] The kingdom as a political entity, that is. The true kingdom cannot ever be at the mercy of a reprobate like Jehoiakim. But once the word of God is deliberately rejected, as in this chapter, the ways of God are going to be increasingly misunderstood, as in chapter 35; and though men may make fitful attempts to do the will of God, they are going to fail, as in chapter 34.

As for the burning of the scroll, was there ever a more pointless gesture of defiance? The prophet and the penman simply 'took another scroll and ... Baruch ... wrote on it at the dictation of Jeremiah all the words of the scroll that Jehoiakim king of Judah had burned' (36:32). And the second edition was bigger, too.

---

12 Verses 2, 4, 10, 13, 15, 20, 21.
13 See 38:17.

12

Endings

(Jeremiah 37–39)

Short messages and long intervals

The three incidents described in chapters 34–36, and dating from various points in the eighteen years between 604 and 586, have summed up the failure of Judah's leadership to bring the kingdom back into line with the mind of Yahweh. Jeremiah and Baruch now return to an account of the last days of the kingdom's capital, and the ending of so much that so many had believed would endure for ever.

Zedekiah is the puppet on the throne, put there by the Babylonians in place of his brother's son, the rightful heir Coniah, *aka* Jehoiachin (37:1); after him there will be no more Davidic kings in Jerusalem. 'Neither he nor his servants nor the people of the land' will heed Jeremiah's prophecies; there will be no more ears willing to hear the word of Yahweh (37:2), though there are still folk who think *his* ears ought to be attentive to *their* words (37:3) – such presumption! And soon there will be no more messages for Jerusalem, because there will be no more Jerusalem to hear them. In all these respects the kingdom is coming to an end.

But before it does, it is going to hear five final prophecies. During the reigns of Josiah's sons it has been given, through the prophet, every possible opportunity to 'turn', to repent, and so to escape its doom. From Yahweh's point of view, there is little to say that has not been said already. So these five 'words from Yahweh' are mostly brief, just a few verses each.

On the other hand, the background to them is the last siege of Jerusalem, and though the account of it which Jeremiah and Baruch give in these chapters is also brief, the siege itself must at the time have seemed interminable to everyone involved, for it was to last two and a half years. The messages which are here recounted in quick succession must, therefore, have been spaced at considerable intervals. In those intervals we find Jeremiah harried from pillar to post by the many in Jerusalem who wish him ill, and each prophecy finds him in a different situation, all more or less unpleasant; discomforts which, as every servant of God knows, are par for the course in times of spiritual crisis.

At the outset, however, he is still at any rate a free man.

Jeremiah at liberty (37:1-10)

The statement that Jeremiah has 'not yet been put in prison' is set in a paragraph (37:1-5) full of significant detail that modern readers may miss. 'Pray for us,' begs the king – a natural request among believers, but in this case the last resort of the disobedient. So far as the international situation is concerned, the sequence of events is plain enough. Zedekiah, 'whom Nebuchadnezzar king of Babylon made king in the land of Judah', has changed sides and thrown in his lot with Egypt, where in 589 an ambitious new pharaoh, Hophra, has come to the throne (his name is mentioned in 44:30). It is because of this that the Babylonian armies (the 'Chaldeans') are in Palestine, to whip Zedekiah back into line. Now an Egyptian army is coming to his rescue, and drawing the Babylonians' attention away from the besieged city. But some uneasiness makes Zedekiah ask for Jeremiah's prayers. Why, we ask ourselves?

Because he has a guilty conscience. Jeremiah's book does not spell this out, but we, like his first readers, know from other sources that the king's actions have deliberately broken Yahweh's law, and that in two respects. It was an oath taken in the presence of Nebuchadnezzar, but (more importantly) in the name of Yahweh, that set him on his throne and bound him to Babylon; and 'if a man ... swears an oath ... he shall not break his word'.[1] Furthermore, ever since the exodus

1 Numbers 30:2; and see 2 Kings 24:20b; 2 Chronicles 36:13; and Ezekiel 17:11-21.

Yahweh's people have been forbidden to look back to Egypt for political or military aid.[2] In his relations with both of these great powers, Zedekiah has shown his contempt for the divine law, breaking one agreement which God had set up and making another which God had banned, and doing so with no sign of regret, let alone repentance. And now he has the nerve to ask Jeremiah to speak to Yahweh on his behalf, while he ignores what Jeremiah is saying to him on Yahweh's behalf. 'There is a God, and He does answer prayers, yours at any rate; so I want Him to listen to what I say, even though I don't listen to what He says.'

How can we get the message through to you, Zedekiah, if you won't listen? The fact is that the Egyptians will let you down, and the Babylonians will return and destroy your city. That is the first of the five words, the word of 37:6-10. If the prophecies of 21:1-7 and 34:1-7 antedate this one, you know these facts already. The point in their being repeated is to underline God's word to the wilfully disobedient: as the old hymn puts it, though in a different connection, 'What more *can* He say than to you He *has* said'?[3]

Jeremiah in the dungeon (37:11-17)
The second of these prophecies from Yahweh is the briefest, again a message for the king which says only what we have heard before and shall hear again. In contrast, the passage that introduces it is full of detailed scene-setting. It seems that once more, as with Jeremiah's 'protests' in an earlier part of the book, our attention is being focused on the prophet personally; not so much on the message he is conveying from the mouth of Yahweh to the ears of Zedekiah, as on the way he comes to embody in his own person the principle that sin always brings suffering. Of course it is Judah's sin, not his own, that causes Jeremiah to suffer. For this envoy sent from Yahweh's council to Yahweh's people does not enjoy a charmed life or carry a safe-conduct. He is like Isaiah's 'suffering Servant'; he bears his people's griefs and carries their sorrows; he is wounded for their transgressions, and crushed for their iniquities.[4]

2 Deuteronomy 17:16; Isaiah 31:1; Ezekiel 17:15.
3 Richard Keen, 'How firm a foundation'.
4 Isaiah 53:4-5.

We are to picture that period in the siege, probably the spring of 587, when the Babylonian forces have withdrawn from Jerusalem in order to confront the challenge from the Egyptian army that is marching up from the south. For the time being, something like normality returns to the streets and homes of the city, there is freedom to come and go, perhaps to replenish storerooms (not that supplies will be exactly plentiful in the surrounding country where the enemy has been so long encamped), perhaps to move away altogether.

Jeremiah had some family business to attend to back in Anathoth, possibly related to the field that he would later buy from his cousin Hanamel (we have already heard about this transaction in chapter 32). Although people were free to move into and out of the city, we can well imagine security forces on high alert, and the jittery atmosphere in which some guard might haul a suspicious-looking individual out of the line queuing to pass through the city gate. It does seem, though, that Irijah, the man on sentry duty, recognized Jeremiah, who was after all a well-known figure in Jerusalem, known moreover as a *persona non grata* with the authorities and one who had publicly opposed the official policy and advised surrender rather than resistance. He jumped to the conclusion that the prophet was defecting to the enemy, and apprehended him as a traitor.

In vain the prophet protests his innocence. 'It is a lie; I am not deserting to the Chaldeans' (who are in any case nowhere in sight). The word that has come instantly to his lips is the one that was the theme of an entire section earlier in the book, chapters 7–10, which dealt with the 'delusions' to which Yahweh's people had sold their souls. When he now says 'It is a lie', he means of course that this is Irijah stating something which is untrue; but he means also that this is the mind of the community at large that can no longer tell truth from falsehood. Yahweh had carried him through that earlier time, when he was bringing prophecies of doom to Jehoiakim's Judah. It had been distressing, but he had survived, and found himself supported by good men who still in those days wielded influence in the kingdom.

If however he had thought that that sort of opposition was a thing of the past, he was now to find it revived. Some things

had changed, but on the whole it was change for the worse. Of those allies in high places who had encouraged and protected him when Jehoiakim first showed his hand as a thoroughgoing unbeliever, most had gone into exile with the deportations of 597, and those now in power were conspicuously lacking in spirituality, integrity, or even ability. Ironically, his only protector would turn out to be (of all people) the new king. Zedekiah had considerable respect, even admiration, for him, but was too afraid of his 'advisers' to show this openly. Jeremiah must have allowed himself a grim smile at the thought that his 'friend at court' in these final days of the kingdom's existence was the king himself, with his stealthy, fumbling attempts to make the great prophet's imprisonment slightly less uncomfortable than it was.

Yet Jeremiah himself had changed, too. For Jehoiakim he had had only prophecies of doom, as that godless man led his nation determinedly down the road to perdition, and it was agonizing to have to watch him do it. For Zedekiah, however, there would be prophecies of hope, even though in the event that unhappy king would never actually close with the offer. And somehow, in spite of the sufferings the prophet had yet to endure, we sense that he was now on an even keel, recognizing and accepting that the political kingdom was in its last days, that much which had been assumed to be permanent was coming to an end, that he himself, 'a fortified city', would find that the kings of Judah would not prevail against him (1:18-19), and that there would in due course be some sort of new beginning for Yahweh's Israel.

We do wonder what it was that so 'enraged' the officials to whose tender mercies he was now committed (37:15). Mindless violence, shrill irrational fury, are familiar enough in our world, even sometimes in our streets, and the only explanation can be that 'it is a lie'; these are people who are seeing everything through a delusional fog, and what they think they see brings out the worst in them. So being 'enraged at Jeremiah, … they beat him and imprisoned him.' He was put in 'the dungeon cells and remained there many days'.

'Many days' in a dungeon – this is one of the long intervals, and at the end of it will come a very short message. King Zedekiah sent for him. Obviously the prison authorities were

involved in facilitating the interview, so some formal reason will have been given for it, but Zedekiah's real object was a private session in which he might learn the latest word from the Lord.

'Is there one, Jeremiah?'

'There is.'

'Then tell me. You are the only person I can trust. Take your time. However much there is to this word, I want to hear it all. Will Hophra's rescue mission succeed? Is the balance of power going to shift? Or must we expect the siege to begin again? What does Yahweh have to say about it? Tell me everything.'

Jeremiah fixes his eyes on the pathetic king. A long pause.

'You shall be delivered into the hand of the king of Babylon.'

Jeremiah in the court of the guard (37:18–38:3)

That is the second of the five words. Brief indeed! Does it come with 'the sensation of a short, sharp shock,'[5] as the prophet foretells yet another ending, in this case the ending of the life of the last king of Judah? No, not quite. The ending of Zedekiah's *reign*, yes. But even now there might be a reprieve of a different kind. Like that earlier Delphic oracle, that he was going to 'die in peace' (34:5), this prophecy is ambiguous. After all, many others have already been 'delivered into the hand of the king of Babylon', not to die, but to be themselves the hope of Israel's future as they start a new life in exile.

After a 'word from the LORD' that does in this way leave the door of hope ajar for Zedekiah, a rather longer word from the prophet, about his own immediate predicament. This is his 'humble plea' to the king, reminding him that he knows very well how much, and how undeservedly, Jeremiah is suffering. The other prophets have been proved wrong, yet they go unpunished; he has been proved right, and suffers for it. Even if Zedekiah is afraid to do the honourable thing and set him free, can he not at least make his imprisonment bearable? Conditions in his damp dungeon are literally killing him.

That Zedekiah can do, and he does. Jeremiah is transferred to the 'court of the guard'. We recall the account of Hanamel's visit, which took place while the prophet was being held here (32:8-12), and we can picture this 'court' as being both a space

---

5 W. S. Gilbert, *The Mikado*.

open to the public, and buildings that house the palace guards; where Jeremiah is kept in custody, yet is able to talk freely with those who come and go; where so far from being left to rot in an insanitary dungeon, he has on the one hand fresh air, and on the other hand shelter, together with a guaranteed official ration of food; and where the conditions of his imprisonment actually protect him from the malice of those who had earlier arrested and beaten him.

Yahweh has brought all this about for His own purposes, hard though it is for Jeremiah to have to live through it; and now He speaks His next word. It reproduces what was said in 21:8-10, where it also included the closing sentence 'He shall burn [the city] with fire', and, significantly, the opening sentence 'Behold, I set before you the way of life and the way of death.' In both places we turn from a message for Zedekiah's ears to one addressed to the people in general. In this present passage, what was veiled in 37:17, the word to the king, is spelt out in 38:2, the word to the people. Implicitly for him, explicitly for them, there is a message of hope. If you accept defeat, and surrender to the besieging forces, you will survive.[6]

Again it is short, this time just two verses. But of course we have here simply the gist of what Jeremiah was given to say in the relative freedom of the court of the guard. No doubt he expanded it, and certainly he repeated it, and everyone who came within earshot would have had the benefit of this third word from Yahweh. But to those who paid only lip service to the God of Israel, and reckoned that in the real world salvation lay not in Him but in the making of shrewd political alliances, it was defeatist talk. We have heard it before (21:7; 32:28; 34:2), but coming at this juncture it determines Jeremiah's enemies to put a stop once and for all to his unpatriotic spreading of alarm and despondency.

---

6 Either the 'Chaldean' siege envisaged in 38:2 has resumed after the lull during which Jeremiah attempted to go to Anathoth while the Babylonian forces were away dealing with the threat from Egypt, or else they are still away, but their return is regarded as inevitable.

Jeremiah in the cistern (38:4-28)

That last phrase comes from British military law, a section of the Army Act of 1879 which might have been tailor-made for Jeremiah's enemies. To them he is a person who 'spreads reports calculated to create unnecessary alarm or despondency', a very good paraphrase of 38:4, though where the Act punishes this offence with penal servitude, these men go further, and are demanding that the prophet be put to death. Alarm, in the sense of panic among the populace, is the last thing they want. But alarm is precisely what Yahweh does want, alarm in the sense of a wake-up call. That is the intention of the word Jeremiah has been proclaiming in the court of the guard: 'Hold out, and you will die; give in, and you will live; for the city is doomed.' This generation is about to see the ending of Jerusalem in its present form, the ending of Israel in its present form, the ending of the kingdom in its present form. Through unimaginable trauma (we have seen it depicted unsparingly in Lamentations) this chapter of their history will close, the page will turn – and he who believes and obeys the word of Yahweh 'shall have his life as a prize of war, and live' (38:2). For Jeremiah is at this point in time the prophet of *hope*.

But at what cost! Zedekiah's scruples are overborne (38:5), the exasperation of his officials at his lenient treatment of Jeremiah carries the day, and back into solitary confinement the prophet goes, for his worst experience yet. Even they dare not actually kill him, but they will leave him to die, now putting him not into a cellar-dungeon below the house of the Secretary of State (37:15) but down a manhole right there in the court of the guard, into a disused water-tank belonging to Malchiah, the king's son.

Let down by his king (and let down literally, into the cistern, by his enemies), Jeremiah turns out to have one more 'friend at court' in the person of Ebed-melech, an Ethiopian on the staff of the royal household. The wording of this man's plea on the prophet's behalf (in most English versions of 38:9) is rather odd, implying that he will starve to death *'because* there is no bread left in the city'. If that were the case, then everyone would already be facing starvation, including Jeremiah, whether in the cistern or out of it; and we know that in fact

it was not the case – not until the very day that the city fell did supplies actually run out.[7] Perhaps, in line with Mackay and the NIV, we should take it that since Jeremiah will, like everyone else, die of hunger anyway '*when* there is no bread left in the city,' the point of Ebed-melech's indignation is that for the prophet to be left to die *there*, ankle-deep in mud in his cistern, is simply outrageous.

One of the most memorable images in the book is that of this courageous African telling the king to his face that the officials were wrong to treat Jeremiah so, and that he, the king, was wrong to let them; then with ropes and rags and a band of stalwart helpers[8] marching to the manhole over the cistern, to pull the prisoner out. But it is important also to try to imagine how it was with the man in the pit before his rescuers arrived. Sitting on the muddy floor, shivering and damp, a circle of daylight above his head only as long as the manhole remained uncovered – did he forfeit even that, perhaps, by continuing to preach to any who might be within earshot, only to have someone silence the voice from the depths by replacing the cover, and so leaving him in total darkness? Was the ration of bread thrown down once a day, to land in the mud and have to be wiped sufficiently 'clean' to be eaten, or did they just forget to feed him? And might he be left there indefinitely? The isolation, the blackness, the cold, the hopelessness, it is the stuff of nightmares.

It is also the stuff of half a dozen psalms, where the Psalmist speaks of 'those who go down to the pit' (28:1, 30:3, 143:7), rejoices at having been pulled out of it (40:2), or in the terrible Psalm 88 finds Yahweh Himself putting him into its depths, and leaving him there where 'darkness has become [his] only companion' (88:18 ESV mg). In all these places we have the same word for 'pit' as Jeremiah 38 uses for 'cistern' or 'dungeon'. It is a kind of dying, even a picture of death itself, and we are reminded of Jeremiah's double calling: he finds himself not only representing God to God's people, but also representing God's people to God. He is willing to 'be' Judah, in God's eyes, sinking into the mire and the darkness,

---

7 See 52:6, with 2 Kings 25:2-3.

8 Three in some translations, enough to haul Jeremiah up from the cistern; thirty in others, a show of strength to face down possible opposition.

to demonstrate what happens to rebellious sinners. Death and destruction await them; and death was what Jeremiah's enemies intended for him, by a slower, crueller, method than execution, and what Zedekiah felt powerless to prevent (38:4-5). The nation's leaders look on, oblivious to the fact that, like *The Picture of Dorian Gray* in Oscar Wilde's novel, the man who seems to be disintegrating before their eyes is in fact a reflection of what is happening to them themselves.

At the same time, Jeremiah must wonder how in the reverse direction he can possibly 'be' Yahweh in the eyes of the nation. A God who speaks, yes; he knows what it means to be the mouthpiece of such a God. But a God who has to endure such shame, such suffering – a God who is scorned and rejected, and is going to *die*? What sort of a God is that?

However, the enactment is enough. Jeremiah is not, in the event, destined to perish in the pit. Even if none of those who expected him to die there grasped the significance of his 'entombment', it would be clear in due course to anyone who had the eyes to see.

So the manhole cover is removed, and silhouetted black against the disc of bright sky is the head of Jeremiah's rescuer – a face that is still black when he is hauled out into the light and can see it! (Did not Yahweh once give him a word remarking on the distinctive skin colour of Ethiopians?[9] Had there been such a thing as a colour bar in that Old Testament world, this would have been a glad encounter across it.) Thanks to Ebed-melech, he will not perish in the pit. He remains in custody, of course, but is now returned to the more humane conditions of the court of the guard.

Zedekiah too, the sad creature, is glad of this turn of events. He still wants Jeremiah's advice, though actually to live by it is beyond him. But before he can put his question to the prophet, the prophet has a word from Yahweh for him. At last, after the harrowing interlude of Jeremiah's 'death in the pit', comes the fourth word of the series. And it is simply the same again, except that this time the hope comes first: 'If you will surrender ... your life shall be spared, and this city shall not be burned with fire... But if you do not ... they shall burn it with fire, and you shall not escape' (38:17-18).

9 Jeremiah 13:23.

The king has yet to put his question. Jeremiah forestalled him with verses 17-18, as if to say, 'All you need to know is what I have told you already, and that I will now repeat yet again.' But Zedekiah refuses to trust and obey. It is the measure of his spiritual obtuseness that he still has to pursue his own agenda, his own anxieties with all their ifs and buts: Suppose this, and suppose that … (38:19). It must be with a mixture of exasperation and pity that the prophet responds, in effect, 'If you are not willing to take on board what has already been made clear to you, there is no point in my following up these suppositions of yours; they are simply so many red herrings.'

The postscript, the last five verses of chapter 38, sets the seal on the rejection of this last king of Judah. It does so in two ways. First, his injunction to Jeremiah not to disclose this private conversation to the officials – 'Let no one know of these words, *and you shall not die*' (38:24) – is deeply ironic, for the prophet has known from the very beginning that though 'the kings of Judah, its officials, its priests, and the people of the land' will oppose him, they will not be able to prevail against him (1:18-19); it is not in Zedekiah's power to decide whether or not Jeremiah shall die. And secondly, what has passed between king and prophet does remain secret, because 'the conversation had not been overheard'. That sentence means literally 'the word had not been heard'; and so the second verse of chapter 37 ('Neither [Zedekiah] nor his servants nor the people of the land listened to the words of the LORD that he spoke through Jeremiah the prophet') corresponds to this one, the second-to-last verse of chapter 38, with its ominous deeper meaning. The two chapters are bound together to brand this reign as the time when the kingdom finally shut its ears to what its divine King was saying to it. The word had not been heard.

Jeremiah in the house of the governor (39:1-18)

There follows in chapter 39 an overview of the entire siege, all thirty-one months of it,[10] which will be rounded off with one more brief message from Yahweh, His fifth and last word

---

10 Jeremiah 39:1-2 appear to indicate a siege of 18 months, but the indications and calculations are not as simple as they look. See Mackay, vol. ii, pp. 364, 612-14; McFall, p. 701, calculates it as lasting from December 589 to July 586.

in this section of the book. It is one which had actually been given to Jeremiah some time before the siege ended.

Before we hear it, we find in 39:1-10 another highly dramatic scene being staged. The walls of Jerusalem have finally been breached. With all resistance at an end, we see the great ones of Babylon enter and take their seats in a central space in the captured city to announce its fate, and we see Zedekiah escape with his bodyguard under cover of darkness, only to be captured within hours 'in the plains of Jericho' (v. 5). He is taken on his last long journey, first to Nebuchadnezzar's headquarters at Riblah in Syria, where his sons are executed and he is blinded, then to captivity and eventually death ('in peace'!) in Babylon. Meanwhile, the victors in Jerusalem put the city to the torch and carry the survivors likewise to Babylon.

So, with great economy of words, the story of the final siege of David's ancient capital is wrapped up. We may recall a notable phrase used by King Abijah, Zedekiah's many-times-great-grandfather, three centuries earlier – 'the kingdom of the Lord in the hand of the sons of David' (2 Chron. 13:8) – and ask ourselves what exactly that would have come to mean in the year 586. Zedekiah was indeed a 'son of David', but in his hand the kingdom fell to pieces, and his line came literally to a dead end. It was terrible for him to have this brought home to him by seeing (and it was the last thing he did see) the killing of his sons. But the line of his royal rule had run parallel to the line of Jeremiah's prophetic word for eleven years without ever really making a connection, and the time came when plainly it never would. Even more significantly, he had no one to blame but himself; it is the man who eats the sour grapes who finds his teeth set on edge (31:29-30). The fact was that in his heart he had chosen the sour grapes, he had chosen not to open his heart to the prophet's word. He and his kind of kingship, in fact the whole concept of Israel as a political kingdom and all that went with that, had run their course. It was the ending of an era, and time for something new.

Jeremiah's prophesying to Jerusalem also comes to an end, as the now deserted city goes up in flames. But his work is far from over. Before the burning begins, while he is still a prisoner in the court of the guard, he finds yet again that

he has a friend at court, even though the court is no longer Zedekiah's in Jerusalem, but a distant one presided over by an alien king. Nebuzaradan, 'commander of the imperial guard' (39:9 NIV), has been given sweeping powers in respect of post-war Judah, the land and the people, and in particular instructions concerning the prophet, whom Babylonian intelligence knows to have advised the government of Judah repeatedly to change its policy and accept its overlord's terms. In fact, the commander acts as go-between not for a plea from Jeremiah to Nebuchadnezzar, but for an edict from Nebuchadnezzar on behalf of Jeremiah. The next chapter will explain more fully what happened, but this one indicates that a very high-powered delegation (39:13-14) was involved in putting things right for a man to whom the Babylonians reckoned that considerable respect was due, for reasons both political and religious. So he was 'entrusted ... to Gedaliah the son of Ahikam,' a good man and an old friend, newly appointed by them as governor of Judah (no longer a kingdom!), 'that he should take him home' (39:14). A touching turn of phrase for one who for years had known little or nothing of domesticity.

So we come to the fifth of the words from the Lord that are grouped together here in chapters 37–39. These verses, 39:16-18, are a promise of protection when Jerusalem falls: reassuring, certainly, but the ESV's phrase 'prize of war' is sufficiently unusual to prompt us to think further about what is meant, who is in mind, and why it is used here.

'Spoils' or 'booty' would be more familiar terms (the old versions have 'prey'). Any soldiers of fortune who might get involved in this conflict in the hope of profiting from it would find that hope dashed, and themselves lucky to escape with their lives (so the NIV translation). Ebed-melech, to whom this word is directed, has had no such mercenary intention, but 'prize of war' is meaningful for him even so, assuring him of personal survival. To see why he, remembered only as the man who rescued Jeremiah from certain death in the empty water-tank, should be favoured with such a promise, we should compare the four occasions where it figures. In 21:9 Yahweh addresses it to the people of Jerusalem: go out to the enemy, hands up, armed with nothing but a white flag, and your lives will be saved. In this present section, in 38:2, it is the

same message, here too offering life to the people of Jerusalem, though at this point the proclaiming of it condemns Jeremiah to a lonely lingering death. Then in 39:18 it is given to Ebed-melech, and finally in 45:5 we shall find it given also to the faithful Baruch.

Repeatedly we have seen Jeremiah not only representing Yahweh to Israel, as he conveys the divine word to the people, but also representing Israel to Yahweh, as he embodies in himself what they are, or might be, or ought to be. If they too are willing to accept 'death in the pit', deprived of everything on which they might pin their hopes except the bare promise of Yahweh, then they too may look for a 'resurrection' to new life. Baruch, who is to be given this promise in chapter 45, will represent all true believers among the prophet's fellow-Israelites; Ebed-melech the Ethiopian here represents all in the wider world who will accept the promise, for Jeremiah was from the beginning 'appointed ... a prophet to the nations' (1:5). In New Testament terms, 'Nothing in my hand I bring, Simply to Thy cross I cling; Naked, come to Thee for dress; Helpless, look to Thee for grace;'[11] the universal plea of the repentant sinner, thankful to escape with his life.

For everyone concerned, then, the end is not yet. We know nothing of what will happen to Ebed-melech, and little of what will happen to Baruch; after all, 'the promise was only that they should escape with their lives, and this they have done,' says McConville. We know much more about Jeremiah. When 'at the end of the book he remains alive,' we are aware that 'in his life the life of Judah is still epitomized. The exile looks like a kind of death, but the nation is merely dormant, awaiting revival.'[12] Much has ended, that is very clear. But the story continues.

11 Augustus Toplady, 'Rock of Ages'.
12 McConville, p.132.

13

Continuations
(Jeremiah 40–45)

Life goes on (40:1-12)
A slight oddity at the beginning of chapter 40 may be meant
as a marker in the overall structure of the book. Verse 1 is
simply a heading, not a sentence: 'The word that came to
Jeremiah'. But in fact in these next chapters Yahweh does
not actually speak to the prophet till 42:7, and it may be that
the 'word' of 40:1 is something more than just meaningful
sounds uttered by a voice. If it corresponds to the 'word' that
came repeatedly to God's people (as we were told at the very
beginning, 1:1-3), from the thirteenth year of Josiah to the
eleventh year of Zedekiah, when Jerusalem fell 'in the fifth
month', we have to recognize that that certainly was not just
a voice speaking. The 'word of Yahweh' for the last days of
the political kingdom comprises the thirty-nine chapters
describing Jeremiah's whole ministry, not only his preaching,
up to that point. Similarly now, in the remaining thirteen
chapters, the last quarter of the book, it is what is done, not
simply what is said, that constitutes the 'word of Yahweh' for
the days when that kingdom is no more. Jeremiah is himself
God's message to His people, after 586 as he was before, and
as indeed he is still today.

Something else, too, suggests that in the book he and
Baruch are putting together there is at this point a break.
One of the many endings described in chapters 37–39 is the
end of his persecution at the hands of 'the people of the Lie'

in Jerusalem. He is rescued, paradoxically, from enemies in Judah by friends from Babylon! But how it happens is described twice: in one way in chapter 39, to round off the 'kingdom' years, and then in another way in chapter 40, to introduce the 'post-kingdom' years.

At first glance there do seem to be differences between 39:11-14 and 40:1-6, but they are more apparent than real, and a careful look at names and dates will help to resolve them. We need to be aware that the city walls were breached on 9th Tammuz (18th July) 586, but only on 10th Ab (17th August), with the walls finally dismantled, was the city torched.[1] With regard to the Babylonian generals who entered the city on the first of those dates, the NIV translation of 39:3 may well be right in proposing that they were three in number, and giving a name and rank for each. If so, it seems that taking precedence over the 'Rab-saris' Nebo-Sarsekim and the 'Rab-mag' Nergal-Sharezer was another Nergal-Sharezer, governor of the province of Samgar, son-in-law of King Nebuchadnezzar and himself a future king of Babylon.[2]

Nebuzaradan, of whom we have already heard (the 'commander of the imperial guard'), oversaw first the evacuation of the city and then the burning of it. Together with the Rab-mag and a new Rab-saris, and following special orders from the highest source (39:11-12), he had traced Jeremiah to the court of the guard. Known to the Babylonians as a prophet and 'holy man', who had moreover advised Judah repeatedly to make peace with them, Jeremiah was freed and honoured and provided for. Everyone else who was left in Jerusalem was to be taken to Babylon (39:9). But while the city was then being methodically destroyed, it seems they were held in a transit camp at Ramah, and Jeremiah, leaving the city with the rest, found that perhaps by some oversight he was for the moment not free after all. Nebuzaradan discovered him there, liberated him this time formally and properly, and, as we know, left him in the care of Gedaliah, the newly appointed Israelite governor of what was now a Babylonian province.

---

1 Jeremiah 39:2, 8; 2 Kings 25:3-4, 8-10. See Mackay, vol. ii, pp. 591, 612-14; but also footnote 6 on p. 230 of this book.

2 Mackay, vol. ii, p. 365.

So as Zedekiah's kingdom expires in flame and ruin, for Jeremiah life goes on. In fact, it is more than a continuation; it is a life considerably changed. What has ended for him is forty years of being ignored, disliked, contradicted, rejected, you might almost say crucified; and what lies before him as Nebuzaradan brings him out of the holding camp at Ramah is, you might almost say, a resurrection. The following verses, 40:7-12, show that life goes on for the land also, and in this case too it is a new kind of life. All who have survived in the city and all who had earlier deserted to the enemy are being taken to Babylon, but the land is not to remain uninhabited. It would not be in Babylon's interest to leave an empty wasteland for the Egyptians to annex. There are the landless poor (40:7), such as the 'slaves' we remember from chapter 34, and others returning after having taken refuge in neighbouring countries (40:11), all of whom now find themselves given 'vineyards and fields' (39:10). And as a hint that someone even greater than the king of Babylon is at work in all this, the horrors of war are followed, incongruously, by an abundant harvest. The dreadful year 586 turns out to be one that in this respect God is going to crown with His bounty.[3]

It won't last, of course. As the Prayer Book puts it, God's people are properly grateful for 'all the blessings of this life', but they recognize that that kind of blessing is temporary, and points forward to 'the hope of glory' in the next life.[4] Gedaliah's governorship will end in tears, and the free choice offered to Jeremiah by the Babylonians ('Go wherever you think it right to go,' 40:5) will be overruled by his own compatriots when they carry him off into Egypt (43:4-7). But the point is made. Although in many respects the world has changed, life goes on.

Trouble goes on (40:13–41:10)

From one point of view you could say that the July of that year saw the kingdom's death, with the capture of Jerusalem and the removal of Zedekiah, and the August saw its funeral, with the burning of the city. Then, it might seem to you, through the September the mourners are dispersing quietly, grieving

---

3 Psalm 65:11.

4 'The General Thanksgiving', in the Book of Common Prayer.

over their loss but hoping never to have to go through such traumas again.

Altogether too decorous, and, sad to say, far too optimistic. By the October (41:1) the true state of affairs is being exposed. New names have begun to appear now that so many of the old ones have been written out of the drama, and among them Gedaliah is outstanding, a man of honour and integrity like his forebears, who have served in high office since at least the days of Josiah: Gedaliah the son of Ahikam the son of Shaphan[5] – there's a pedigree for you! But this good man (an excellent choice, it has to be said, on the part of Nebuchadnezzar and his generals) seems to believe that in Isaiah's words Jerusalem is finding 'that her warfare is ended, that her iniquity is pardoned, that she has received from the LORD's hand double for all her sins.'[6] Having been so humbled, surely Judah has learned her lesson, and everyone fortunate enough to have survived will be only too keen not to risk another such calamity. All will be pulling together, to make the much-reduced nation the community it ought to be. This optimism is ill-founded, as we shall discover.

As Gedaliah sees the situation, there is no denying that the city has been destroyed, the countryside ravaged, half the population deported, and the monarchy overthrown. A dismal outlook. But on the other hand, life goes on, land has been reallocated, the harvest is plentiful, and, though he is no Davidic king, he has a good standing in Israel and the confidence of his overlord in Babylon. Hoping that this really is a new start with a clean slate, he sets up his headquarters in the historic town of Mizpah, eight miles north of Jerusalem, and it becomes the focal point of the post-war community, as we have seen in 40:7-12.

Among those who converge on Mizpah to identify with the new regime are the leaders of guerrilla bands that have kept clear of the conflict around Jerusalem. Two of these men at once come to the fore in Jeremiah's narrative. Johanan ben-Kareah is a loyalist, and brings unwelcome news concerning the leader of another guerrilla group, Ishmael ben-Nethaniah. We remember from chapter 27 the conference (held a few

---

5 See 2 Kings 22.
6 Isaiah 40:2.

years earlier, and interrupted by Jeremiah wearing his yoke) between six of the small kingdoms of Western Asia, debating how best to face the Babylonian threat. They may have been united against Babylon, but are not necessarily friendly to one another. The king of Ammon has been delighted that in the event Judah has been trounced while his own kingdom has gone unscathed, and now he hopes to take advantage of Judah's present weakness.

This is what lies behind the exchanges of 40:13-16. Ishmael has family connections with Zedekiah (41:1), and Johanan knows him to be plotting with the king of Ammon to oust this non-royal upstart Gedaliah and take over what used to be the kingdom of Judah. It will soon become obvious that in Ishmael we are dealing with a power-mad psychopath, who has big ideas about destabilizing the region to his own advantage and no idea at all about what might actually happen if he were thus to thumb his nose at imperial Babylon. Of all this Johanan warns the governor, and offers to act (in the jargon of gangster movies) as the hit man who will 'take out' the villainous Ishmael before he can do too much damage.

Gedaliah does not believe him, and refuses to sanction the assassination. 'You shall not do this thing, for you are speaking falsely of Ishmael' (40:16). It is hugely revealing that in that last phrase he uses the word we have heard so often in this book, particularly in chapters 7–10: '*It is a lie,*' he says. He has heard Jeremiah in earlier times repeatedly warning against *the* Lie, the grand Delusion, and not wanting to be taken in by such falsehood he assumes that Johanan's warnings are part of it. His naivety results in his own murder at the hands of Ishmael, together with that of the rest of his household and even of the Babylonian bodyguard provided for him as governor.

The very next day, before news of the murders at the governor's residence can get out, there comes past Mizpah the group of pilgrims of whom we heard when we first embarked on our reading of Lamentations. For reasons which are unclear to us but which no doubt make sense to Ishmael's twisted mind, they too are slaughtered, all but a few who offer him access to caches of foodstuffs they know of. After that, he and his brigands return to the town, round up the citizens, and march everyone off in the direction of Ammon.

But, we may ask, on what grounds did Gedaliah judge Johanan to be telling lies, a misunderstanding that was to result in a whole series of tragic events? How was it that he, on the alert against delusion, was himself deluded into thinking Ishmael could not possibly be as black as Johanan painted him? And once we start asking that kind of question, a further question comes to mind, suggested by a book of a very different kind from a very different age. One of Agatha Christie's murder mysteries takes its title from the last words uttered by the victim, which are the central puzzle that drives the whole plot: 'Why didn't they ask Evans?' Just so, as we see the troubles that spread like ripples on a pond in the chapters before us, we must find ourselves wondering 'Why didn't they ask Jeremiah?' The prophet had gone to live with Gedaliah at Mizpah (39:14, 40:6; somehow he escaped the massacre), and one would have thought that a servant of Yahweh whose credentials had been proved to the hilt by the time Jerusalem fell would be the first point of reference for a leader wanting to discern between truth and lies, especially a leader who had grown up in the godly family of Shaphan and knew Jeremiah from of old.

That familiarity however was his downfall. To his mind, having the prophet available was enough; you need not bother him in cases where you reckoned you could trust your own judgment. Gedaliah had assumed that a new age had dawned, and in that he was right. But when the kingdom had come to an end, which from one point of view was of course a great tragedy, he seems to have assumed also that all the sins and follies which had led to its demise had been dealt with too. No, no. He should have asked Jeremiah. After the great catastrophe, as after every great change in human history (and indeed in the individual's experience), life would go on, *and troubles would go on as well.* Until the last great awakening we shall always need the prophetic word of Yahweh to call us repeatedly to penitence and faith, and to guide and teach us in His ways. If only the governor had thought to consult the prophet, the prophet would have told him how to distinguish the truth from the lie. The God-given word was readily available.

Worldly wisdom goes on (41:11–42:6)
The day of judgment which had destroyed Zedekiah's
Jerusalem was a fulfilment of Jeremiah's very first prophetic
visions, the almond branch (the 'wake-tree') and the boiling
pot. Yahweh's wakeful eye had seen everything that had been
going on throughout the days of the kings, and now at last His
judgment had boiled over from the north upon the wicked
and unrepentant nation. It had swept away the 450-year-
old monarchy, and a new era had begun. But Gedaliah had
learned the hard way that there was just as much wickedness
and folly in this new world as there had been in the bad old
days of Jehoiakim and Zedekiah. 'Paradise Regained'? Not
by a long chalk. The excesses of Ishmael might have been
designed expressly to show how many rampant evils there
are still, only just under the surface, even when a variety of
improvements have taken place above it.

In fact, the evil breaks through again and again, and not
just in the horrific form which has blown Gedaliah's optimism
to pieces. The two guerrilla leaders who have been united in
resistance to the Babylonian invaders are here pitted against
each other; but though at first glance one belongs with the
'baddies' and the other with the 'goodies', neither is, in fact,
an admirable character. While Ishmael is the more obvious
example of the sinfulness that still bedevils even this 'brave
new world', Johanan too represents it, and indeed does so in
a more subtle and more dangerous way.

In connection with chapter 17 we turned the name of a bad
character in *The Pilgrim's Progress* to good account, describing
Jeremiah as being in the most positive sense Mr Facing-both-
ways. Another uncomplimentary name in John Bunyan's book
is that of Mr Worldly Wiseman, and in the case of this one we,
like Bunyan, are going to use it in an uncomplimentary sense,
and apply it to Johanan.

Imagine yourself in his shoes. You are well aware that
pious people are trying to make sense of all these events from
the religious point of view; but (you say) let's leave religion
out of it for the present, and ask what needs to be done in the
way of practical politics. Though you are a soldier, you are
not a cold-blooded killer like Ishmael, and to you the wisest
course of action seems to be to accept that Babylon has won

the war, and to make the best of the new situation. You arrive too late to prevent the series of murders for which Ishmael is responsible, but when you discover that he has now rounded up the people of Mizpah, his own fellow-Israelites, and is marching them off to work for their historic enemy the king of Ammon, obviously the right thing to do is to catch him and stop him. Ishmael himself escapes, with a few of his men, but at least you have achieved your humanitarian aim of preventing yet another mass deportation (a grubby imitation of Nebuchadnezzar's grand designs). Now it stands to reason that the authorities in Babylon will learn soon enough about the massacre at Mizpah of the governor they have appointed, and of his staff, and of the Babylonian garrison of the town. To your way of thinking their next move is bound to be a punitive military expedition to restore their control over Judah. So clearly the sensible thing to do is to get out of the area as quickly as possible, and organize an evacuation of the local populace, not against their will to servitude in Ammon, but very much to their advantage to safety in Egypt. The first stage of the journey takes you all southwards past the ruins of Jerusalem to a temporary encampment near Bethlehem.

All this is the very sensible, reasonable, logical kind of thinking that one would expect of Mr Worldly Wiseman. There are a dozen turns of phrase in that last paragraph which betray Johanan's trust in his own judgment rather than God's. He has even recognized that the historic religion of these people, which means a lot to some of them, though he himself manages pretty well without it, may be helpful in selling them these proposals. So he enlists the help of the well-known prophet Jeremiah, who will presumably confirm the wisdom of them.

His invitation, though carefully worded to appeal to Jeremiah's sensibilities, contains one word which completely gives the game away. 'Pray to the LORD your God for us.' Does not the word I have in mind stand out like a sore thumb? 'The LORD *your* God.' Johanan's wisdom is the wisdom of this world, paying lip service to religion when it suits its purposes to do so; but the God of Israel is not in any real sense *his* God.

Jeremiah sees through all this worldly wisdom, and his reply is a rebuke, which reminds Johanan's company that his

God is supposed to be their God too (42:4). Still, he promises them that he will nonetheless pray as requested, even though their sanctimonious response (42:5-6) is the last word in bad faith and insincerity.

The word still follows you (42:7–43:13)
The six chapters from 40 to 45 are telling how the story of Old Testament Israel continues even after it has in one respect come to a dead end in the year 586. They have at their centre this weighty passage, twenty-nine verses long, which in turn has at *its* centre (43:1-7), the account of a notable journey. (This central paragraph is like the hinge of a palindrome or chiasmus. Yet again the Scripture yields special treasures when we are on the alert for its shape and structure.)

The journey is from Geruth Chimham to Tahpanhes. The names may mean nothing to us, but their locations are explained, one being 'near Bethlehem' (41:17) and the other being the first significant place you reach when you come 'into the land of Egypt' from the north (43:7). The people who have chosen to take refuge in Egypt will be no more out of reach of the words of Yahweh than the people who have been carried off unwillingly to Babylon. The latter will find they have taken prophets with them – Daniel, Ezekiel – and the former, of course, have Jeremiah himself, for Yahweh will continue to speak even in Egypt (where He did, as we remember, have quite a lot to say back in the days of Moses).

It is ten days before Jeremiah is clear in his mind as to what Yahweh would have him say to Johanan and his people. Then he summons them (42:8; no question about who is really in charge!), and delivers a twofold message: first an open choice, then a closed decision. The choice is what it has always been, again going right back to Jeremiah's original call (1:9-10), and based upon the great 'If'. 'Show us the way we should go,' they have said (42:3), and Yahweh replies, '*If* you are prepared to stay here in Judah, you shall be built, not pulled down; planted, not plucked up. Conversely, *if* you insist on going to Egypt, the sword and famine and pestilence that have already destroyed your kingdom here will follow you and destroy you there. You ask where you should go, and the answer is nowhere. But the choice, the responsibility, is yours.'

Before they can reply, 'the LORD of hosts, the God of Israel,' speaks again (v. 18), because they have, in fact, made their choice already. No more 'ifs'. They have said they will obey, but in practice they do not obey 'in anything' (v. 21), and the doom will fall upon them even in the supposed safety of Egypt, as they are about to hear.

So having asked what Yahweh has to say, and having promised to abide by it whatever it may be, they promptly reject it. 'It is a lie,' says Johanan, which was exactly what had been said to him when he had told Gedaliah the truth about Ishmael. But how needle-sharp is Yahweh's challenge to him and 'all the insolent men' that surround him! To stay in Judah in spite of the possibility of Babylonian reprisals after Ishmael's bloody deeds – that would be a real test of confidence in the word of Yahweh; and it is a test that these arrogant people fail. Someone spins a yarn about Baruch having an agenda of his own and manipulating poor feeble old Jeremiah (!) so as to further it: the all-too-common, and all-too-effective, alliance between malicious troublemaking and ludicrous fantasy. They believe what they want to believe, they go where they want to go, and by verse 7 the journey from Geruth Chimham to Tahpanhes has been completed.

'Then (43:8) the word of the LORD came to Jeremiah in Tahpanhes', and we have an obvious case of the word being something more than simply things that the prophet says. It is of a piece with the many instances we have found already of plain statements from Yahweh that are enhanced not only by vivid picture-language, but by objects and actions, and witnesses called to particular places to observe them. In the classic ABA pattern of Hebrew poetry (we have just noticed it yet again in this very section), the pivotal event of Jeremiah's whole ministry is the death of the kingdom-dream in July 586, and balanced on either side of that event are two place-names, one in the land of today's enemy and the other in the land of yesterday's enemy: in chapter 13, the river Euphrates in Babylon, and here in chapter 43 the town of Tahpanhes in Egypt. And at each place attention is drawn to a significant object, a memorable visual aid: the pre-586 Israel is a loincloth rotted by the waters of a foreign river, the post-586 Israel is a layer of paving-stones under the weight of a foreign throne.

Debate over 13:1-7 has to do with the location of 'Euphrates', whereas debate here in 43:8-13 is not about the place-name Tahpanhes, but about the meaning of the words translated 'mortar', 'pavement', and 'palace', and the likelihood of a visitor from another country being allowed to dig around in the forecourt of whatever this official building was. But imagine this acted prophecy how we will, there is no debate over its meaning. It pictures Nebuchadnezzar of Babylon enthroned at Tahpanhes, having come to 'strike the land of Egypt' (v. 11). Still to be found in our hymn-books are lines perhaps too flowery for the taste of some – 'I know not where His islands lift Their fronded palms in air, I only know I cannot drift Beyond His love and care';[7] they certainly tell a truth, but they have a grim corollary: it is equally impossible to evade His judgment.

The people of Judah who have been forcibly exiled to Babylon are actually going to be better off than those who are now deliberately exiling themselves to Egypt. For Yahweh's use of Nebuchadnezzar as His instrument[8] cuts two ways. Those who are wise accept the discipline, whether settling in Babylonia or submitting to the Babylonian occupation of Judah, and will emerge remade from the seventy years of it. Those who are foolish reject the discipline and try to escape from the power of Babylon, but will be pursued by it even into Egypt. That is the word given through Jeremiah in Tahpanhes.

The word still finds you (44:1-14)

It may be news to the modern reader, but would have been well known at the time, that there was already even in those days a 'Dispersion', a network of Israelite communities settled in foreign countries, and the prophetic word that in the person of Jeremiah was following the latest group of emigrants into Egypt was also going to find and challenge these earlier settlers. In 44:1, more unfamiliar place-names appear, in this case indicating how the Israelite incomers had spread across the country, from the frontier post at Migdol, by way of Tahpanhes, the first considerable town they would have reached, to Memphis, the chief city of Lower Egypt and the Delta, and on up the Nile valley into Upper Egypt, the

---

7 John Greenleaf Whittier, 'Who fathoms the eternal thought?'

8 Compare Isaiah 10:5, 'Assyria, rod of my anger.'

land of Pathros. Furthermore, it seems that time has passed
since the events of chapter 43, and the refugees led by Johanan
have settled down too, adapting to the Egyptian culture as the
longer-established expatriates have already done.

So Israelite colonies right across the country, old and new,
are being addressed in chapter 44. If you are Israel, this is your
God speaking, Yahweh of hosts. So He announces Himself at
the beginning of each of the three oracles in the first half of
this chapter (vv. 2-6, 7-10, 11-14).

First (He says), I have to confront you with the facts. You
have all heard, and many of you have seen, the state your
homeland is in. If you ask 'Who is responsible?', the first
answer will probably be Nebuchadnezzar king of Babylon.
But there is a second, much more important, answer. *I am.*
I put him up to it, as the only way that in the end I could
bring home to you what a destructive thing your sinfulness
is. And that means there is a third answer, because ultimately
it is you yourselves who are responsible. In spite of all I have
said through My prophets to warn you, you have persisted
in rating all sorts of other 'gods' (and I don't just mean those
ridiculous idols) as more important than Me. You do not
love the Lord your God with all your heart, soul, mind, and
strength. Hence the desolation of Judah.

Secondly (He says), I have to ask you for the reasons. (He
drops into the familiar three-question pattern that we recall
from earlier passages like the 'balm in Gilead' verse, 8:22.)
Why are you so keen to destroy yourselves? Why are you
provoking Me so that I will destroy you? Have you forgotten
just how flagrantly, for years now, the leadership of your
nation has ignored My law?

Thirdly, therefore (He says), I have to condemn you to the
punishments which have fallen upon the land of Judah, and
which you think you have escaped by coming here. I do have
a remnant that will be preserved through all these troubles,
but 'the remnant of Judah who have set their faces to come to
the land of Egypt to live' is not it. The scourge of sword and
famine and pestilence which has decimated Judah will come
here too, and will destroy you. For the penitent, the 'death'
of exile in Babylon is the way to resurrection life. For the

impenitent, the attempt to escape death by self-exile in Egypt will end in death indeed.

The word still condemns you (44:15-30)

Linger for a moment over that heading. Who is meant by 'you'?

Obviously Jeremiah's book as a whole is intended in the first instance for the people of Israel as they are at the time of writing, with these present chapters reporting what he says particularly to the émigrés in Egypt in the mid–580s. It is to one community intermingled with another, foreigners among natives, that he is here speaking and writing. In this latter-day 'Israel in Egypt', the sharp contrasts between master and slave, between home-born and immigrant, that obtained when Israel was last in Egypt,[9] no longer obtain. Just the opposite, in fact. Here in chapter 44 is an Israelite community increasingly drawn into the culture of Egypt, especially into its religion. Deprived of the structures of their own religion, not just the Jerusalem temple but also all that went with it, they have had to work out what it means to worship God in these changed circumstances. The result has been a return to the whole 'queen of heaven' mishmash of superstition and complacent folk-religion, already commonly practised in Judah in the days when Jeremiah preached his famous 'temple sermon' (7:17-18).

In the providence of God, Jeremiah has been brought from an Israel whose holy city and temple have been destroyed to an Israelite community in another land which has no holy city or temple anyway. He comes with the message that Yahweh is nevertheless still alive and active and *speaking*, with a word that continues to home in on heart and mind and conscience. Holy places or no holy places, where you hear Him speak, there you know He is.

So he tells all who hear him even in Pathros (44:15), the 'southern land' at the far end of Egypt, that the word still follows them, and finds them, and condemns them. What it condemns is one of the most breathtaking rejections of the truth even in this most confrontational of books. Hear the response of the 'great assembly' in Pathros to Jeremiah's

9 See Exodus 1:8-14.

threefold message from Yahweh: 'As for the word that you have spoken to us in the name of the Lord, we will not listen to you' (44:16). And like a child determinedly forcing a piece of a jigsaw into the wrong place, they make out that the prosperous times in Judah belonged with the worship of the 'queen of heaven', and the bad times came when they were compelled by narrow-minded King Josiah to give up that kind of religion.

Jeremiah responds as he did to Hananiah, when that prophet likewise flatly contradicted the word of Yahweh (28:15-17): 'I am watching over them,' says the God of the 'wake-tree' whom we first met in 1:11-12, 'for disaster and not for good. All the men of Judah who are in the land of Egypt shall be consumed by the sword and by famine, until there is an end of them' (44:27). Time will tell, and as Elijah once made the same point though with a different sign, 'the God who answers by fire, he is God.'[10] And before that actually happens, there will be a preliminary sign that it is going to happen: as certain as the downfall of King Zedekiah in the recent past, will be the downfall of Pharaoh Hophra in a few years' time. When the news comes that the ruler of this land where you have taken refuge has died, and not of old age in his bed, you will know that your own doom is on its way.

In some ways the world of Jeremiah 44 has closer affinities with our world, even though we are centuries further down the line, than it has with the world that had ended only months earlier with the sack of Jerusalem. Not, of course, in the sense that the people of God today have unanimously and explicitly abandoned their historic faith and sold out to the modern equivalent of 'queen of heaven' worship (though many have). The fact is that Egypt – what John calls 'the world'[11] – presents herself as congenial and welcoming, unlike the 'foe from the north', the aggressors from Mesopotamia. The church is always in danger from the lure of 'Egyptian' values, their pervasive influence, their acceptance by all civilized, sensible, modern people, the ease with which the church absorbs them and settles down with them, until one day she finds herself confronted with a hard message from

10 1 Kings 18:24.
11 1 John 2:15-17.

some faithful but unfashionable preacher, and responds, 'As for the word that you have spoken to us in the name of the LORD, we will not listen to you.' Against such a betrayal of principles Jeremiah speaks trenchantly today as he has always spoken. The paradox is that those who choose to live in Egypt will die there, whereas those who are willing to accept the 'death' of invasion and exile at the hands of Babylon – in New Testament terms, the way of the cross – will find it the way to life.

Yet there is still a remnant (45:1-5)

If the new reader looks ahead and realizes that the last big section of Jeremiah's book (commonly called his 'oracles against the nations') is about to begin at 46:1, the little chapter 45 is likely to puzzle him. What is it doing here? The writing of Baruch's scroll 'in the fourth year of Jehoiakim', in our terms the year 604, has already been described in chapter 36. Why now, nine chapters later, would this further mention of it be tacked on to the account of Baruch's journey to Egypt with Jeremiah nearly twenty years afterwards? From theories about the rearranging of sections of the book by later editors, various answers emerge; what follows here is one that seems to emerge if we assume that Jeremiah and Baruch were themselves responsible for the order of the material. It is hard to imagine why chapter 45 should be where it is, so far from where you would think it ought to be, unless it had been put here intentionally; and though it may be difficult to make sense of the text as it stands, we should at any rate try to do so. So let us remind ourselves of the theme of the previous five chapters, and then consider five illuminating points made in the five verses of this one.

The storyline since 40:1 has been all about what continues to move on down the track of history once the Zedekiah train, the political kingdom, has fetched up against the buffers at the end of a siding. Life goes on, and troubles go on, and worldly wisdom continues to be as influential as ever, and takes Johanan and Co. to Egypt; and the power of the word of God continues to do its work among the survivors, for good or ill, wherever they are. We are reminded that among the most important of those survivors were the prophet and his

friend and colleague. It further registers with us that we are being taken back several years to that winter's day in 604, when the first edition of Jeremiah's book came out in the form of a public reading – a book which would likewise continue down the years to convey timeless lessons to generations yet to come.

That is 45:1. From 45:2 we learn that among the words of Yahweh given to Jeremiah and recorded by Baruch was one, the only one, addressed to Baruch himself. And equally unique is 45:3, the words of Baruch to which Yahweh is about to respond, the only point anywhere in the book at which he speaks on his own account, as distinct from reading out Jeremiah's prophecies as he did in chapter 36.

The verse is an intriguing one. It is a cry from the heart. Of the twenty-odd verses, spread over four chapters, that mention Baruch by name, none gives any explicit reason for the extreme distress conveyed by the half-dozen words used here: woe, pain compounded by sorrow, weariness, groaning, restlessness. By and large, the commentators take it that he is overcome by the enormity of the fate that is about to befall Jerusalem. This is no doubt true, as far as it goes. But when in a moment we arrive at verse 5, what is said there may add a further dimension to our understanding of Baruch's troubles.

Before that, we look at verse 4, which begins the Lord's message to him. Instead of dealing at once with his sorrow and pain, Yahweh first opens up the big picture for him. He takes him back to the beginning, and reminds him of some of the very earliest words he wrote down. According to Jeremiah's original call, there would in due course be building and planting (1:10), but only after there had been the kind of plucking up and breaking down that Baruch is finding it hard to cope with. It is indeed hard, but necessary, to stand back from present troubles, however large they loom, and see that they may be an inevitable part of the best solution to an even larger problem.

Along with that important lesson there comes in verse 5 a personal challenge. The question with which the verse begins is of great interest precisely because it says so little. Baruch is seeking great things for himself, is he? This is the first we have heard of it, and the last we shall hear, too. The

only sidelights that other scriptures might shed on the matter are a name going back two generations instead of the usual one (in 32:12, Baruch Neriah's-son Mahseiah's-son, which one might fancifully compare to a double-barrelled English surname), and the mention of Seraiah (51:59, apparently his brother, and quartermaster for King Zedekiah's journey to Babylon in the mid–590s). Would these connections really have given Baruch ideas above his station? A pretty slender basis on which to build delusions of grandeur, one would have thought. All we can say is that Scripture presents him as capable, reliable, efficient, faithful – and a man who needed to be warned against personal ambition. Yahweh chooses not to tell us why.

Which may shed light on verse 3 also. Why was Baruch so deeply upset? The coming disaster that he was having to write about presumably had a lot to do with it, but he does seem to have been quite extraordinarily distressed; surely there must have been other factors aggravating his misery? If so, these too Yahweh chooses not to tell us.

This is not the only place where Scripture 'forgets' to explain something we should really like to know, and leaves a tantalizing gap in the story. But taking Paul's 'thorn in the flesh' as a classic example,[12] because it is never defined I can the more readily apply the phrase to my own equivalent problem, whereas if I knew the details I might say 'That situation is not like mine.' The same elliptical kind of reference here enables me to identify the more readily with Baruch's unexplained distress in 45:3 and his unexplained temptation in 45:5.

How will it all end? With him, the representative home-born Israelite, alongside Ebed-melech, the representative adopted Gentile, each being given his life 'as a prize of war', the phrase which figures four times in Jeremiah (21:9, 38:2, 39:18, and here), and which we considered in connection with the third of those verses.[13] These two men, with all who closed with Yahweh's offer of rescue by surrendering to the Babylonians, escape destruction by the skin of their teeth.[14]

---

12 2 Corinthians 12:7.

13 See pp. 189-90

14 One of the many phrases that modern English owes to the King James Version of the Bible (Job 19:20)!

Stripped of every pretension and everything that might be identified with the dying kingdom, they are, to use an old-fashioned term, trophies of grace. And they find themselves to be still part of the company that will take the stage as the curtain rises on the next act of the continuing drama.

14

The View from Tahpanhes
(Jeremiah 46–51)

The death of a dream, and what came after

The core of Jeremiah's message is the covenant, and the context of it is the kingdom; and his book has been showing how both the covenant and the kingdom in their Old Testament form come to a dead end, and have to be renewed in a different form. Not that either the Mosaic covenant or the Davidic kingdom was a mistake on the part of Yahweh. In each case the renewing is like the emerging of a butterfly from a chrysalis; the earlier stage is a necessary preliminary, and the later one is its intended outcome – each assumes the other.

People of insight in Old Testament times were given hints and pointers enough for them to realize that there must be something more to both the law of Yahweh and the rule of Yahweh than they had yet experienced. The latter was the more obvious disappointment, as one king after another let them down, and the glorious kingdom they dreamed of seemed ever more elusive. And of course the reason Israel could not experience the glories of the kingdom was that she would not, could not, keep the terms of the covenant.

Jeremiah saw practically no response to his preaching of repentance in the days of Josiah, and moved on in the days of Jehoiakim to the preaching of doom. 'Sin when it is fully grown brings forth death,'[1] and the only hope for the sinful nation was to accept the 'death' of 586, Jerusalem destroyed

---

1 James 1:15.

and Israel exiled to Babylon. There would be a 'resurrection' after the seventy years of 25:11f.; the 'good figs' of 24:5, whether that generation or the next one, were going to return to the homeland (though it would still be many a long year before the faithful would see the unveiling of what they hoped for, a kingdom and a covenant that would actually work).

Meanwhile, overarching everything that Jeremiah has taught and everything that is now gathered into this compilation of his writings concerning the covenant and the kingdom – overarching all that is the prophet's divine calling. We go back forty-five chapters, and as many years, to hear again Yahweh's brief but pregnant statement: 'I appointed you a prophet to the nations' (1:5). We remember that it reappears at the centre of his book: 'everything … which Jeremiah prophesied against all the nations' (25:13). And as the book draws towards its close he devotes six whole chapters to 'the word of the Lord that came to Jeremiah the prophet concerning the nations' (46:1).

These are the three texts, spaced out across Jeremiah's fifty-two chapters, which I suggested at the outset might be pegs on which the whole tapestry hangs. Notice the wording: 'to the nations', 'against the nations', 'concerning the nations'. Chapter 46 is obviously a prophecy 'concerning' Egypt, and is sufficiently negative to be also a prophecy 'against' Egypt. In what sense could it be a prophecy 'to' Egypt?

Again and again the God of Israel speaks to other nations besides His own (through Jonah to the people of Assyria, for example, and through Daniel to the kings of Babylon), and He gives similar messages to other spokesmen besides the 'writing prophets' of the Old Testament. In fact there are repeated revelations of this kind, which climax in Christ's command to 'go … and make disciples of all nations',[2] and begin with Moses, the first and greatest of the prophets, telling the pharaoh of Egypt to his face 'Thus says the Lord'.[3] But though Jeremiah's original call was to be 'a prophet to the nations', there is no hint here in chapter 46 of his having direct access to the pharaoh of his day. His intended audience, or readership, is first and foremost Israel, and this chapter

---

2 Matthew 28:19.
3 Exodus 5:1.

is what Israel needs to know about Egypt. Nevertheless Yahweh's further intention is for Israel then to learn to relate to Egypt in the light of that. In other words, the revelation of God is given to His church, for the church to make known to the nations.

Where the dream has yet to die (46:1-28)

It is now from Tahpanhes in Egypt that Jeremiah, who with his colleague Baruch has, as we know, been taken there against his will, looks out across the world of his day. From there he speaks with great boldness, as these six chapters begin, of the nation where he and his fellow-refugees are now 'resident aliens'. There is no reason why the substance of chapter 46 should not have been first heard as a word from Yahweh for the Judah of Jehoiakim's time, linked with the writings in the scroll, mentioned just now in 45:1, that Baruch had made back in 605/604. At that time it would have been a warning to Jehoiakim and his policy-makers about the unreliability of Egypt as an ally, and the unwisdom of trying to resist the rise of Babylon. Twenty years have gone by and, while in some respects the world has changed radically, the word (need we doubt it?) is as relevant as ever.

Like all these 'oracles against the nations', as they are commonly called,[4] the words relating to Egypt combine descriptions of what has already happened with predictions of what has yet to happen. First, in 46:2-12 the account describes Pharaoh Neco's northbound expedition ('rising like the Nile') to aid his Assyrian ally against their common enemy Babylon, and their combined armies coming to grief beside another river, the Euphrates, in 609 (vv. 5-6). With what pride the pharaoh had marched north (vv. 7-9)! In what shame he retreated south! Gilead with its famous balm[5] would have been a good place to stop and lick his wounds on the way home (vv. 10-12).

In 46:13-24, a second word from Yahweh describes Nebuchadnezzar's retaliation with a southbound expedition,

---

4 'There are oracles against the nations in all the prophetic books except Hosea (e.g. Isa. 13–23; Ezek. 25–32; Amos 1–2)… Forty such prophecies [are each] about the destiny of one distinctly named foreign nation' (Mackay, vol. ii, p. 439).

5 See 8:22.

for which various dates have been suggested. In verses 14-
17 we find that Yahweh is behind this. The pharaoh's foreign
mercenaries abandon him,[6] calling him rude names as they
go.[7] In verses 18-19 the king of Babylon looms on the northern
horizon like Mount Tabor to your right or Mount Carmel
to your left, and will be in Memphis before you know it. In
verses 20-24 a colourful array of metaphors, recalling some of
the chapters at the beginning of the book, depicts the shaming
of Egypt.

A third word from Yahweh completes this oracle. Brief
and emphatic are the points made here in 46:25-28. Amon
and Pharaoh and Egypt, the gods and the kings and the
people, for all of them punishment is decreed at the hands
of the Babylonians. Alongside that is decreed also, perhaps
to our astonishment, an eventual restoration for Egypt! But
the chapter ends with the guarantee, repeated from 30:10-
11 where it stands as one of the great gospel promises, of
the restoration of Israel. If even a humbled Egypt, of which
Yahweh had made 'a full end', could nevertheless be restored
one day, it would be a death-and-resurrection scenario to blow
the mind. Why should not the same thing be possible for His
own beloved though rebellious people? What wonders does
Yahweh have stored up for the future?

But for the present, two things come across loud and
clear. One is that the policies of the rulers of Egypt, which to
their mind have nothing whatever to do with the God who
is worshipped in Israel, are actually being supervised and
manipulated by that God. The other, more subtle but even
more important, is that the Israelite refugees in Tahpanhes
who think they are preserving the kingdom of Judah by
keeping themselves out of the clutches of Nebuchadnezzar,
are, in fact, refusing the only way that it *can* survive, which
is by their abandoning the dream of a political kingdom,
dying to that old life, letting themselves be 'buried' under the
domination of Babylon for seventy years, and then coming
back to life in a new and changed world after the exile. Or,
to revert once more to the modern metaphor I used earlier,
the people in Tahpanhes (with the exception of Jeremiah and

6 Cush/Put/Lud in 46:9 are likely to mean in modern terms Sudan/Libya/Turkey.
7 'King Bombast, the man who missed his moment' (46:17, NEB).

Baruch) are still sitting in the Zedekiah train, which is going nowhere. Alternative transport has been arranged for the onward journey, but will they be on board?

Where the dream never was (47:1-7)
For the second of these 'oracles against the nations', Jeremiah moves up the map from Egypt to Philistia, a name familiar even today in the modern term 'Palestine'. More specifically, chapter 47 takes us northwards along the Mediterranean coast from his place of exile, Tahpanhes in the eastern Nile delta, to the cities of Gaza and Ashkelon, in the same latitude as southern Judah. The 'lords of the Philistines' long figured in Israel's history much as the pharaohs of Egypt did – occasionally friendly, much more often a troublesome nuisance – except that they lived that much closer: you might think of them as the irritating people-next-door.

Like the nations in the following chapters, they were Israel's neighbours; but unlike them, they were not her relatives, and that made a difference, as we shall see. Interestingly, Jeremiah brackets the Philistines, living along the southern section of the Levantine seaboard, with the Phoenicians, who occupied the middle section. Unlike the Israelites, who with rare exceptions shuddered at the thought of sea travel, both nations had the sea in their blood, and therefore a western outlook; the one had originally come as migrants in ships from the islands of Greece, and the other sent ships out to trade all around the Mediterranean and beyond, and to plant settlements like their own cities, Tyre and Sidon, wherever they went. Both Philistines and Phoenicians organized themselves as federations of city-states, each city with its own government. That in itself set them apart from the other nations which were targets of Jeremiah's prophecies.

And of course, by the same token, it set them apart from Israel also. A monarchy? A single nation, a people united around a king, one king, who rules everyone from his capital city on a mountain in the middle of what is these days a land-locked country? Not our style at all. And we really cannot see why the prophet next door should want to foist his alien ideas on us. Israel's kind of kingdom, whether in its present form or

in any other, is of no interest here in Tyre and Sidon and Gaza
and Ashkelon.

That should not prevent the man who knows telling
what he knows to the people who need to know it. Always,
today more than ever, the people of God are surrounded by
'neighbours' who may be quite willing for them to pursue
their religious concerns privately, but cannot see how such
topics can be of sufficient interest, let alone importance, to
be addressed to them across the garden fence. The eyes glaze
over, the subject is changed, a prior engagement is suddenly
remembered. When from the south Pharaoh does strike at
Gaza (v. 1), or when 'out of the north' come the Babylonians
in 'an overflowing torrent' (v. 2), the Philistines will not see
the connection with what Jeremiah has been saying, if indeed
they have paid any attention to it. But, if he is to be faithful to
his calling, he has to make his voice – Yahweh's voice – heard
wherever he finds the need and the opportunity.

Where the dream has been glimpsed (48:1–49:6)

The oracle against Moab is long (the whole of chapter 48), and
the one against Ammon is short (only six verses of chapter
49), but in other respects these two have much in common.

As before, they describe hard experiences that arise from
the international power struggles of the seventh and sixth
centuries BC in the Middle East. And again as before, it is often
unclear whether when the prophecies were given they were
describing what had already happened, or what was currently
happening, or what was yet to come; nor is it always possible,
in the case of something already past, to identify which of two
or three similar events is in mind.[8] None of this should bother
us. We should picture Jeremiah and Baruch being guided,
consciously or not, to put their book together in such a way
that (as with the rest of Scripture) matters of importance
would be clear, while what was less clear would be taken to
be less important.

So now from Philistia on the west we move across Israel
to Moab on the east, and to a scene of coming devastation

---

8 For example, for the Babylonian attack on Egypt mentioned in 46:13 three
different dates have been suggested, 604, 582/81 and 568. See Mackay, vol. ii,
p. 449.

at the hands of invaders there also. The bulk of chapter 48 is one long lament, but every so often the prophet levels an accusation (for example, 'You trusted in your works and your treasures,' v. 7), or states a consequence ('Therefore, behold, the days are coming, declares the Lord, when I shall …,' v. 12), or, remarkably, shows Yahweh grieving even as He punishes ('I will bring an end to Moab … Therefore my heart moans for Moab,' vv. 35f.).

Even more remarkable is the threefold declaration by Yahweh that ends chapter 48. Here in verse 42 is the accusation: Moab has 'magnified himself against the LORD'. Here in verse 44 is the consequence: 'I will bring … upon Moab the year of their punishment'. And in verses 46-47 there is doom ('Woe to you'), but now it gives way to a promise of blessing: 'Yet I will restore the fortunes of Moab in the latter days'.

Verses 1-6 of the following chapter are a brief summary of the very similar message Jeremiah is given for the people of Ammon. Their country lay to the north of Moab, both nations facing Israel across the Dead Sea and the Jordan valley. The Ammonites were not only neighbours but also relatives of the Moabites, and the peculiar interest is that both nations had family connections with Israel also. The original Moab and Ammon were the two sons of Lot, Abraham's nephew, so there was a real though distant relationship. When Moabites and Ammonites, now with kings of their own, looked across the valley towards Israel, they were being given a glimpse of the dream kingdom, however unworthy it might become by the days of Zedekiah, and however great the antagonism between it and them. And beyond that, we cannot help wondering what Yahweh had in mind when He promised that He would one day 'restore the fortunes' of these two nations, so often enemies of His people (48:47, 49:6).

This kind of word from God has an obvious ongoing relevance. Wherever His church has been long established there will be people round its edges, distant cousins to the family of Israel, as it were, who have had a glimpse of Yahweh's kingdom. But they have an ambivalent attitude to much of its activity and no commitment to its God; they talk a debased version of its language, and they are by no means prepared to let it put them out or shake them up. The prophet's reproof

takes a metaphor from a speciality of the region: Moab, vine-grower and winemaker, 'has been at ease from his youth and has settled on his dregs; he has not been emptied from vessel to vessel' – he has never been decanted – 'nor has he gone into exile' (48:11). He doesn't want to be disturbed. And when he looks across to the west bank of the Jordan, life there does seem to have more than its fair share of disturbances, especially in the present state of Middle Eastern politics, with the Babylonians constantly making trouble. Moab and Ammon see nothing terribly attractive about Zedekiah's kingdom, and probably envied it even less in Jehoiachin's day when that young man found himself removed from the throne and packed off to Babylon by Nebuchadnezzar. Clearly Yahweh was not a god who could be relied on when really powerful people were throwing their weight around.

Yet there is hope for folk like these. Some remnant of the old faith of Abraham, even in Lot's inadequate version of it, may yet be reawakened in Lot's modern descendants, and Yahweh may yet restore the fortunes of these distant relatives. Indeed, He has declared (as we have noticed at the end of each of these two oracles) that in some sense He not only may but will.

Where the dream has been misunderstood (49:7-27)

Edom, away to the south-east, and Aram, beyond what used to be Israel's northern territories, are two nations which have had more opportunities than most to see how the concept of an Israelite kingdom develops over the years. Jeremiah speaks to the first in 49:7-22, and to the second in 49:23-27.

Edom was more closely related to Israel than Moab and Ammon were. Members of those nations could have no place in the Israelite community, but (said the law) 'You shall not abhor an Edomite, for he is your brother';[9] in a sense it was literally true, and no mere figure of speech, because Edom traced its ancestry to Esau, a grandson of Abraham, a son of Isaac, and twin brother of the Jacob who became Israel.

---

9 Deuteronomy 23:7. One obvious exception to Deuteronomy 23:3 was Ruth, who married not only into Israel but into what would become Israel's royal family, David being her great-grandson.

There was frequent contact between Edom and Israel – Esau and Jacob, you might say – throughout the days of the kings. It was something of a love/hate relationship. Often they clashed, occasionally they cooperated; and it is interesting to notice how many of these encounters were in the reigns of the more significant of Israel's kings, David and Solomon, Jehoshaphat and Uzziah, so that Edom had the opportunity to see the model of Israelite kingship at its best.

Not that it did the Edomites much good. They had a reputation for clear thinking, but it seems they did not live up to it: 'Has counsel perished from the prudent? Has their wisdom vanished?' (49:7). It was true that Yahweh had made no such covenant with them as He had with Israel, but they could not plead ignorance of His standards, and had not lived up to them either. Verse 12 is a difficult one, because it seems to say that Israel 'did not deserve to drink the cup' of punishment (which she manifestly did). It should probably be understood to say rather that she 'had the right not to drink it,' under the terms of her covenant with Yahweh.[10] But she flouted those terms, and so she has after all been punished; and covenant or no covenant, Edom will suffer a similar fate.

As Jeremiah's long Moab section was followed by a short Ammon section, so now sixteen verses addressed to Edom are followed by a mere five, the briefest of these oracles, addressed to Damascus. The name of the city stands for Aram, or Syria, the nation whose capital it was. It is entirely unclear what Aram's punishment was, and when it happened, and what she had done to deserve it, which is a reminder that there are some statements in Scripture which we do not need to understand in detail; we get the general picture.[11] What we do know about Aram is that although not related to Israel as Edom was,[12] she had had the same sort of contacts: not indeed with the southern kingdom in Jeremiah's day, but with the northern kingdom before it was destroyed a hundred years earlier. The Aramean kings in Damascus had had repeated encounters

---

10 Jeremiah 49:12f. See McConville, pp. 140f.

11 See above, on 45:3.

12 There is, however, the curious connection that the two names, Aram and Edom, look very alike in Hebrew; the careless writer or reader might easily confuse them.

with half a dozen of the Israelite kings in Samaria, and with the prophets Elijah and Elisha, and indeed with their God. Like Edom, therefore, Aram knew about Israel and Yahweh in a way that Egypt and Philistia and Moab and Ammon did not. The two nations were (at one level) well aware of how Yahweh's kingdom worked. But Jeremiah did not on that account assume that they had no need of a message from him. On the contrary, they were only too likely to fall for the idea that in Israel 'the kingdom' meant, and would always mean, simply the political kingdom. That, as we know, was a dream that would die with Zedekiah.

But religion did, all the same, loom large in both halves of the kingdom of Israel. With that sort of community the present-day heirs of Edom and Aram are (or think they are) well acquainted. They probably call it 'The Church'. Theirs is not the paganism of the Philistines next door, or the nodding-acquaintance religion of Moab and Ammon. These people have an interest in 'The Church', opinions about it, advice for it, even involvement with it. But of its inner heartbeat they know nothing, and they cannot conceive what it would look like if its buildings were to go up in smoke and its personnel disappear into captivity. Still today Jeremiah is telling them that on the contrary it is their cities, not the city of God, that have no future. Both the Edomite capital down south and the Aramean capital up north are doomed: 'I have sworn by myself, declares the Lord, that Bozrah shall become a horror, a taunt, a waste, and a curse' (49:13); 'I will kindle a fire in the wall of Damascus, and it shall devour the strongholds of Ben-hadad' (49:27). The true kingdom is somewhere else. Something else.

Where the dream has yet to come (49:28-39)
With the next two oracles we are, in a manner of speaking, in uncharted territory. It is not that we don't know the whereabouts of the nations Jeremiah is now addressing, 'Kedar and the kingdoms of Hazor' (49:28) and Elam (49:34), for it is easy enough to find them on the map. Trace a straight line eastwards from Israel to the head of the Persian Gulf, and it will cross a large expanse of what looks like desert. And it is desert of a kind, in that if you wanted to travel by

land between those two places while keeping within reach of civilization and the usual amenities, you would take a wide detour, curving round to the north, as travellers have done for thousands of years, following what is called the 'fertile crescent'. But the empty space south of the curve is not actually deserted. There are tents and flocks (v. 29), camels and herds of livestock (v. 32); there are isolated unfortified settlements (v. 31) which the King James Bible memorably calls 'the villages that Kedar doth inhabit.'[13] But the Bedouin nomads in these parts are wild men – Midianites, the 'people of the East' – and their raids on the cultivated lands of surrounding peoples have been serious enough to provoke retaliation over the years, all the way from Gideon in the days of the judges to Asshurbanipal in the seventh century and Nebuchadnezzar in the sixth.

It was only a year or so after his campaign against Kedar that Nebuchadnezzar returned to Judah and installed Zedekiah as king in place of his nephew Jehoiachin (vv. 28, 34). That was the point at which the true Israel was taken away into the 'death' of exile, leaving this ineffectual puppet to preside for eleven more years over what was now nothing but the husk, the empty chrysalis, of the kingdom. And it was the point at which 'the word of the Lord ... came to Jeremiah the prophet concerning Elam' (v. 34).

Elam. Where was Elam? Beyond Kedar; beyond Babylon; on the extreme outer edge of the Bible lands. And what did Yahweh intend to do with the people of Elam? 'I will bring disaster upon them, my fierce anger, declares the Lord. I will send the sword after them, until I have consumed them, and I will set my throne in Elam and destroy their king and officials, declares the Lord' (vv. 37f.).

And why would He want to do that?

We have no idea. That is the 'uncharted territory'. He has a quarrel with this remote nation which so far as we can tell has nothing whatever to do with His dealings with Israel. But Israel, we thought (and surely we were right to think it), is at the centre of His master plan for humanity, is she not? How do far-away Kedar and even farther-away Elam fit into that plan?

13 Isaiah 42:11.

This, we have to conclude, is Jeremiah fulfilling his calling right to the end. First, he has a ministry to God's people Israel, leading them through the vital stage of their history in which they learn what 'kingdom' means by actually *being* a kingdom, to the point at which they now have to progress to the next stage. The experience has taught them much about the kingship of Yahweh, and much about the sinfulness of the human heart. But to imagine that the Hebrew monarchies are themselves the 'real thing', Israel's final destination, is only a dream that dies at the opening day, as the hymn puts it.[14] In that new day there will be new lessons to be learned, about a new kind of kingdom based on a new kind of covenant.

That, however, is only part of Jeremiah's calling. While Israel has been busy at her lessons, Yahweh, for whom the horrid modern term 'multi-tasking' might have been expressly designed, has simultaneously been pursuing His plans for Egypt and Philistia, Moab and Ammon, Edom and Aram, and even for Kedar in the depths of the desert, and Elam at the end of the earth. In all of these the prophet has been involved, and latterly we have had the fascinating experience of overhearing prophetic messages which will have been quite clear to those to whom they were addressed but in some respects leave us totally in the dark. Why should we be told everything, though? So far as we are concerned, it is not important to know exactly how Elam had angered the Lord God of Israel, or how she might learn about His kingdom, or how it is that she (like Egypt and Moab and Ammon, but unlike Edom and Aram and Kedar) is promised the eventual restoring of her fortunes. What is important is to know that God is as intimately concerned with people I know nothing about (and, what is more, with each and every one of them) as He is with me.

Where the dream has died (50:1–51:58)
Finally, in these mind-stretching oracles, we confront the 'big one', with 110 verses (nearly as many as all the rest put together) which form 'the word that the Lord spoke concerning Babylon.' What Jeremiah saw from Anathoth in chapter 1 was simply nations bringing trouble from the north. What he saw

14 Isaac Watts, 'O God, our help in ages past.'

from Jerusalem in chapter 25 was Babylon foremost among those nations, coming forth first to punish and then to be herself punished. What he is now seeing from Tahpanhes is a vast opening-out of the same subject in nine oracles, the last of which – this one, against Babylon – he is moved to express in a complex and detailed sequence of six poems.

It soon becomes evident what kind of poems they are. If we first allow 50:1-3 to be an introduction to the whole Babylonian oracle, then secondly recall the poems of Lamentations which we used as an introduction to Jeremiah, and thirdly notice the repeated phrase 'In those days and in that time, declares the LORD' here in verses 4 and 20, we realize that we are back among the palindromes, the chiastic there-and-back-again pattern so prominent in that other Bible book.

Each of these poems is a kind of optical illusion. It looks complicated, but as our eyes adjust it clicks into focus as a relatively simple ABCBA shape, its balancing halves framed between the As and pointing inwards to the central C. Setting out such a pattern schematically would have taken up a lot of space with the poems in Lamentations, but these are perhaps a little more manageable. We might set out the first of them as follows, with numbers indicating of course the verses of chapter 50:

(4) Repentance/pardon and
   (5) return;
      (6-7) sheep lost/devoured, with impunity.
         (8) Flee from Babylon, where –
            (9-10) a new foe comes!
               [*(11-13) Babylon's
                  triumph/disaster*]
            (14-15) A new foe comes –
         (16) flee from Babylon!
      (17-18) Sheep lost/devoured; now with punishment following.
   (19) Return, and
(20) repentance/pardon.

At the heart of this first poem, then, is the paradox that Babylon has been raised up to bring about Yahweh's purposes for His own people, and is then to be thrown down for the arrogance with which she has done it.

The second poem follows the same pattern, and comprises the twelve verses 50:21-32, which pivot on the fate of Babylon: at their central point, destruction commanded (v. 26), punishment decreed (v. 27), vengeance declared (v. 28). 'Punishment' looks back to verse 21, where it figures as the place-name Pekod, and forward to verse 31. 'Destruction' in this context is specified as the 'devoting' of things to Yahweh, to show how completely they are under His dominion.[15] 'Vengeance' makes explicit the connection between the fall of Jerusalem and the eventual fall of Babylon – *this* is because of *that*, an eye for an eye: justice not only done, but seen to be done. Right at the start of this oracle against Babylon, in 50:3, the parallel was drawn, for she who was herself the 'foe from the north' would find that she in her turn would be laid waste by another nation 'out of the north'.

We move on to 50:33-46. Where at the heart of the second poem Yahweh threatens destruction, punishment and vengeance, this third one has at its heart a picture in just two verses (39-40) of the desolation of Babylon that will ensue. Nebuchadnezzar's kingdom, at present so strong, will meet its match in the person of Israel's Redeemer. In the picture's outer frame, verses 33-34 and 44-46, the 'unrest' He causes to Babylon at the beginning turns out by the end to be an earth-shaking disaster. In verses 41-43, the inner frame will show the new foe from the north to be 'a mighty nation and many kings' – it would all come true with the Medo-Persian empire of Cyrus seventy years later – with bows and spears, cavalry and armour, all of this to be recognized, as verses 35-38 have already described it, as the sword of Yahweh. Echoes from the past resonate: Jeremiah is moved to repeat from only one chapter earlier the doom of Edom as being equally applicable to Babylon (compare 50:40, 44-46, with 49:18-21); the Babylonians now, like the Egyptians in Moses' time, refuse to let God's people go (50:33); the overthrow of Sodom and Gomorrah in the days of Abraham should still be a warning to Nebuchadnezzar (50:40).

The fourth poem is much longer, and constructed differently. Topped and tailed by metaphors of harvest, the winnowing

---

15 Hence, for example, everything in the city of Jericho (Josh. 6:17f.) and every heathen nation in the land of Canaan (Deut. 7:1-5) were 'devoted' to destruction.

of 51:2 and the threshing floor of 51:33, it is a sequence of prophecies, each one contrasting the punishment of Babylon with the loving purposes of Yahweh for His people, which Babylonian wickedness has been made to serve. In 51:1-5 Babylon is 'full of guilt', yet for Israel and Judah their suffering through these wars has been an opportunity to learn that they 'have not been forsaken by their God.' In 51:6-10 Babylon is deservedly punished for the damage she has done to the nations, and to herself, yet because of it God's people have been vindicated as they have learned to look to Him in the midst of it. In 51:11-19 Babylon's destruction is brought about by Yahweh as 'vengeance for his temple'. The facts about 'the one who formed all things', as they were earlier set before the people of God in chapter 10, are now set before the rulers of this world, for His was the house they had treated with such blasphemous disrespect when they sacked Jerusalem. I think it likely that in 51:20-26 Babylon is hearing again Yahweh's original appointing of Nebuchadnezzar to a necessary task, and is having to grasp that one can be used in God's purposes and yet commit great sins in the process. Finally in 51:27-33 we see this greatest of godless nations, the Bible's classic example of worldly power, surrounded by enemies – the next generation of the 'kingdoms of this world', eager to bring it to its knees and take its place. But it is 'the LORD of hosts, the God of Israel', who is masterminding all this.

The fifth poem, 51:34-44, reverts to the more concise pattern of the earlier ones, but now with a rapid series of images so varied that they contradict one another (Babylon both a land of drought and submerged beneath the waves), unless we regard them, like those way back in chapter 2, as a kind of kaleidoscope. Yet there is a chiastic shape to this patchwork of pictures: an outer frame, at the beginning Babylon swallowing her victims and at the end being made to disgorge them (vv. 34-35 and 44), an inner frame (sea, heap/waves,[16] horror, uninhabited, all in vv. 36-37 and again in vv. 41-43), and the concentrated core of it in verses 38-40, from which metaphors for Yahweh's vengeance shoot off in all directions.

---

16 'Heap' (v. 37) and 'waves' (v. 42) both represent the same Hebrew word *gal*. See footnote 17 below.

Attempts to find the same ABCBA pattern in the verses that follow seem to produce a tangle of unhelpful complications, until you realize that the shape of this sixth poem is not after all more complex, but actually simpler, than that of its predecessors. Its pattern is ABA, covering the nine verses 51:45-53. The pivot is verse 49, and the two sets of four verses on either side echo each other quite remarkably. The Hebrew words for 'go', 'heart/mind'[17], 'therefore behold the days are coming', 'punish/execute judgment on images', 'the whole land/all the land', 'slain/wounded', 'destroyers come against', 'declares the LORD', follow in the same order down each panel, on either side of the deeply significant facing-both-ways pivotal verse that sums up the entire oracle against Nebuchadnezzar's city and all that it stands for: 'Babylon must fall for the slain of Israel, just as for Babylon have fallen the slain of all the earth.'

A five-verse summary, verses 54-58, punches home the message of this ninth and last of Jeremiah's oracles against the nations. All of them have been Yahweh's royal declaration, and He has the last word – a fitting conclusion, in fact, to these six chapters. 'The peoples labour for nothing, and the nations weary themselves only for fire'; all their antagonism to God and His people is destined to go up in smoke.

We may picture Jeremiah and Baruch in Tahpanhes, some time in the late 580s, slotting the oracles in almost at the end of their long manuscript. They add a note (51:59-64) to say how a copy of the final oracle had actually gone to Babylon back in 594, taken by Baruch's brother Seraiah, who was one of the party accompanying King Zedekiah when he was summoned there by his overlord Nebuchadnezzar. Seraiah made its contents known among the exiles from Judah, for their encouragement (though only the youngest of that generation would still be alive when the prophecies of restoration came true), before acting out a very Jeremiah-type parable by tying a stone to the manuscript and throwing it into the river Euphrates: 'Thus shall Babylon sink, to rise no more.' Whatever would the exiles from Judah have made

---

17 'Heart/mind', etc., means that in every such case there is (unfortunately) variety in the English translation where there was (designedly) repetition in the original Hebrew.

of it at its first reading, surrounded as they were by a pagan empire at the zenith of its power and glory? No doubt some of them at any rate, like Mary, 'treasured up all these things, pondering them in [their] heart'.[18] At what point might they begin to dare to talk about its contents in the hearing of their Babylonian neighbours? They had seventy years stretching ahead of them in which to do so. They had certainly been given an extraordinary glimpse of a spiritual empire of even greater power and glory than Nebuchadnezzar's.

The acted prophecy of Babylon's sinking to rise no more raises a question of considerable interest. When Babylon fell to the Medes and Persians in 536,[19] it was not in fact destroyed as the prophecies promised, and as Jerusalem had been. Its capture, described in Daniel 5, left it intact, and it became a regional capital within the Medo-Persian empire. So were the prophecies not fulfilled?

Scripture itself answers the question, in two ways. Jerusalem was literally torched (52:13), but fire was also a very good metaphor for any such total victory. It is used here for the downfall of Babylon (51:58) alongside a completely different metaphor, a drowning in the 'tumultuous waves' of the sea (51:42): both of them picture language, apparently contradictory but very telling, for what actually happened,[20] namely the obliteration of Babylon as a political power.

The other answer is that Babylon itself becomes a metaphor, and in the New Testament stands for the world, that is, the whole world system that organizes itself independently of God. The prophecy of the fall of that ongoing Babylon has indeed not yet been fulfilled, and God's people are still anticipating the day 'when I will punish the images of Babylon; her whole land shall be put to shame, and all her slain shall fall in the midst of her. Then the heavens and the earth, and all that is in them, shall sing for joy over Babylon' (51:47f.). The Book of Revelation is speaking of our own age when it describes a 'mighty angel' who takes up a great stone

---

18 Luke 2:19.

19 Cyrus, king of Persia, (aka 'Darius the Mede', Dan. 5:31) became king of Babylonia in 539/538, but did not capture Babylon city till 536 (McFall, 'Sixty-Nine Weeks', pp. 688-93, 713). See p. 131, footnote 11.

20 Psalm 18:6-19 uses similar hair-raising metaphors to describe what was at the time, to all appearances, simply the evaporating of Saul's vendetta against David.

and throws it into the sea, 'saying, So will Babylon the great city be thrown down with violence, and will be found no more ... The smoke from her goes up for ever and ever'[21] – the same two metaphors, burning and drowning, set side by side.

Meanwhile Nebuchadnezzar's Babylon has served its purpose in the plan of Yahweh, and effectively brought to an end the dream that the monarchy which has now ground to a halt with the sack of Jerusalem might be in any full and final sense the kingdom of God.

---

21 Revelation 18:21, 19:3.

15

Destinies

(Jeremiah 52)

'The end of the matter'

We have arrived at the end of chapter 51, and at the end of 'the words of Jeremiah', but not yet at the end of his book. So where do we go from here? What is the destination towards which the book as a whole has been moving?

For a word to suit the train travel anecdote that for me illustrated chapters 24 and 25, 'destination' would have been exactly right. But the only people who are going anywhere in chapter 52 are the victors and the vanquished marching away from the ruins of Jerusalem, and there is considerably more to the book's closing paragraphs than that. The word that applies throughout this chapter is not 'destination' but 'destiny', which has to do with 'what' rather than with 'where' – not so much where people go as what happens to them – and which can furthermore apply not only to people but also to places and institutions.

Another term which does not quite suit chapter 52 is 'epilogue'. Prologues and epilogues are usually the author's own way of topping and tailing his work, whereas here 51:64 states 'Thus far are the words of Jeremiah', and as good as tells us that someone else wrote the rest. But we are not on that account to treat this final chapter as being of less significance than the previous fifty-one. Like the headings that we find in the book of Psalms, it may be by a later hand, but is still an integral part of the Hebrew scriptures, and whoever did write

it, the 'divinity that shapes our ends'[1] was concerned likewise in the case of this book to shape its end in a meaningful way. What now completes it is a narrative which is almost exactly the same as 2 Kings 24:18–25:30, which corresponds to the latter part of the Chronicler's summary of Zedekiah's reign (2 Chron. 36:11-21), and which we have already seen expressed in different words in Jeremiah 39. That does not make it superfluous: we have found several such repeats within the book, all of them in my view intentional.

'The end of the matter', in the phrase with which the writer of Ecclesiastes concludes his book,[2] is that here we have 'the *words* of Jeremiah' destined to end with chapter 51, but the *book* of Jeremiah destined to be completed by this anonymous postscript, through which it has four final points to make.

The king's destiny (52:1-11)

The Victorian middle classes used to flock to picture galleries to see the works of the artist John Martin, who wowed his public with the equivalent of modern blockbuster disaster movies. I could imagine a vast painting of his, depicting the scene 'at Riblah in the land of Hamath' (52:9), with a cast of thousands, naturally, and entitled 'The Condemnation of Zedekiah'. Having gasped at the overall effect, we should then want to move in close and peer at every significant detail. The whole thing focuses of course on Zedekiah himself, a woebegone figure so different from his arrogant brother Jehoiakim, about to have his eyes put out. (The ladies squeak with horror, and have attacks of the vapours.) We feel sorry for him. Yet in his own pathetic, timid way, he chose to do 'what was evil in the sight of the LORD, according to all that Jehoiakim had done' (52:2). It was in his day that God's patience with His people finally expired – had Zedekiah, like so many then and now, assumed that it was unlimited? – and things 'came to the point … that he cast them out' (52:3). Escaping from Jerusalem as Nebuchadnezzar's forces entered it, he and his soldiers scattered and disappeared into the badlands of the Arabah, as hard to find as a needle in a haystack; 'yet even in that wilderness the Babylonians found him … "they had

---

1 Shakespeare again, with his surprising grasp of Bible truth (*Hamlet*, V.ii.).
2 Ecclesiastes 12:13.

God, as it were, as their guide"' (52:7-8).[3] Our account records
the death of his sons, and adds to the one in 2 Kings a note of
the execution also of 'all the officials of Judah' (52:10); this is
the end not just of the king but also of his posterity and of his
kingdom. He is taken, blinded but alive, to Babylon, 'as another
living proof of Nebuchadnezzar's might';[4] but alongside his
life we are told also of his death, for he eventually dies there
as a demonstration of Yahweh's intention to restart the story
of His people in a different way (52:11). Finally, having been
given material for half a dozen different sermons, we are given
the text for one more. The picture as a whole is a warning that
there is always more to God's purposes than our limited and
often presumptuous thinking will allow for; because 52:11
shows how Jeremiah's prophecy in 34:3-4 was fulfilled. Hear
again those words from Yahweh, full of irony for a man who,
though a failure in everything else, did succeed in one thing,
namely a stubborn refusal to repent and be saved: 'You shall
not escape... You shall see the king of Babylon eye to eye (!)
and speak with him face to face. And you shall go to Babylon...
You shall not die by the sword. You shall die in peace.' And so
he did, blind and imprisoned, in a tragic way that could not
possibly have occurred to him at the time of the prophecy.

It was his destiny to represent to the bitter end all who
persistently anger God by their folly and sin. Both the church
and the world outside the church should take warning from
Zedekiah. We might say that the unbelieving world knows no
better. But it does have the light of reason and of conscience
and of the testimony of God's people to illuminate it if it will
only open its eyes to these things. Instead we find on every
hand a fatal reluctance to face facts and acknowledge sins,
and should not be surprised when 'because of the anger of
the LORD' (52:3) our much-vaunted civilization begins to fall
apart. As for the church, which does know better, its sin is that
much less excusable and the divine anger that much more
understandable. For us who say we believe, to be 'cast ... out
from his presence' means that our churches become ineffectual
and irrelevant, looking outward with a ghetto mentality and

---

3 John Calvin, quoted in John Goldingay (1984), *God's Prophet, God's Servant*
(Exeter: Paternoster), p. 71. I am much indebted to Goldingay's comments on this
particular chapter.

4 *ibid*, p. 69.

inward with a club mentality, deserving the criticism they so often receive, and sooner or later dying.

In the ever-relevant pages of Scripture it is Zedekiah's destiny to embody this abandonment of the divine law. What is more, he represents the frightening connection between sin and punishment, in that for all his indecisiveness he did in the end choose to rebel against Nebuchadnezzar, and so by his own free choice brought judgment down on himself and his people. 'Men's own free decisions are the means by which God works out his purposes.'[5]

The city's destiny (52:12-16)

So far as the people of that time were concerned, Jerusalem was destined for destruction. From Riblah in Syria, the headquarters for his western campaigns, Nebuchadnezzar would have had in view the punishing of past disloyalty (especially of Zedekiah's broken oath), and the preventing of future uprisings. He would in any case want to demote Jerusalem from its status as a capital city, and as it was known to be also the focal point of Judah's fierce attachment to her historic religion, to destroy it altogether would be even more satisfactory, not least because such a course of action would apparently have the backing of what Israel's own God was supposed to have threatened (40:2-3)! Of the commander of the guard, Nebuzaradan, we have probably already formed a quite favourable opinion. Soldier though he is, he figures in chapters 39 and 40 not as a bloodthirsty warrior but as an efficient and very fair-minded organizer. He it was who was given the task of overseeing the destruction of the city, briefly noted already in 39:8.[6] Once the tumult and the shouting had

---

5 *ibid*, p. 71.

6 The parallel passage in 2 Kings 25:8 has him arriving in Jerusalem on 7th Ab, which may seem to contradict Jeremiah 52:12. But this latter verse may be read differently, viz: 'On the 10th day ... Nebuzaradan *stood before* the king of Babylon in Jerusalem' (as in the Masoretic Text and the RV, though almost all other translations have *served/entered*, or the equivalent). On this reading, the sequence of events is as follows:
— the walls breached and the city taken, 9th Tammuz (52:6-7);
—Zedekiah captured and taken to Riblah, where the king of Babylon is based (52:9);
—Nebuzaradan arrests 74 leading citizens and takes them too to Riblah (52:24-27);
—four weeks after Jerusalem's capture he arrives back there, 7th Ab (2 Kings 25:8);
—the king of Babylon arrives in Jerusalem, 10th Ab, and Nebuzaradan, 'standing before' him, is given the order to burn the city (52:12ff).

died down and the survivors had been moved out, he set most of his troops to the methodical dismantling of its walls, while he, presumably with a team of specialist 'firemen', set about the burning of the buildings within them.[7]

As in other such fires, the burning of some structures would in any case soon become a general conflagration enveloping them all. But Nebuzaradan seems to have had three particular objectives. The wording of 52:13 in the NKJV points to this: he burned (a) the house of the Lord, (b) the king's house, and (c) all the houses of Jerusalem, that is, all the houses of the great. With temple, palace and a score of mansions in flames, none of the meaner dwellings would survive. The destruction of the house of Yahweh might signify to people of other faiths that Judah's God was less powerful than the gods of Babylon, but to His own believing people (and apparently to others like Nebuzaradan) that Yahweh had Himself brought about what He Himself had threatened. The destruction of Zedekiah's palace obviously meant the end of the monarchy, and the destruction of the homes of everyone of importance meant the end of the nation. So it would be reasoned, and so it would appear. And the stage would be set for the new thing that Yahweh was preparing, the next act of the drama He had written so long before.

For when the seventy years of exile came to an end, Jerusalem would rise again. It would rise with painful slowness, and some things would never be as they had once been, but God's people would return as real flesh-and-blood people to a land that was the same real hills-and-valleys land. Jeremiah had prophesied that they would when he bought the field at Anathoth, as we remember from 32:13-15. And the temple would be built again, as we read in Ezra 1:1-4, and the city would be walled again, as we read in Nehemiah 1:1-3, 6:15-16, though there would be no royal palace because there would be no king. Long before, Jeremiah had told of a day when even that loss would be made good: 'There shall enter by the gates of this city kings and princes who sit on the throne of David, riding in chariots and on horses' (17:25). But that was an 'if' prophecy, theoretical and provisional, dependent

7 In the dystopian future world of Ray Bradbury's novel *Fahrenheit 451*: 'Is it true that long ago firemen put fires *out* instead of going to start them?'

on certain things which in the event did not happen. In the end, all would turn on the coming of a new kingdom with the coming of Christ, who was to speak of it in Mark 1:15 and continually from then onwards, and on the making of a new covenant through the death of Christ, who would speak of that in Luke 22:20.

So everything takes on a new dimension when the days of the New Testament dawn. Jerusalem, destroyed by fire in Jeremiah 52, was rebuilt, only to be destroyed again in A.D. 70 – significantly, just at the time when the gospel of the new covenant and the new kingdom was beginning to spread worldwide. Then in that physical, geographical form, its fortunes have continued to fluctuate as the centuries have gone by. The people of God, however, have learned to base their understanding of the city on what Hebrews 12:22 tells them: 'You have come,' whoever you are and wherever you live, 'to Mount Zion and to the city of the living God, the heavenly Jerusalem,' your changeless, universal, everlasting home.

What a crucial point of Old Testament history is this, as Jeremiah sees Jerusalem destroyed and Babylon triumphant. We his readers see how from here onwards the latter becomes the Bible's name for the whole world of evil that sets itself against Yahweh and His people, while the former becomes its name for them, the church of Jesus Christ, whose message is the only power that can overcome that evil. For triumphant Babylon shall in the end be laid waste, and the tale of her doom in Jeremiah 51 answers to that in Revelation 18; while suffering Jerusalem, for all the woes that will have befallen her in the meantime, shall in the end be raised to the everlasting glory that we see in Revelation 21.

The temple's destiny (52:17-23)

When Nebuzaradan set about the burning of Jerusalem the house of Yahweh was at the top of his list. As with the rest of his brief, he embarked on the task methodically, and the month's delay between the capture of the city and its final destruction shows that the latter was no mindless orgy, but a planned operation. Nebuzaradan could demolish Jerusalem as the political heart of Judah without massacring its inhabitants,

and by the same token he could destroy Yahweh's temple as the religious heart of the nation without sacrificing the wealth of valuables that it contained. Hence the inventory of temple furnishings in 52:17-23 and the statistics of the deportees in 52:28-30, things and people all duly taken away to Babylon.

We should not run away with the idea that the long inventory of items removed from the temple represents the very articles listed in 2 Chronicles 3–4 and in even greater detail in 1 Kings 6–7, where the construction and furnishing of Solomon's temple 400 years earlier are described. For one thing, as Solomon had added to what was already in use in the tabernacle that dated from the days of Moses,[8] and in various cases replaced the old with the new, so were further replacements and other additions on various occasions in the centuries that followed. The temple also became the home of many other items of value, a kind of national treasury. In good times a generous king might give it new adornments, but in bad times one who was strapped for cash might use its wealth to pay the bills or to buy off demanding enemies. In Rehoboam's reign, Shishak of Egypt attacked Jerusalem and took away all these treasures,[9] and in Amaziah's reign, Jehoash of Israel did the same[10] (we assume the temple had been re-endowed with the appropriate goods in the meantime!). Major refurbishments by Hezekiah at the end of the eighth century B.C., and by Josiah at the end of the seventh, meant that by 586 there was once again a lot worth taking, and here it is, listed in some detail.

All this makes us aware that in respect of the temple a paradox is being set up for the attentive reader. Whether or not the exiles now on their way to Babylon, and those already there, are aware of the enormous wagon train that is transporting all this paraphernalia from Jerusalem (and we notice that according to 52:18 it comprises specifically the things 'used in the temple service', not the temple's other treasures or adornments), Israel in exile is not going to have

---

8 Exodus 25–30, 36–39.

9 2 Chronicles 12:9.

10 2 Chronicles 25:22-24. I regret to say that I find this a source of guilty amusement; it reminds me of the old soldier in Hilaire Belloc's poem reminiscing about his exploits in the Napoleonic wars, who 'lost a leg at Waterloo, And Quatre-Bras, and Ligny too.'

all this set up for her on some dedicated site in Babylon, by a benevolent government that wants to make her feel at home. Far from it; literally, far from it. All this gold and silver and 'bronze … beyond weight' (52:20) is going to be stashed away by Nebuchadnezzar 'in the house of his gods',[11] while for seventy years Yahweh's people have to work out how to worship their God without all the aids that they had been taught were indispensable, and far from the place on which He had set his name, and of which He had said '*This* is where you and I are going to meet.'

Yet at the same time the temple's day is not over. Just as exiles will eventually return to their own land, and the city will rise again, so too the temple will be rebuilt. The day of the political kingdom is over; that will not come again. It is true that for a short while in a later century this repatriated Israel will be ruled by self-styled kings, of a sort, based in this rebuilt Jerusalem, the most notorious being the Herods. But there will now be no king of Israel of the line of David until the coming of the Christ. Only with Him will the new kingdom come. The day of the Jerusalem temple, though, is not over; nor will it be, until the new covenant is established, and that too awaits the coming of the Christ, whose sacrifice of Himself will finally do away with the need for the old temple and its sacrifices.

So the paradox for the people of the exile is that they have to learn both that the temple is necessary, and that it is not. They are going to be deprived of it as long as they are living in Babylon, to teach them that even there, without priest or altar or sacrifice, they can know the presence and blessing of God. Daniel and his friends, and Ezekiel, and Ezra and Nehemiah, and many, many others among the exiles, are witnesses to the fact that personal, loving, trusting, obedient contact with the living God is not restricted to one particular holy place and one particular religious ritual. But that same God also requires that the Jerusalem temple be rebuilt in due course, because for another five hundred years they will need to be reminded that the new covenant is not yet in operation. As soon as the exile ends and the rituals of Old Testament worship can recommence, this other lesson, not contradictory

11 Ezra 1:7.

but complementary, comes into play. 'By this the Holy Spirit indicates that the way into the holy places is not yet opened.' Only with the advent of the Christ, 'a high priest of the good things to come', 'the mediator of a new covenant,'[12] will that happen.

How fascinating, then, that Jeremiah 52 devotes this seven-verse paragraph to pots and snuffers and shovels and basins, a temple furnisher's shopping list: 'Item, Two pillars; One sea; Twelve bronze bulls, etc., etc.' Here were gold and silver and 'bronze ... beyond weight'. Where is all this going? What is it for?

Perhaps you are there before me, turning up the first chapter of the book of Ezra! 'In the first year of Cyrus king of Persia, that the word of the LORD by the mouth of Jeremiah might be fulfilled, the LORD stirred up the spirit of Cyrus' not just to repatriate the exiles, but positively to encourage them, with funding and every facility, to go back to Jerusalem explicitly to 'rebuild the house of the LORD, the God of Israel.' To which end, 'Cyrus the king also brought out the vessels of the house of the LORD that Nebuchadnezzar had carried away from Jerusalem and placed in the house of his gods.' Thereupon 'Mithredath the treasurer ... counted them out to Sheshbazzar the prince of Judah. And this was the number of them...'[13] Bronze items taken from the temple had been broken up, and were now simply a vast amount of scrap metal; little point in taking that back. But the returning exiles did take home more than five thousand items of gold and silver. Nebuchadnezzar's treasurer had checked them out from their temporary storehouse, but in respect of the place where they really belonged, Jeremiah 52 had counted them out and Ezra 1 would count them back in, as the saying goes.

The kingdom's destiny (52:24-34)

Four hundred years before these events, when the idea of Israel as a kingdom was still a new thing, David's glittering career had made it a force to be reckoned with in the Middle East. With its satellites and allies it was duly inherited by Solomon as a dominion which might almost be called imperial. But their mini-empire was to be quite eclipsed by

---

12 Hebrews 9:8, 11, 15, (ESV mg).
13 Ezra 1:1, 3, 7ff.

the rise of Assyria in the eighth century. Here was something on a different scale. This was the real thing. Assyria might in due course be elbowed out of the way by Babylon, but with Egypt always to be taken into account on their southern flank, these were now the days of the great empires. It became increasingly difficult for the smaller kingdoms of earlier times to remain independent.

Even so, the Judah into which Jeremiah and Josiah were born was still a compact little realm. Only after the death of the latter did it finally begin to crumble, till eventually foreign troops were tramping to and fro over it with impunity. With its economy in tatters, its leadership in disarray, half its population holed up in a besieged city and the other half trying to carry on ineffectual guerrilla warfare or eking out an existence in a devastated countryside, it breathed its last on that night in July 586 when the Babylonians broke into Jerusalem.

As Babylon would have seen them, the events at Riblah in Syria described in 52:24-27 signed the kingdom's death certificate. We have to reckon with the fact that within verse 9 of this chapter, between the capture of Zedekiah and his appearing before Nebuchadnezzar at Riblah, there has to be time enough for a 180-mile journey, and considerably more if the people listed in verses 24-25 were rounded up and taken north to be executed on the same occasion. With seventy-four individuals specified for Nebuzaradan to arrest, we cannot see this as indiscriminate slaughter. These were not deaths inflicted in the heat of battle. This is the elimination of the nation's official leadership, and by it Babylon is declaring Yahweh's kingdom dead and buried.

But the record then goes on to tell us, again quite specifically, with statistics, that many of Judah's people were not killed, but 'carried away captive' (52:15) to join the many others who on previous occasions had already been exiled to Babylon. They were the 'good figs' of chapter 24: 'I will set my eyes on them for good, and I will bring them back to this land' (24:6). In seventy years' time it would be Nebuchadnezzar's kingdom that would come to an end, while the kingdom of Yahweh, which he assumed he had destroyed, would rise from the dead, although no longer in the form of an oriental monarchy.

So, says the book of Jeremiah in its last eleven verses, this is how through all kinds of vicissitudes the political kingdom finally perishes, its last monarch (as we know already) in lingering misery, and now its representative leaders by summary execution (vv. 24-27). This is how under the very noses of its enemies – indeed, all unwittingly, by their agency – the true kingdom survives and is purified and strengthened and prepared for new things (vv. 28-30). And now we learn (vv. 31-34) that the line of David, its first great king, also survives, and with it the promise of the kingdom in a new form, to emerge one day from this Old Testament chrysalis. A prophet like Moses, only far, far greater. A judge like Samuel, but immeasurably greater. A king like David, but greater beyond all imagining. Not some non-human angelic figure, though, parachuted in from a different dimension; rather, the great-great-many-times-great-grandson of the exiled boy-king Jehoiachin. Even if the Old Testament were a closed book to us, we might have noticed that name in its other form, Jechoniah, in the very first chapter of the New, in the family tree halfway between David and 'Jesus ... who is called Christ.'[14]

From the study group in which this book first began to take shape came also a delightful piece of work by one of its members, a letter purporting to be sent by Jehoiachin from Babylon in his old age to his grandson Zerubbabel, governor of Judah and leader of the returned exiles.[15] No doubt the latter, important person though he had become, would have smiled at the (imagined) pet name from his childhood!

'Dear Grandson, my dearest Zubbable,

'Greetings from Babylon, your Grandmother and I are both well and send you our love and felicitations, and our best wishes for your continuing good health.

'The news from Jerusalem has pleased us beyond measure, you and Joshua are achieving great things and are well thought of, and we hear that you have started to rebuild the Temple; I can't tell you how delighted we both are to hear of this.

---

14 Matthew 1:12.

15 1 Chronicles 3:17-19; Haggai 1:1. Extracts from the letter are reprinted here with the permission of the author, Linda Hallums.

'You will bring back the honour to this family that your great-great-uncles and I so thoughtlessly and foolishly threw away. Your great-great-grandfather Josiah would have been so proud of you; with God's help you will give back to the people of Judah their rightful inheritance.

'When you were a little lad you used to ask me to tell you all about King Josiah, and your great-great-uncles, and of course about the Prophet Jeremiah, and I always answered that I would tell you all about it when the time was right. Well, that time has come ...'

Jehoiachin continues with a vivid narration, in brief, of the whole story of sin and punishment, repentance and forgiveness and lessons learned, and near the end he writes:

'If you ever hear any news of what happened to Jeremiah I would be pleased to hear it, I hope that he eventually managed to return from Egypt, as he was forced there against his will, and after all our family did to him I should like to think that he had some ease in retirement.'

Well, Jehoiachin, we still don't know. But we do know that he has left us all, God's people in every succeeding age, an extraordinary legacy: a book which is in every sense one of the Bible's greatest. And with you the very last person named in it! Even if it is not Jeremiah himself who dictated this final chapter, it will be one anonymous editor, at any rate, of whom he would have approved.

For we cannot miss the parallel obituaries that mark the book's ending. 'The day of his death', in 52:11: that is, Zedekiah's death. He lost his throne, he lost his freedom, he lost his posterity, and he lost his sight. Whatever faith he may once have had, he had long since lost that too. He died in prison in Babylon, which could be a thought-provoking epitaph for every unbeliever, in every age, the world over.

But when the book's final verse, 52:34, also includes the phrase 'the day of his death', Jehoiachin is the man in view. What a nonentity, we might think. Though he did once rule the kingdom of Judah (for three months!) you could scarcely call him an important figure in Bible history, could you? We know, though, from 1 Corinthians 1:26-29, that not many 'big names' are called and chosen by God, and some of the

most apparently insignificant people have very special places in His scheme of things. We might note four ways in which Jehoiachin's experience stands in contrast to that of his tragic uncle Zedekiah. The first is that he escaped all the suffering and the trauma that Judah went through in the 580s. The second is that he was both freed from imprisonment and honoured by Nebuchadnezzar's son Evil-Merodach when that prince inherited the crown of Babylon. The third is that for the exiles he was still, thirty-seven years after he had been taken there, regarded as King Jehoiachin (52:31), so they assumed that the royal line of David would after all continue, whether or not any future members of it would ever reign enthroned in Jerusalem. And the fourth is, as we have noted, that One of that line eventually would; but from a higher throne, in a greater Jerusalem, as He does to this day and will do for ever.

Some inkling of that glorious future must have registered in Jehoiachin's mind away there in Babylon. After all, he was one of the exiles, the 'good figs' of chapter 24, true believers with true prophets among them being prepared for the next chapter of the ongoing story. As for Zedekiah, back in Judah, the walls of God's city in Jerusalem would not protect him from the final assault on it by the 'foe from the north', and the word of God's prophet Jeremiah, right here in the city with him, could not save him if he refused to take it to heart and act upon it. But as the great Delusion closed in around him, the words of truth were already on their way to the world outside, to other nations near and far, for that time and for centuries yet to come, having within them (as Yahweh had said, 23:28-29) power to nourish the soul like wheat, to burn the conscience like fire, to break hard hearts as the hammer breaks the rocks. The only real difference between the world as Jeremiah knew it and the world as we know it is that in the meantime Jehoiachin's most famous descendant, great David's greater Son, has come into His inheritance, bringing such new depth to the meaning of the words 'kingdom' and 'covenant' as will be surpassed only when this world comes to an end and we see Him as He is.

STUDY QUESTIONS

1. LAMENTATIONS (Lam. 1–5)

A lamentable state of affairs (1:1-22)
In what circumstances might a Christian community suffer deservedly?

A lamentable chain of consequences (2:1-22)
What might have prompted the Writer's choice between 'Yahweh' and 'Adonai' in particular verses?

Two lamentable cries of distress (3:1-66)
Are there in this chapter other verses less well-known than verse 23 that might be turned into modern song?

A lamentable loss of privileges (4:1-22)
What good purposes might be served by God's withholding promised blessings?

A lamentable lack of prospects (5:1-22)
What other Bible passages end in unmitigated gloom? What is their value to the believer?

2. THE VIEW FROM ANATHOTH (Jer. 1)

Many nations:
To what other non-Israelite nations besides those mentioned here do Israel's prophets speak?

Three kings:
The prophet's story is entwined with that of the kings who were his contemporaries. Do we already have pointers to how they are going to relate to one another?

Two visions:
Consider the declarations about what Yahweh has done, and will do, that accompany the visions of 1:11-13.

One God:
How does this picture of 'one God' bear on relationships today between the great religions of the world?

3. JUDGMENTS (Jer. 2–6)

Arraignment: God puts His people on trial (2:1-37)
Which of the many word-pictures in this chapter relate particularly clearly to events in Israel's story?

Appeal: God pleads with His people (3:1–4:4)
Trace the occurrences of the 'turn' words through this passage, and note the different meanings.

Assault: God brings punishment on His people (4:5-31)
What place is there in the Christian ministry for a cry like that in 4:10?

Accusation: God specifies His people's sins (5:1-31)
It is Jerusalem that here stands accused. Look for modern equivalents not in today's world but in today's church. Of what sins in particular might Yahweh accuse it?

Assay: God puts His people through the fire (6:1-30)
'Sometimes,' an experienced preacher once said, 'a text will leap off the page and grab you, and say "Preach on me!"' Which verses in chapter 6 might do that?

4. DELUSIONS (Jer. 7–10)

The nature of the delusions (7:1–8:3)
What delusions beset today's 'man in the pew', 'man in the street', and 'man in the Valley of the Son of Hinnom'?

The cause of the delusions (8:4-17)
In what particular ways were the nation's leaders saying 'Peace, peace', when there was no peace (8:11)?

The effect of the delusions (8:18–9:11)
How far is 9:1-9 a picture of the world we live in?

The delusions blown away (9:12-26)
Think over Derek Kidner's comment on the two Hebrew verbs in 9:24: 'There is a nuance of practical good sense in [the word] *understands*, while to 'know' God is life itself, even to eternity.'

The gods of delusion and the God of fact (10:1-25)
How radically does the 'God of fact' challenge the assumptions of present-day society?

5. PROTESTS: THE FIRST GROUP (Jer. 11–15)

The setting of the first protest (11:1-17)
The relationship between Yahweh and His people over the years between the exodus and Jeremiah's time: what has changed, and what has not changed?

The first protest: Jeremiah in the firing line (11:18-23)
Compare these verses with the passage in Isaiah 53:7-8 that foresees the sufferings of Christ. Is it right to see Jeremiah's trials also prophesied there?

The second protest: Jeremiah under a darkening sky (12:1-6)
What at this point is clear in Jeremiah's mind about Yahweh's plans, and what is not yet clear?

The setting of the second protest (12:7–13:27)
How might Jeremiah have understood the destiny of Yahweh's 'evil neighbours' (12:14) in relation to that of his own 'evil people' (13:10)?

The setting of the third protest (14:1–15:9)
Consider how thorough the confessions of 14:7-9 and 14:19-22 seem to be, and how they might nonetheless prove ineffective.

The third protest: Jeremiah the object of calumny (15:10-21)
Note the mixed emotions of a servant of the Lord now in the thick of a hugely demanding ministry, and note how the original call of 1:17-19 had warned him in advance.

6. PROTESTS: THE SECOND GROUP (Jer. 16–20)

The setting of the fourth protest (16–17:13)
'Look at me, because I represent Judah. This is what our nation is soon to become.' Does God set up such scenarios in our own day as warnings of coming woes?

The fourth protest: Jeremiah facing both ways (17:14-18)
Set out these five verses as a chiasmus, as in the diagram of 18:19-23 on page 99, noting the parallels which focus attention on its important points.

The setting of the fifth protest (17:19–18:18)
'It is up to them to decide what their future shall be ... Whatever He may have intended, they can make Him do the opposite.' Discuss!

The fifth protest: Jeremiah at the end of his tether (18:19-23)
How can a prayer like that of 18:21 be justifed?

The setting of the sixth protest (19:1–20:6)
In what sense will Yahweh 'break this people and this city' so that they 'can never be mended' (19:11)?

The sixth protest: Jeremiah in agony (20:7-18)
Consider further the calling to 'face both ways'. Do we see it in other Bible people besides Jeremiah and David and Samson?

7. BETRAYALS (Jer. 21–23)

Speaking prophet, listening king? (21:1–22:9)
Every Israelite king was expected to 'enquire of the Lord' (21:2). In this respect, was Zedekiah following in the footsteps of his father Josiah? Or in Hezekiah's? Or in David's? Or in Saul's? (See 1 Chron. 10:13-14; 13:1-4; 2 Chron. 31:21; 34:21).

Kings who betray their trust (22:10–23:8)
How does this series of royal 'drop-outs' affect Yahweh's commitment to the house of David (22:30, 23:5)?

Prophets who betray their trust (23:9-40)
How does modern church leadership measure up to the demands set forth here, relating to the Lord's law, and His council, and the 'burden' of His message?

8. THE VIEW FROM JERUSALEM (Jer. 24–25)

The call / The place
Would each of the three calls have been recognized as the voice of Yahweh? How would the 'cup of the wine of wrath', and the command to drink it, reach 'all the kingdoms of the world' (25:15, 26)?

The time / The end of the line
Why are the exiles of 597 regarded as 'good figs' and those of 586 as 'bad figs'?

All change / The view from Jerusalem
The events of 586 marked the end of Israel as a political kingdom. What bearing does this have on the modern state of Israel? How should Jeremiah's world-view in 25:30-38 colour the church's teaching in the world of today?

9. INTENTIONS (Jer. 26–29)

Jeremiah and Uriah (26:1-24)
How should we react to events like the scandalous treatment of Uriah?

Jeremiah and Hananiah (27:1–28:17)
What would be the modern equivalent of Hananiah's false prophesying?

Jeremiah and three prophets in Babylon (29:1-32)
What does it mean for us today to 'pray for the peace not only of Jerusalem but also of Babylon'?

10. PROMISES (Jer. 30–33)

The days of understanding (30:1-24)
'Watch how Yahweh works, and it really does begin to make sense.' Does it?

The days of covenant (31:1-40)
How and when might believers today see the five 'scenes of hope' become a concrete reality?

The days of wrath (32:1-44)
Consider some major disaster for which God might be blamed, and how it might prove eventually to have some constructive purpose.

The days of fulfilment (33:1-26)
Kingdom, priesthood, nation, family – what sort of new version of each should we see in this present age, and what belongs only to the next world?

11. FAILURES (Jer. 34–36)

A goal not achieved (34:1-22)
Can you recall being set a task in which (as you realized afterwards) God's intention was not so much to get the task done, as to teach you something through the doing of it?

A lifestyle not understood (35:1-19)
Were there other plus points about the Rechabites' lifestyle besides their loyalty to the rule of their founder?

A word not accepted (36:1-32)
What might have been going through Jehoiakim's mind as he destroyed Baruch's scroll?

12. ENDINGS (Jer. 37–39)

Jeremiah at liberty (37:1-10)
How clearly do people understand that when God seems not to listen to them, it may well be that they are not listening to Him?

Jeremiah in the dungeon (37:11-17)
Do you agree that as times get tougher, so, it seems, does Jeremiah?

Jeremiah in the court of the guard (37:18–38:3)
Notice that while accepting bad treatment, Jeremiah does not hesitate to speak out against the injustice of it. How would we know when to act thus, and when not?

Jeremiah in the cistern (38:4-28)
The journalist Hugh Redwood once preached to a vast crowd in Toronto on the 'old rags and worn-out clothes' of 38:11! What would you preach on from this memorable chapter?

Jeremiah in the house of the governor (39:1-18)
Summarize what is destroyed in that fateful summer of 586, and what survives.

13. CONTINUATIONS (Jer. 40–45)

Life goes on (40:1-12)
What was, and is, the prophetic message for those who try to picture the world beyond the present crisis?

Trouble goes on (40:13–41:10)
How should Gedaliah have acted in respect of Johanan's warning? And is there any point in asking this kind of question?

Worldly wisdom goes one (41:11–42:6)
List the 'dozen turns of phrase' that brand Johanan as a real-life Worldly Wiseman.

The word still follows you (42:7–43:13)
Consider the privilege of being able both to hear and to pass on God's Word in such an alien environment as Tahpanhes.

The word still finds you (44:1-14)
Who are today's equivalent of the Israel-in-Egypt here addressed by Jeremiah?

The word still condemns you (44:15-30)
Suggest some of the effects of 'Egyptian' values on modern politics and the media.

Yet there is still a remnant (45:1-5)
What might be the main points of a sermon on Baruch?

14. THE VIEW FROM TAHPANHES (Jer. 46–51)

Where the dream has yet to die (46:1-28)
How in practical terms would Egyptian people get to hear this message from Yahweh?

Where the dream never was (47:1-7)
What do you reckon the 'sea peoples' would have known about Israel's God, remembering how they figure in the stories of (for example) Samson, David, and Ahab and Elijah?

Where the dream has been glimpsed (48:1–49:6)
Consider the responsibility of God's people to those around them who reckon they already know 'the church' and don't much care for it.

Where the dream has been misunderstood (49:7-27)
Find instances in earlier times of Israelite contacts with Edom and Aram. What effect might the experience of someone like Naaman have on his fellow-Gentiles?

Where the dream has yet to come (49:28-39)
'God is as intimately concerned with people I know nothing about ... as He is with me.' How should that thought affect the way we pray?

Where the dream has died (50–51)
How do we square the prophecy of Babylon's fall with the command in 29:7 to 'seek the welfare of the city'?

15. DESTINIES (Jer. 52)

The king's destiny (52:1-11)
Reflect on the character of Zedekiah. 'Sad rather than bad'?
At what points in his career might he have made different
decisions and so come to a different end?

The city's destiny (52:12-16)
Consider how the meaning of Psalm 122:6 ('Pray for the peace
of Jerusalem') has developed in the course of the city's history.

The temple's destiny (52:17-23)
Do we have any clues as to how godly people among the exiles
coped without temple worship?

The kingdom's destiny (52:24-34)
What bearing does this account of the Old Testament kingdom's
last days have on the gospel account of (a) popular expectations,
(b) Jesus' teaching, on the New Testament kingdom?

Subject Index

Scripture Index

Focus on the Bible Commentaries

Focus on the Bible Commentaries

Genesis: The Beginning of God's Plan of Salvation – Richard P. Belcher
ISBN 978-1-84550-963-7

Deuteronomy: The Commands of a Covenant God – Allan Harman
ISBN 978-1-84550-268-3

Joshua: No Falling Words – Dale Ralph Davis
ISBN 978-1-84550-137-2

Judges: Such a Great Salvation – Dale Ralph Davis
ISBN 978-1-84550-138-9

Ruth & Esther: God Behind the Seen – A. Boyd Luter/Barry C. Davis
ISBN 978-1-85792-805-9

1 Samuel: Looking on the Heart – Dale Ralph Davis
ISBN 978-1-85792-516-6

2 Samuel: Out of Every Adversity – Dale Ralph Davis
ISBN 978-1-84550-270-6

1 Kings The Wisdom and the Folly – Dale Ralph Davis
ISBN 978-1-84550-251-5

2 Kings: The Power and Fury – Dale Ralph Davis
ISBN 978-1-84550-096-2

1 Chronicles: God's Faithfulness to the People of Judah – Cyril J. Barber
ISBN 978-1-85792-935-5

2 Chronicles: God's Blessing of His Faithful People – Cyril J. Barber
ISBN 978-1-85792-936-2

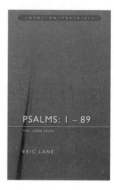

Psalms 1-89: The Lord Saves – Eric Lane
ISBN 978-1-84550-180-8

Psalms 90-150: The Lord Reigns – Eric Lane
ISBN 978-1-84550-202-7

Proverbs: Everyday Wisdom for Everyone – Eric Lane
ISBN 978-1-84550-267-6

Ecclesiastes: The Philippians of the Old Testament – William D. Barrick
ISBN 978-1-84550-776-3

Song of Songs – Richard Brooks
ISBN 978-1-85792-486-2

Isaiah: A Covenant to be Kept for the Sake of the Church – Allan Harman
ISBN 978-1-84550-053-5

Jeremiah and Lamentations: The Death of a Dream, and What Came After – Michael Wilcock
ISBN 978-1-78191-148-8

Daniel: A Tale of Two Cities – Bob Fyall
ISBN 978-1-84550-194-5

Hosea – Michael Eaton
ISBN 978-1-85792-277-6

Amos: An Ordinary Man with an Extraordinary Message – T. J. Betts
ISBN 978-1-84550-727-5

Jonah, Michah, Nahum, Habakkuk & Zephaniah – John L. Mackay
ISBN 978-1-85792-392-6

Haggai, Zechariah & Malachi: God's Restored People – John L. Mackay
ISBN 978-1-85792-067-3

Matthew: The King and His Kingdom – Charles Price
ISBN 978-1-78191-146-4

Mark: Good News from Jerusalem – Geoffrey Grogan
ISBN 978-1-85792-905-8

Acts: Witnesses to Him – Bruce Milne
ISBN 978-1-84550-507-3

Romans: The Revelation of God's Righteousness – Paul Barnett
ISBN 978-1-84550-269-0

1 Corinthians: Holiness and Hope of a Rescued People – Paul Barnett
ISBN 978-1-84550-721-3

2 Corinthians: The Glories & Responsibilities of Christian Service – Geoffrey Grogan
ISBN 978-1-84550-252-2

Galatians: God's Proclamation of Liberty – Joseph A. Pipa Jr.
ISBN 978-1-84550-558-5

Ephesians: Encouragement and Joy in Christ – Paul Gardner
ISBN 978-1-84550-264-5

Philippians: Rejoicing and Thanksgiving – David Chapman
ISBN 978-1-84550-687-2